The Aspiring Psychologist Collective:

Reflective Accounts of Mental Health Professionals on their way to Qualification

by

Dr Marianne Trent

The Aspiring Psychologist Collective: Reflective Accounts of Mental Health Professionals on their way to Qualification

First published in the UK by KDP, 2022.
Copyright © Dr Marianne Trent 2022.
All rights reserved.
ISBN: 9798354311026
Imprint: Independently published.

Also available in e-book and hardback formats.

The right of Dr Marianne Trent to be identified as the author of this work has been asserted by her in accordance with the Copyright Design and Patents Act,1988. Marianne has asserted that individual case study contributors will maintain the copyright for their own unique stories. All contributors have signed a waiver to allow their work to appear within this book.

This book is sold subject to the condition that it shall not, by way of trade and otherwise, be lent, relent, resold, hired out or otherwise circulated without the publisher's prior consent in any form, binding or cover other than that in which it is published and without a similar condition being imposed on the subsequent purchaser.

Created, Compiled, Indexed and Edited: Dr Marianne Trent
Proofread: Chrissie Fitch
Cover Photographs: Damien Trent
Cover & Book Design: Dr Marianne Trent
Author Photographs: Damien Trent

About the Lead Author

Dr Marianne Trent is a Clinical Psychologist in Private Practice. She specialises in Trauma, Grief, Anxiety & Depression. She supports the needs of Aspiring Psychologists and also helps coach psychologists to develop their own passive income streams.

This is Marianne's third book, with her first being *The Grief Collective: Stories of Life, Loss & Learning to Heal* and her second being *The Clinical Psychologist Collective: Advice & Guidance for Aspiring Clinical Psychologists.*

Marianne is a media regular, writing about mental health related topics and concepts. She has been interviewed live on BBC News and has written for the British Psychological Society's magazine The Psychologist, The Guardian, Platinum Magazine, Huff Post, The Telegraph and more.

Marianne is the host of The Aspiring Psychologist Podcast which launched in December 2021.

She is also an ambassador for AtALoss.org and a clinical advisor for 'Our Time' a charity who support young adults who have experienced parental loss.

Website:	www.goodthinkingPsychology.co.uk
Instagram:	@DrMarianneTrent
Facebook:	Good Thinking Psychological Services
YouTube:	Dr Marianne Trent
LinkedIn:	Dr Marianne Trent
TikTok:	@drmariannetrent
Twitter:	@DrMarianneTrent

Dedication

From the back of our car a few months ago my kids decided it was about time I dedicated a book to them. And so, to you, my darlings Boo & Rama, who are not actually called Boo or Rama, and to my husband Damien, this one is for you.

It's also for all of you reading this book who are out there striving to further your careers and, in the process, helping so many people. You're wonderful.

Contents

Contents

Foreword

By Dr Chris Irons

B eing a qualified psychologist is one of the biggest privileges of my life. I really love my job, the people that I've worked with, and the huge variety of things I'm able to do as a Clinical Psychologist. But it's fair to say that the path to becoming a psychologist is often exceptionally hard and stressful, with regular setbacks, and rejections and disappointments a common experience along the way. Irrespective of how great the destination may be once we get there, why should anyone put themselves through such pain to get there? Well, there are many reasons why people want to be a psychologist. Sometimes this might even link to a desire for status, appreciation and the 'Dr' title. But for most people, we are willing to put ourselves though hardship *because we care*. We are bothered about other peoples' pain and distress and are training ourselves as psychologists to be best equipped to try and alleviate these difficulties in various ways.

So, the motivation at the heart of becoming a psychologist is compassion.

Given all of this, what might help us through the difficult process of becoming a psychologist? One interesting idea emerges from Compassion Focused Therapy (CFT), and relates to the direction that compassion can flow in.

Compassion for Others

When asked about compassion, most people immediately think of this being towards someone else. And as a psychologist, we often think about this as compassion for the clients we work with. But what about having compassion for your fellow Aspiring Psychologists? If you think about it, having compassion here isn't always easy, especially when we're in direct competition with each other for a limited number of opportunities.

Although it's not easy, research has found that when we purposefully open ourselves to be caring, supportive and compassionate to others, this not only helps the person that we're being compassionate to, but also benefits us as the giver. When we're compassionate to others, it also helps to build a sense of connection and safeness and makes it more likely that they'll respond in turn with care towards us in the future.

So how do we practice compassion for our aspiring Psychology colleagues? Well, the key here is that we don't see compassion as an emotion linked to liking, kindness or positive feelings. Whilst these can be part of the process of compassion, it's more important to hold in mind that compassion is linked to a motive – to be sensitive to others' distress, and to try and do things that might be helpful. In that sense, it can be useful to hold in mind that if you were going through a similar struggle to your colleague, what you might find helpful. Or, instead of it being a colleague you imagine instead that it's your friend going through the difficult time, how would you try to be helpful with them? And then with this in mind, you can try and do something similar with your colleague that's struggling.

Humans are the most social of species. Whilst compassion for others can bring many benefits, we didn't evolve to just to give care, but also to need and require care from others. In fact, a huge amount of research has discovered that being cared for by others has a major  beneficial impact on a variety of physiological and psychological processes. It leads to lower stress and anxiety, a greater sense of connection and wellbeing, and can help us to navigate difficulties in life.

But it turns out that when we're an Aspiring Psychologist (and even when we become a Qualified Psychologist), it might not always be easy to seek out and allow in the kindness, care and compassion from other people in our life. In fact, our research in CFT has found that when we're blocked to receiving compassion from others, this is associated with higher levels of stress, anxiety, shame and self-criticism.

There can be lots of reasons why we end up being blocked to the care of others. For example, rather than feeling that the people around us are supportive and helpful, we might feel instead that we're in competition with them for an Assistant Psychologist role or place on a training programme. We can feel that we 'should' be strong and resilient, and that other people need to see this, as signs of vulnerability and stress might somehow represent weakness or inadequacy. Outside of the Psychology world, friends and family might be unaware of how competitive, challenging, drawn-out and stressful the process of becoming a psychologist is, and therefore lack empathy for what you're going through.

So, one way that you can support yourself through the process of becoming a psychologist is by learning how to reach out to others and receive their kindness. Whilst this isn't always easy, courage and practice can help this become more familiar, and it will ultimately help you to feel more connected, safe and supported. And whilst this might not erase the stress you're going through, like having good suspension on a car or a bike, it definitely helps!

" Self Compassion "

Alongside learning how to seek out and receive compassion from others, there's growing evidence that learning how to be compassionate with ourselves may play a central role in helping to navigate stressful situations and life experiences. Think about it for a minute – you'll spend far more time in relationship with yourself than you will anyone else in life. In fact, if you were to add up every minute that you're in relationship with another person through your life to date, it'll come nowhere close to how much time you've been in relationship with yourself. But here's the thing: what type of relationship do you have with yourself? When you're having a stressful time – maybe if you've been turned down for that assistant job or trainee interview - how do you respond to yourself and your distress? Do you offer yourself the same empathy, kindness and care as you would your best friend or loved one?

Just like there's lots of ways to get physically fit, in CFT there's lots of ways to develop your compassionate mind, and from this, learn how to cultivate compassion to others, from others and to yourself. Recently, I've started to do research on how using ideas and exercises from CFT benefit trainee psychologists and therapists and the results are looking good! So alongside reading the helpful chapters in this book, you might find it helpful to look into some of these too. You can find free audios at www.balancedminds.com, learn more about the Self-Compassion App, and some of our compassion self-help books.

Wishing you well for your future careers,

Dr Chris Irons
Clinical Psychologist & Author

Introduction

Self-care isn't all face masks & pedicures

In writing this book, I was mindful of the words of my friend and fellow Clinical Psychologist, Michaela Thomas. She wrote the book 'The Lasting Connection,' which is a wonderful resource for helping you understand how to work compassionately with couples and also how to have healthy relationships yourself[1]. Anyway, so, within her book she talks about the process of writing her book and doing so with compassion to herself. This meant actually planning in diary time for it rather than squeezing it around other activities. Reading this was like a foreign language revelation for me. When The Lasting Connection was first published, I'd not long completed The Grief Collective.... within the space of a month! Now, you may be wondering how and why on earth I did this so quickly. I'll level with you that now I'm a further two books in, I often wonder the same. The truth is that it was part of a 'write and publish a whole book in a month' challenge[2]. I most definitely didn't apply these self-care principles to book number one, or for that matter number two. But I really wanted to see how I could implement them into *this* book. So, I gave myself the longest recruitment time yet, with it starting in March 2022 ahead of publication in October. I also blocked out time in my diary in September to be able to work on the book during daylight hours rather than still tapping away on the sofa at 11pm. I also chose to aim for publication in October rather than September because I knew that having the children off over the Summer was not commensurate with being likely to have free time available to me. As I type this chapter it is the Queen's

---

[1] The cover is also pretty beautiful with an embossed copper foil which has stroke appeal!
[2] Which I won!

Funeral Bank Holiday. Now, you might be thinking "Well working on a bank holiday isn't terrific self-care, Marianne!" To which I would usually agree. But you see, with only 2 weeks until publication, things are hotting up! I had always planned to use all of today for writing and editing. Then a bank holiday was announced and whilst it then meant I'd have two kids at home it didn't alter the need to meet my deadline. And so, I have made myself a cup of my very poshest tea[3], and I am listening to my kids laugh with their cousin on Facetime as they play Roblox for the millionth time this year. The Queen's funeral is in the background as the guards march with her to Windsor. And so, you see, this is self-care, because if I'd chosen to take this out of my diary, I'd then have needed to find an extra 8 hours in the next fortnight to do the work I was going to do today. If I'd put myself out to spend time with the kids instead of writing, I'm also confident they would have told me at the end of the day that they would have preferred to have just played Roblox! Oh, the frustration of trying to plan 'golden time' and then it being underappreciated! So, on this occasion I thought I'd miss out the middleman and just write my book as planned. Some may call this 'mean Mummy syndrome'. I call it real life and what being a human and business owner is like.

In your own career ahead, you might also find some of these strategies helpful. This might be especially useful around case report deadlines, exam prep and thesis work.
The next pages are laid down to my top tips for self-care.

---

[3] A Fortnum & Mason's Apricot, Honey & Lavender Tea, I bought myself with my Christmas money!

Ideas for Psychology career self-care

Use Your Diary

Get deadlines into your diary as soon as they're given and then plan backwards. Create the time to do the work. Make sure you create an earlier deadline for yourself if you'd like someone else's opinions on what you've created. Also factor in jobs you can do whilst waiting for their feedback.

If possible, try to plan things for you to look forward to once each milestone activity is ticked off. For me, I always used to relish a week of annual leave at the end of each placement. I also used to plan two weeks of non-client time before moving jobs. This allowed me to mindfully write closing reports and to have proper endings with clients.

Planned Down Time

Communicate your Deadlines

Tell those closest to you about your deadlines in advance. Ideally, they should have access to them in a shared calendar or in their own diary. This reduces the chances of any conflict when you say, "I've got to work".

It might sound silly but if you are given study leave, try to use it as such rather than just napping through it or watching Netflix! If you don't get study leave within your role or it's not scheduled at the right time for any deadlines it never hurts to ask for it! Don't forget that, technically

Use Your Study Leave

speaking, if you're already working for the NHS and are in the process of applying for another NHS role or interview that you can do this within company time. It is of course polite to discuss this with your management, but certainly worth considering!

Move Your Body

Exercise and productivity are most definitely linked. It is, also, most definitely self-care. If I am going for a run, then I like to get it done as soon as I wake. I often get out of bed and straight into my running gear. When I was a Trainee Clinical Psychologist, I used to like a swim. I now do strength training and yoga too. Where I can, I also walk for shorter journeys rather than drive. Move your body however feels good to you and in whatever way your body allows. As an Aspiring Psychologist, I used to attend some wicked seated yoga classes with my clients so do explore other options if your mobility is more limited.

Keep talking to people around you. Supervisors, placement supervisors, friends and family. Be honest about the impact of the work upon you and your life. People are not mind readers and it is much better for you to be able to communicate your needs early rather than do so in

tearful, shuddering sobs because you're already burned out. Team work most definitely makes the dream work and you don't need to do everything alone.

If I could go back and make one change in my career it would be to have learned about and embraced the practice of self-compassion sooner. Since discovering it in 2018, it has changed my life. I wish I'd said yes when I was offered the chance to borrow the Paul Gilbert book in 2011 but to be honest it was offputtingly large! Thankfully, audiobooks are now widely available and so I used commutes to learn more. Had I been using its principles sooner I would have been a better clinician sooner as well as kinder on myself as a mother, partner, wife, friend and daughter. There's most definitely a reason I invited Dr Chris Irons to write our Foreword for this book and it's because this self-compassion malarkey really does work!

Writing Induced Injuries

Thishis morning whilst watching Aladdin[4] with my kids I told them:

"Mummy once rode an elephant. Oh, and actually a camel too when I spent some time in the desert in India but that was so uncomfortable, I wouldn't recommend it cos I ended up with open wounds on my bum from how uncomfortable it was!"

The kids found that hilarious of course. "Mummy hurt her bum!!!!!! "Mummy hurt her bum!!!!!!" They will be amused by that for a good long time yet.

Now that you and I know each other a little better and I've already gently introduced the concept of my bum, I feel I can share with you that I also injured myself whilst writing and editing this book.

It's hard to describe how many hours of work this project has taken because I haven't counted. I might do next time! But trust me, it's a lot and usually squeezed in around other activities too, so often not written at my desk. Whilst the project commenced in March 2022, it was largely completed during the super-hot summer months of that year. On a warm day my go to summer outfit is usually an old pair of denim cutoffs. They work perfectly for all activities aside from, it seems, book writing whilst laying on the sofa. In that attire and that position on a hot summer's

---

[4] The one with Will Smith in case you're wondering.

day, it seems you can expect to give yourself bottom wounds comparable to having spent a whole day on a camel.

So, there you go, that explains why I am now writing this in an almost fully reclined position on my bed whilst wearing a pair of pyjama shorts and a bit of a wince. Lesson learned.

About this Book

In March 2022 I started recruiting people to feature within this book. This took the form of creating a nifty little survey for interested parties to briefly summarise their ideas for their chapter. I then kept on chatting about it on my socials and in the podcast. Reading through the proposals was a real joy. From the submissions 53 people were invited to write their account for this book. Of those 53, 46 submitted a story and we were able to get 43 of them across the line as published accounts. I'm currently aged 41 and for a little while I was quite excited that it looked like we might accidentally happen upon 41 stories within this tome. Then I found I'd accidentally given 2 of the stories in the spreadsheet document the same number. This opened me up to chase up 2 stories I particularly liked who had completed a survey but not responded to my reminder emails since. With days to spare we managed to get 1 of these finished in time to get it here for you to read.

All contributors have consented for their work to appear within this book and have been sent a free signed copy with my warmest thanks.

Please read the stories with kindness in your heart as they are real people.

About the Name of this Book

I was really struggling to name this book. Even as I type this on 20/09/2022 the subtitle is still blank.

Towards the end of July 2022, I asked my social networks for help coming up with a subtitle.

I really fancied including the words 'Assistant Psychologist' in the title and said as much in my appeal[56]:

Dr Marianne Trent (She/Her) • You
Author & Podcaster Supporting Aspiring Psychologists in Highly Competitive...
2mo • 🌐

The Aspiring Psychologist Collective book is coming together so nicely!

It's now 110 pages long so probably about 1/3 - 1/4 of the way done!

Spearheading this project is such an incredible privilege and I am blown away by the wisdom, compassion and tenancity of people who have so far submitted stories.

I could do with some help though. What should the sub heading be?

The Clinical Psychologist Collective was: advice and guidance for Aspiring Clinical Psychologists

The grief collective was: stories of life, loss & learning to heal.

What suggestions would you put forward for the aspiring Psychologist collective?

Bonus points if it uses the words assistant psychologist!

Let me know your ideas in the comments. If you are the first to suggest the winning one I'll send you a free signed copy when published!

If you'd like to join the waiting list to be notified when the book is published please head here: https://lnkd.in/dnjqs_Jh

#Dclinpsy #psychology #assistantpsychologist #competition

---

[5] I also spelled tenacity wrong. That's embarrassing.

My network firmly told me that they thought focusing on one specific route was not cool. Comments included:

"I wonder why you want to include "Assistant Psychologists"? I do feel that including "Assistant Psychologists" is limiting as there are so many other routes and often people feel frustrated and disappointed with the challenges of getting AP roles and the landscape is so much broader and I think that should be embraced".

Thank you for everyone for helping me see the light on this one and as a result of the posts...... Drum roll please, my 2 favourite title suggestions were:

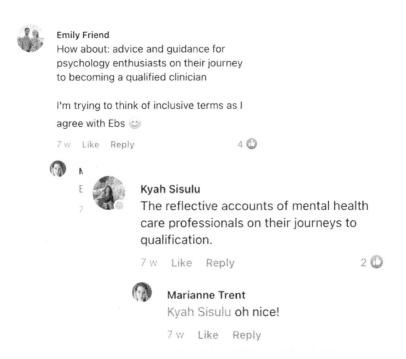

Emily Friend
How about: advice and guidance for psychology enthusiasts on their journey to becoming a qualified clinician

I'm trying to think of inclusive terms as I agree with Ebs 😊

7 w   Like   Reply   4

Kyah Sisulu
The reflective accounts of mental health care professionals on their journeys to qualification.

7 w   Like   Reply   2

Marianne Trent
Kyah Sisulu oh nice!

7 w   Like   Reply

So, let's award Kyah and Emily a free book each! And now I'll play around and find the exact title I like. Hold the line caller. Add your own sound effects to this picture[7]:

Ok, so it won't surprise you because you're holding the book, but I decided upon:

The Aspiring Psychologist Collective:
Reflective Accounts of Mental Health Professionals on their way to Qualification

So, there we go, what a corker! If you think I need to get better at giving the books shorter titles you're probably right! The person I feel most sorry for is my podcast jingle guy who comes up with and sings the book titles for me. He's worth his creative weight in gold.

---

[7] If you didn't grow up bored, in the U.K. in the mid-afternoon you might now know that this is a popular Channel 4 game show called Countdown with a very catchy song to distract you whilst the clock ticks.

About the Cover Image

Right from when I first started talking about this book, I thought I'd try and make it seem like a more tangible entity. I decided that a sure-fire way to do that was for it to have a temporary cover during the production stages. I figured that would make it look 'a bit more bookish' right from the get-go. So, I popped on over to Canva and played about on there for 10 minutes. I came up with a cover mock-up which I thought looked pretty cool and demonstrated a kind of solo journey. It was only ever supposed to be a holding cover until I could get my usual cover creator, a.k.a , my husband, on the case. Except it turned out you'd all had your heads turned by the working one and it already felt like part of the family, so I decided to stick with the 'temporary' cover. I hope you like it. Even the random bird at the top who also makes guest appearances throughout.

About the Book Design

When the Clin Psych Collective was published I ran a competition to win a 1:1 coaching session with me. To enter, people just had to send me their verified purchase review from Amazon. I recall one of the entries specifically because it was a slight puzzle to me. The contents of the review were glowing, superbly positive stuff, but it only had 4 stars rather than 5. I gently enquired:

"What could the book have done to win that final star?"

The reviewer responded that the layout and book style had been a bit uninspiring. The design had been all my own but to Chrissie, My Editorial Assistant, it felt like a bit of a kick to us and went to lick her wounds, but it set me thinking:

"How can I do better next time?"

So, this time around I decided to jazz it up a bit. I've really gone to town on the memo style and thought more about the aesthetics of the stories too. Where they lent themselves to it, I've added graphics to some of the accounts. As I write this it's also my intention that the hardback version is available in full colour because some of them are a thing of beauty!

I hope you like the content as well as the style.

Amazon and Good Reads reviews are always so humbly received as they:

1) Help books be shown higher up in search rankings
2) Tell me that you like the content I'm creating and I'm pitching it at the right level for where you're at right now.

14

About the Stories

I have always been drawn to people and their stories. When my husband and I went on our first date[8] he was amazed that I chatted freely and happily to people working in shops, people serving in stores, people on beauty counters. Wherever I go I love speaking with people and learning about them and the way they see the world. Even outside of therapy situations it's not uncommon for people to say,

"I can't believe I told you that – no-one else knows that!"

In fact, that happened as recently as last week with someone I've so far only met socially twice.

When I put The Grief Collective book together it felt like such a privilege that so many people trusted me with some of their most painful reflections and observations about incredibly difficult times in their lives. At the time I wanted the stories to be so incredibly authentic and unless what authors had written didn't make sense, I was reluctant to change much at all.

With the next book came a little more editorial input but because the majority of the contributors were themselves qualified psychologists it didn't necessarily feel too appropriate to go to town on suggesting big edits and re-writes.

However, this time around I felt that it was really important to have each story be the best it could be. Some of the stories were golden nuggets of reflective prose that required little more than

---

[8] Shopping and lunch in Stratford-Upon-Avon in case you're wondering!

formatting and some support in reducing repetition. Turns out in a book about our wonderful profession the words:

- Job
- Master's
- & undergraduate

Can get pretty samey!

It was important to me that each account was as engaging as possible and often that it was reading like a conversation to you, the reader. I wanted you to be able to get a feel for each individual Aspiring Psychologist so that you got a flavour for how they see the world and what shaped their experiences.
Therefore, upon reading some of the originally submitted stories I could see there was beauty within them, but they needed a little, and sometimes a lot, of tweaking to help them really come to life in glorious Psychology-technicolour. So that's the way this book has come together.

If you ask anyone who has worked with me as an Assistant, Honorary or Trainee Psychologist what I'm like about reports and letters they might well do the 'plumber's tooth suck' sound they do when you ask them how much that leaky tap is going to cost to fix. Yep, I have pretty high standards, which is ironic considering I just started that sentence with the word 'yep'. However, if you then ask the same person whether they had become a better writer by the time they finished working with me then I would say, based upon my own little review system, and the feedback they've given me, that the answers would be a unanimous yes. I make these points here because I firmly believe that anyone advancing into higher level professional

Psychology needs to be able to write well. This stuff matters. We have the honour and privilege of conveying incredibly important and complex information to our clients. We must be able to do so sensitively, coherently, and concisely. I think that the standard of the published narratives in this Collective demonstrate a good standard of written work. I hope that they will hold your attention well, feel like a pleasure to immerse yourself in and that you'll be able to easily comprehend the take home points from each story. You should also be able to see the author jump off the page at you and have a sense that only they could have written it because it's uniquely about them.

This is not to suggest that if you are dyslexic or have other additional needs that you can't make a wicked psychologist. You most definitely can, in fact, my LinkedIn buddy and podcast guest Dr Deborah Kingston, was diagnosed as dyslexic and is a glorious psychologist. Her advice in the podcast was that if you need extra support with your written work that you firstly acknowledge that and secondly ask for the help you need in order for you to meet the required standards. This might mean that you have to start your assignments and reports ahead of schedule to give yourself the additional time to get it all sorted. My own top tips in this area are:

- When you're really in the flow for report writing you might well find it helpful to create a template with sentences to complete for each client. This can prompt you to at least start paragraphs and sentences in a way you already know stands a good chance of making sense.
- Setting your word or pages language to British rather than American English is going to save you so much time if you're working in the U.K.

- Consider using a computer programme such as Grammarly, Linguix or WordTune. In a nutshell they automatically take what you've written and make it better! As an added bonus I believe they also check plagiarism for you!

I contacted Dr Deborah to check she was okay with me mentioning this and she also wanted to add:

"I think some courses are harder on those with a difficulty and in some way want to "make them better" and it's "tough love". I've learnt loads. I am a better writer. But on a bad dyslexic day that all goes in the bin, and I struggle to put a sentence together.

I just think we have to remember that although good writing skills can be taught, the brain doesn't always support that learning. On days like this: step away from the keyboard or put the note pad down. Reconnect with your body. Try grounding techniques/breathing exercises. Whatever works for you to get your diaphragm to work. Notice what you're stressed about. For me, if I go for a run or a brisk walk it's like I've re-regulated my brain and I stand a better chance of writing. Personally, I always get reports proofread."

I am so grateful to Dr Deborah for her warmth and support of me and my work and for her kindness in allowing me to share this with you.

Speaking of the written word and high standards..... In this book, you will notice that a few stories have used the word 'gotten'. Generally speaking, I'm not down with that, because I think it's an American word and not one we typically use in the

U.K. However, it seems it's something the cool kids are doing and because I wanted this book to contain authentic accounts, I've turned a blind eye to it. I also used to be hot on never using a comma before the word "and".[9] Sorry to all of my previous assistants, turns out I've broken my own rules on that left right and centre in this book!

We've also kept the tone well written but conversational so usual rules for formal writing most definitely don't apply. I seem to recall we've started sentences with "and's", had proper noun faffs, and all sorts. I so hope that you will enjoy this book and that our grammatical transgressions will make it all the more human and 'eat with a spoon straight from the tub' in style.

---

[9] Chrissie, my Editorial Assistant, loves the Oxford comma!

Autoethnography

In October 2021 I was delighted when Professor Jerome Carson of Bolton University got in touch with me. He told me that he loved The Clinical Psychologist Collective book and that it was wonderful to see autoethnography being used in this way. Well, I gave that a quick google and Wikipedia informed me that:

*"**Autoethnography** is a form of qualitative research in which an author uses self-reflection and writing to explore anecdotal and personal experience and connect this autobiographical story to wider cultural, political, and social meanings and understandings."*

Well! I was just blown away and so pleased – that's exactly what The Clinical Psychologist Collective and Grief Collective books have been all about. Totally hit the nail on the head and yet it was a term I either was never taught or it's fallen out of my head somewhere over the years since I qualified – quite possibly the latter!

So, whilst taking part in research has been on the to-do list since qualification but not yet been ticked off, it is wonderful to be doing something which might aid people's understanding of this wild but wonderful ride we call Psychology.

Thank you so much Professor Jerome!

Why Support Aspiring Psychologists?

I loved being an Aspiring Psychologist and since qualifying I have always loved spending time and spreading wisdom and compassion to more junior staff members. When I worked in the NHS, it was imperative for me that I spend time with new trainees and assistants so that they felt supported. In 2019, I did a series of free Q&A sessions to support the DClinPsy application season. It was well received and so after a while I gave myself permission to go ahead with the idea which had been rattling around in my head for a while. That idea was The Clinical Psychologist Collective book and that was also met with lots of great feedback.

I have always believed that people striving for a career in Psychology should have access to really great content which is free. So, before too long I started to think about creating a podcast.

Thereafter, people began asking how they could work with me and benefit from the way I think about things. This led to the birth of the Aspiring Psychologist Membership.

The warmth and appreciation of my work in this area has been one of my greatest professional pleasures to date. I love hearing that particular parts of book or podcast episodes have really resonated with you. People often contact me after watching the lives to let me know that they tried out one of the strategies I suggested and that it really helped them to generate great ideas for cracking on with their form or preparing for an interview or application. I love knowing that what I am doing is meeting you at the right level for where you are and for where your pain points are. Don't be shy – if you'd like me to create some specific content either as a podcast episode, reel or LIVE slip into my DM's and I'll do my best to make it happen!

Free Essential Guide to DClinPsy

To accompany this book, I have written a free downloadable guide.

It is called 'The Essential Guide to The DClinPsy Application Process'.
To get your hands on a copy head to:

https://www.goodthinkingPsychology.co.uk/free-dclinpsy-guide

Free Supervision Shaping Tool

I also have a free supervision shaping tool available. This can help you to set up supervision relationships optimally right from the start.
To get your hands on a copy head to:
https://www.goodthinkingpsychology.co.uk/supervision

The Clinical Psychologist Collective

The Clinical Psychologist Collective book is the elder sibling to this one. You absolutely don't need to have read one to enjoy the other though.

When The Clinical Psychologist Collective was published, I loved it and I think it is wonderfully useful. However, as time went on, I was conscious that I didn't only want to tell one side of the story and I was aware that the people likely to also be reading it in their homes also had very important stories to tell. It also watered some seeds I'd planted earlier in my career.......

When I was an Assistant Psychologist (AP) at St Andrew's Healthcare I came up with the concept of "The Assistant Psychologist Skills Exchange". It was born upon my realisation when watching monthly presentations at our AP meetings and:

 a) being totally blown away by the skills, talent and aptitude of my incredible colleagues working in the same hospital but within different directorates,
b) being kind of in awe;
c) feeling not good enough...

I reflected that as an AP I was also doing pretty cool stuff too and that to an outsider perhaps I looked equally competent? So, I came up with the idea that it would be great to arrange a shadow rota to share best practices and exchange skills and tips.

Like what often happens to best laid plans, by the time this was agreed by management, I was ready to start a new job for a different employer. But I think the very first seeds being planted for this book were sewn at that time. I even toyed around with the idea of calling this one "The Assistant Psychologist Skills Exchange' but very firmly was told by you guys that AP roles are NOT the only route to becoming a qualified psychologist and so I wanted to make this more inclusive.

Interestingly, when I first mentioned this current project on LinkedIn one of the first comments I received was "Yes! I knew this would be your next book!" I was like "I wish you'd told me, cos I'd have started it sooner!"

The Aspiring Psychologist Podcast

In late Autumn 2021, I suddenly thought "I could probably start a podcast for Aspiring Psychologists. Oh! But what should I call it? Oh yes, let's not sweat that one – let's keep it simple and transparent:

The Aspiring Psychologist Podcast

At the time of writing this section there are 42 episodes of the podcast. All episodes can be found on your favourite podcast hangouts including:

- Apple Podcasts
- Spotify
- Google Podcasts
- Amazon Music
- My website!

I know you lead busy lives, so I'll list them here in case you want to listen to a specific one you've missed.

Ep	Title / Content
1	Making the most of 'not that relevant' experience
2	Making the most of supervision and the supervisory relationship
3	Navigating life events as an Aspiring Psychologist
4	Self-compassion as an Aspiring Psychologist
5	Creating opportunities for teaching, training & consultation
6	Developing skills in non-invasive history taking
7	Using outcome measures

If you'd like to submit a request for a specific episode or suggest a guest for me to approach then please head to:
www.goodthinkingPsychology.co.uk/podcast

The Aspiring Psychologist Membership

Gaining the right experience on your journey to becoming a qualified psychologist is not always easy. It's often about the opportunities close to you and also the quality and compassion of the more senior people you'll meet along the way.

If you could dream of being optimally supported and to be able to gain the opportunities to be able to gain insight, confidence and experience along your journey it might well feature:

- A non-judgmental space
- The chance to learn professionally but informally
- A chance to reflect and to watch others do the same
- The chance to learn and gain exposure to key approaches including:
- Cognitive Behavioural Therapy CBT)
- Compassion[10] Focused Therapy (CFT)
- Cognitive Analytic Therapy, (CAT)
- Psychodynamic Frameworks
- Formulation
- Research
- Reflection
- Wellbeing activities including mindfulness

---

[10] Spooky, just as I typed the word 'compassion' I heard some archive footage of the Queen saying the same word on the TV in the background as I'm working.

Hold on, shouldn't all this be free?

W hen The Clinical Psychologist was published I was asked by a fellow qualified psychologist:

"Hold on, shouldn't all of this stuff be free?"

Well, this is a bit of a prickly pear.

I am first a foremost a human and a pretty nice one at that, I am next a Clinical Psychologist and also a wonderfully proud business owner. Since April 2021 I have been solely self-employed. I'm also the Mummy of 2 young boys. As much as I would love all of the things I need to raise them, and to feed, clothe and stop myself from shivering to be free, they're also not.

Even for my free content there are costs incurred by me such as:

- Software
- Transcribing
- Virtual Assistant Support
- Assistant Psychologist Support
- Media Coaching fees
- My own time

It's difficult to begin to estimate how many hundreds of unpaid hours I have spent working on this one book alone. I've also hired my editorial assistant to proofread it all for me too. When running a business there are always costs and if profit is not made then a business will fail. I don't wish for my business to fail because I love what I do, and I want to be able to keep doing it.

I pledge to always offer free content, including the podcast, my free Q&A sessions and my social content. It's entirely okay if people want to access the free stuff and can't afford or don't want to engage with the paid options. But if it's your time and you're ready for support to get to the next step, then I have a variety of options to help you to strive for your goals.

Anonymity

Some contributors were happy for their full names and contact details to be listed whilst others preferred just their first name or a pseudonym. All contributors have consented for their story to appear within this book.

Use of Acronyms

If there's one thing you'll soon learn in the Psychology field it's that there are a LOT of acronyms. Sometimes no matter how much you scratch your head you can't for the life of you figure out what the heck it might mean.

For that reason, within each story in this book all terms are first used in full and then immediately placed in brackets as the acronym. If used again within the story in most cases just the abbreviated letters will be used.

We have added a handy reference guide called Acronym Busting, which you will find at the end of this book.

A Note on ASD/ASC Acronyms

The acronyms ASD and ASC relate to:
- Autistic Spectrum Disorder
- Autistic Spectrum Condition

When I worked in CAMHS[11] we tended to speak about ASCs with parents as to refer to people with disorders could seem quite pejorative.

Within this book, I wanted to reflect the current themes for these titles within the services which support clients and their families. To that end I checked with a friend and previous colleague who advised:

---

[11] Oh look, how ironic that I didn't add the full title here, it does of course refer to Child & Adolescent Mental Health Services.

"I use the DSM 5 term autism spectrum disorder to reflect that I work in healthcare settings, and that is the diagnostic term that professionals use.

ASC describes the same 'condition' but some people with ASD, or teachers, or professionals in social care settings use ASC as they do not like the word 'disorder'. They often say it has a negative connotation as this reflects 'difficulty' rather than highlighting a persons' 'strengths.' So, maybe which term you use will depend on who the book is for?"

I decided that I would leave the author of the story to decide whether to use ASD or ASC, so the terms are used interchangeably within this book. In future, you can use the term which sits best for yourself and for the clients you work with.

The Stories

1

- Georgina's Story -

You Can Do It Too!

My name is Georgina, I am 27 years old and this is the story of how I achieved my dream of securing a place on the Clinical Psychology Doctorate 2022 intake. Now I know what you are thinking – why has she pulled a Hamilton and told us how the story ends in the introduction? Well, I think as Aspiring Psychologists we are often so focused on the end goal that we don't take the time to enjoy the journey; I know I am certainly guilty of this. Being human is complicated and non-linear, and there have been many bumps, obstacles, and nuances along the way that I doubt I can give justice to in this chapter. But my hope is that in starting this way, we can all appreciate the road a little more, myself included.

My journey into Psychology started in childhood. My interest and passion for mental health was sparked by experiencing mental illness and the toll this has taken upon my own family. During my teenage years, I wanted to understand and help them, and it was during this time I also began experiencing anxiety and depression. I became fascinated with documentaries on mental illness and when the opportunity arose for me to study Psychology formally at A level I jumped at the chance. My passion for Psychology only grew with age and in 2017 I graduated with a BSc in Psychology with Sociology.

Upon graduating, I knew that I wanted to work in mental healthcare, a desire that was strengthened by my own lived experience of mental illness and admiration of the support I have received from services in various stages throughout my life. Upon graduating I struggled to know where to start in terms of gaining work experience to fulfil my dream. I was also in need of a stable job to financially support myself and my family, so I ended up working full-time in a customer service role at a stockbroker. Didn't see that coming? Me neither... Whilst this was never a career I envisaged myself in, it paid the bills and helped solidify in my mind that I wanted to pursue Psychology. Psychology called me like the ocean called Moana. I missed the subject so much that alongside my work I decided to study a part-time MSc in Forensic Psychology and Crime. This turned out to be a fantastic decision and a pivotal moment in my story as I made a friend on the course who was working as a Healthcare Assistant (HCA) in a mental health hospital. This experience opened my eyes to how I could start working towards a career in Psychology. When I told my employer at the stockbroker that I was leaving to work as an HCA they said it was the first time they had someone leave for that type of role – something I feel sums up this period of my career perfectly.

I changed roles a few times whilst continuing to study for and completing my MSc, with my progression looking like this:

- In 2018, I started my first clinical role as an HCA in Child & Adolescent Mental Health Services (CAMHS) inpatient units in a private mental health hospital.
- I then went on to work as a Senior Support Worker in the NHS on a forensic male medium secure unit.
- I then began working as a Support Time Recovery Worker in a community mental health team.

Were these the most glamorous or stimulating roles? At times no, but they gave me a great foundation, teaching me invaluable skills and allowing me to work with professionals from multiple disciplines. I experienced what it is like working on the 'frontline' and learnt how to manage the emotional and physical impact of shift work. I've been led to believe these skills will also come in handy in future when navigating the Doctorate and motherhood. It was within these roles that for the first time I experienced our service users seeming to demonstrate increased trust towards me. In turn I was rewarded with some of my most interesting conversations yet. I truly believe these types of roles are wholly relevant and essential to Psychology and that they helped shape the clinician I am today. I so wish they were valued more both financially and professionally. It was also during this time that I decided Clinical Psychology was the particular Psychology route I wanted to strive for. This was not an easy decision as I have always been acutely aware of how competitive Psychology is, and Clinical Psychology often feels like the most competitive of all, but I knew that was where my passion truly lay.

In June 2021 I secured my first Assistant Psychologist position working within a new wellbeing hub set up to support NHS and Social Care Workers during the COVID-19 pandemic. This is the role I am in as I write this in August 2022 and I'm still thoroughly enjoying it. This post has been incredibly rewarding both personally and professionally. I have been very lucky to be surrounded by an incredibly supportive team and this gave me the confidence to apply for the clinical Doctorate for the first time. I'd heard stories about how difficult the process would be, so I had mentally prepared myself for this being a 'practice run.' I received three straight rejections and one remote interview. In the weeks leading up to interview I found out I needed to find a new place to live, and I was also very unwell with COVID. It felt like the odds were stacked up against me, but as Dolly Parton taught us:

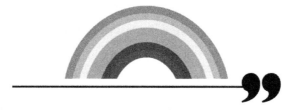

If you want the rainbow, you gotta put up with the rain.

There were many times when I thought about giving up and the self-doubt really began to creep in, but with the support of my colleagues, friends, and family I was able to persevere.

Boy was there a rainbow heading my way because incredibly that remote interview materialised into an offer of a place on the course. Just after receiving the acceptance letter, I facetimed my boyfriend and squealed with delight for what felt like an instance and a lifetime at once. I actually found out this life altering news when I was at work and about to go into a meeting. Well, the squealing continued because I couldn't contain my excitement and had to tell everyone immediately! To say I was shocked would be an understatement.

Here's the things I did in my disbelief:
- Read and re-read the offer letter multiple times
- Asked my boyfriend to read the letter and confirm I hadn't imagined it.
- Logged into my clearing house account to do a definite check!

The answer seemed unanimous: I had been offered a place. But it was A LOT to assimilate to! With some time to process what happened and reflect, it de-mystified the DClinPsy application process for me; I always saw the Doctorate as this unattainable and magical thing, and I never thought I would be successful after one interview. But I did it and you can too! I know I am the exception, not the rule, but I do think it is important to highlight the positive experiences too so that it does not feel like such a scary endeavour.

So, here I am preparing to start the Doctorate, to move again for the second time this year and uproot my life to a new city – honestly, I haven't ever lived outside my little town let alone the county! As the interview was virtual, I didn't even get to visit the university and it is odd to accept a job/place on a three-year course in these circumstances. I am nervous and scared and there is a lot of uncertainty and unknowns, but I am so excited to embark on this next chapter of my life and see what this adventure brings. Who knows, maybe I'll write about that one day.

Now for the serious part. Something I really wanted to convey with my story is that lived experience of mental illness should not be a stumbling block in working with Psychology, but rather should be seen as an asset and unique contribution to psychological services. As I have mentioned, I have experienced mental illness since adolescence, and I have had periods of ebbs and flows with my mental health. I often feared I was too 'broken' to work in Psychology. However, I have learnt that my own lived experience has helped me in many ways on my voyage into this world. It has helped me to see the amazing work that is being done within mental health services, but also the gaps, from a service user perspective. It allows me to relate to my clients in ways I otherwise wouldn't be able to and gives me insight into how they may be feeling on the receiving end of psychological support. And my experience and expertise can be used to help shape and improve services. Don't get me wrong, it has been a difficult journey, my mental illness has felt debilitating at times, and I have had many nights where I have felt like I was not good enough. However, with the right support in place this has never had a detrimental effect on my work. Unfortunately, there is still stigma around disclosing mental health conditions and some teams are less accommodating than others, but my experience has generally been positive. My employers have for the most part welcomed me and made reasonable adjustments to support me in optimising my unique skillset, whilst also looking after myself and our service users. My experience of applying for the Doctorate this year has been equally supportive and I am hopeful this will continue when I begin the course. I hope that this may give someone in a similar position the hope and confidence they need to keep pushing forward by sharing my story.

If someone told me even a year ago that I would be writing a story for a book I never would have believed them. I am sure I will look back on this in years to come with joy, with pride, and with many, many critiques. I feel like I have achieved a lot in my 27 years, but I am sure this is just the beginning and as a wise person[12] once sang, 'there's just no telling how far I'll go!' But for now, I am excited to add writer to the list of roles I adopt, alongside daughter, musical theatre aficionado, partner, begrudging gym goer, exceptional cook[13], aunt, true crime enthusiast, incoming trainee Clinical Psychologist, board game player[14], friend, Olympics lover (I know curveball), yogi, and Lin-Manuel Miranda superfan, to name but a few.

Anyway - enough about me, mine is just one in a sea of billions of stories. What about you? Where is your path headed? What awesome things have you done on the way? I hope I get to hear about it one day. Celebrate every small victory and milestone. Psychology can be a tough industry, but you got this.

---

[12] Oh, go on then…. It's totally Moana again, but she's right!
[13] If I do say so myself – which I do!
[14] Marianne's little note: I'd totally beat you at Downfall!

MEMO

Dear Georgina,

Thanks so much for your story and for helping others to have faith and hope that first time application successes are indeed possible.

Even within the last 2 weeks since we've been collaborating on the edit for your story it's been such a pleasure to watch you grow. You've really seemed to develop your confidence for your new upcoming role and in being yourself and holding your head high. I have to confess that I am now listening to the Moana soundtrack all over again, it's a lovely blast from the past from when my boys were small! I find myself thinking about you:

"Our people will need a chief and there you are!"
and
"And when we look to the future, there you are!"

I hope you really enjoy your training and getting to know the new place you will be moving to! It sounds pretty exciting!

Thanks again, Marianne

DR MARIANNE TRENT
www.goodthinkingpsychology.co.uk

44

2

- Kai's Story -

Balancing a Dual Career in Psychology and Sport

"Hi, I'm Kai and I'm the new Assistant Psychologist!"

This is a sentence I have repeated a lot over the last couple of weeks and one that every time I say it, it doesn't seem real. I have recently been appointed to my first Assistant Psychologist (AP) role and at the time of writing this I am two weeks into it. Imposter syndrome is high, but I am equally excited to get stuck in. How did I get here? It all seems a bit of a blur, but I will try to give a summary.

I did pretty rubbish in my GCSEs, but I did just scrape by and get what I needed to study my A levels. I originally picked:

- Psychology
- Sociology
- Business
- Biology

But I dropped Business for Geography and then also dropped Biology. This was because I felt unable to balance my sporting career with my education. But don't worry, we'll get onto sport later! So, I ended up studying:

- Psychology
- Sociology
- Geography

When it came to education, I was a bit of a late bloomer achieving AAB in my A levels. This was enough to get me into the University of Warwick to study BSc in Psychology. Unfortunately, during my second year COVID-19 struck and my university experience quickly sucked. But I saw an opportunity and whilst studying from home I also volunteered at a local Dementia Day care service. This then turned into a paid job. In total I worked here for 8 months until I moved back to university to focus on the last two terms of the third year. During this latter stage of my degree, I was also a research assistant looking at the effects of the pandemic on Key Workers. It was a great experience because it was international research which meant we had to communicate with researchers all over the world.

Like all people in my year group, I finished university by clicking the 'submit exam' button. In my case it was on a random Wednesday at 2am (24-hour exam) but I WAS DONE. I graduated with a 2:1 which I was happy with as I got what I needed but I also got 68.8% in total and with most Universities moving you up a grade within 1%, I see this as being 0.2% off a first class. I applied to a master's in Clinical Psychology which offered a placement opportunity as an Assistant Psychologist. I was placed on the waiting list but was eventually unsuccessful. My feedback advised that at interview I hadn't given enough depth in my answers. This highlighted for me that I didn't have enough experience to be able to go into depth. So, I accepted it and moved on.

Then came what seemed like application and interview season:

- Straight out of university I applied for Assistant Psychologist jobs and although I knew they were competitive, I quickly realised that I wasn't going to get one based on my experience so far.
- I then started applying to support worker (SW) roles. I got an interview at a stroke unit but was rejected as another candidate had more experience. It's like the Groundhog Day paradox: how am I going to get experience without someone giving me experience?
- Next came a SW interview at a local medium secure forensic hospital. I don't mind telling you that this was the worst interview of my life! With hindsight I think I was overwhelmed by the setting with all the airlocks and

security. It was all so unfamiliar it just exacerbated my nerves. Somehow and I mean SOMEHOW, I was successful in this interview and started a couple of months later. Upon reflection, although this was my first full-time mental health job, I learnt an unfathomable amount and I would happily say I learnt more about mental health in this role than during the three years of my degree and I only worked here for a year!

- I also joined the bank service and worked in Children and Adolescent Mental Health Services, (CAMHS) and Psychiatric Intensive Care Unit (PICU).

After a year had gone by, I applied to the same Master's, this time with more experience but once again I was put on the waiting list again. Slightly different feedback this time being that my academic interview answers were weak. After a year of not being at university I accepted this but was of course frustrated. At this time, I had read some advice which said for your first Assistant job it's about the quantity of applications, so I took this on board and applied to 43 posts! At this point I metaphorically stuck two fingers up to this master's and I began applying to every Assistant Psychologist job under the sun. I felt like I had the right experience by this point so I wanted to see if I could even get at least one interview! I did this by having draft applications (supporting information) saved in categories dependent on the settings on the job. For example, if the job I was applying for was forensic, I had a draft forensic application saved and then after a few small changes to mention the job specifically, I was able to send off the application. Although this was a long process, I landed 6 interviews in total. Some I couldn't attend and so turned them down and some I was on shift at my job so had to do them from my car. I'm sure you can imagine that this didn't go too well but it was all good experience! Happily, I finally had an interview which I could do from my home on a day off and it went like a dream: I gave good answers and had robust examples of my experience for most of the questions asked. When I tell you luck was on my side, I mean it. I didn't get offered this role but a few days later I got an email saying another AP role has become available in the service and I would be the next employable candidate. They did have to open the role up again though due to it being new and because it was internal only, they didn't have many to interview (in fact they had one). After an incredibly anxious few weeks (and after this other candidate dropped out the day before their interview) I WAS OFFERED MY FIRST ASSISTANT PSYCHOLOGIST JOB!!!

I started two weeks ago and am loving being in my first job on the Psychology career ladder. I am in a community learning disability team. My initial impression is that it is a hell of a lot slower than working as a support worker in an inpatient ward but as we have a huge Psychology waiting list, I am sure I will soon be very busy. My advice for those wanting an Assistant Psychologist job would be:

- For your first AP job, apply to as many as you can. Rejection is pretty par for the course. I was rejected 45 times before landing my first[15].
- Whilst you're at university seek as many opportunities as possible. Be a research assistant if you can, go to talks by practicing psychologists, do whatever you can to learn.

---

[15] Wow! That seems weird writing that haha!

- Be a support worker or something similar – if I had the option to redo my journey so far, I would join my NHS bank team close to university and do a few shifts a month to get some money whilst gaining valuable experience too.

What makes my story a bit different from others is that this isn't my only career. During all of this I have been balancing a dual career as a semi-professional athlete in Archery.

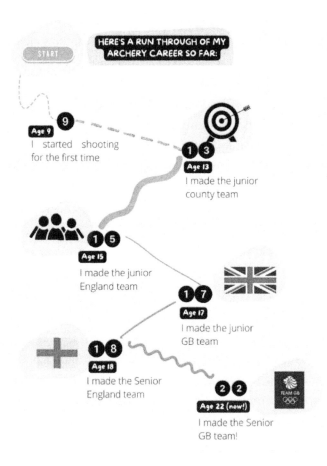

HERE'S A RUN THROUGH OF MY ARCHERY CAREER SO FAR:

START

Age 9
I started shooting for the first time

Age 13
I made the junior county team

Age 15
I made the junior England team

Age 17
I made the junior GB team

Age 18
I made the Senior England team

Age 22 (now!)
I made the Senior GB team!

I can't lie to you, trying to balance achieving a career in the stupidly competitive career of Clinical Psychology and also trying to make the British team in the sport I love has been disgustingly hard, but so far, I have done it! If there were clashes in the two, I have always put my education first (which at times has been hard) but my parents have always happily supported this. Like me, they see that if I were to be injured or anything else happened which meant I couldn't shoot anymore I would need a backup option. Luckily, a lot of the international competition calendar has fallen during the summer holidays. Where events have fallen within term time my schools and Universities have been supportive and flexible. They have allowed me to move deadlines or miss classes to be able to attend the competitions. Currently I am ranked 2nd in Britain and am lined up to hopefully compete at the 2026 Commonwealth Games and the 2028 Olympic Games.

So, if you are also into sport and manage to find yourself in the same position as me here is some advice for wanting to get into Clinical Psychology:

- If you do find yourself talking about your sporting career in Psychology interviews, link the s**t out of it to how it will help you in the role! A question I tend to put this in is surrounding time management skills, or if they are interested in what you do outside of work to see if you can "switch off from Psychology". Aside from these areas I would probably say avoid speaking about it and focus on your clinical/educational experiences.

- Unfortunately, as you already probably know your social life will have to suffer a bit. You will see your friends going out on nights out and having fun whilst you're busy preparing for or being at a competition. It's probably worth saying here that alcohol is a banned performance enhancer in Archery so as a young man I understand this even more! I know on paper it sounds boring, but it makes winning those medals so much sweeter.

- Have SMART[16] goals in both your Psychology career and in your sporting career and use your time management skills to figure out exactly how you're going to hit those goals. If you struggle at any stage, don't panic! Keep at it and you will get there even if you have to prioritise it in front of other things.
- Have a to do list; a weekly or yearly planner and make sure you're achieving what's most important to YOU and not anyone else.
- If you go away to a competition, make sure that you are fully organised for when you leave and that you have a plan to get back on track when you return.
- Finally seek advice from everyone and anyone. Anyone can help you in their own way, it doesn't matter if it is a big or small. Any advice is good advice.

I hope that something in this ramble about Psychology and sports helps someone out there and I wish everyone reading this the best in their careers.

Kai Thomas-Prause
Assistant Psychologist & GB Athlete

---

[16] Specific, Measurable, Achievable, Realistic, Time Focused

Dr Marianne Trent (She/Her) • 3:32 PM

Dear Kai,

Thanks so much for your story and for connecting with me on LinkedIn. I love that you just casually drop in there that you're ranked second in Great Britain! This is incredible and alongside another fiercely competitive career in psychology you really are doing great things. I once worked with someone on the English Deaf Cricket team, and I used to love chatting with him about it all and seeing how he managed to jostle it alongside his traditional career too.

Wishing you so well for everything you do, especially remembering everyone's names at your shiny new AP job - that's something I used to lose sleep over! I will watch your archery career unfold with eager interest and everything crossed for you and Team GB!

Thanks again,
Marianne

3

- Lydia's Story -

A Healthy Balance

For many professionals in a position of care, empathy is one of the most important skills they display. On the surface, it is easy to assume that caring professionals have the answers and solutions for every problem; that their optimism, empathy, resilience, and calming nature is a natural born skill. It is easy to assume that people who show these skills could not have ever experienced difficulties; that they have no true understanding of hardship. The reality is that we never truly know someone else's story. We never know the experiences that have shaped someone whether that's joyful memories or disastrous ones.

My journey towards becoming a psychologist has not been straightforward. I did not even know that is what I wanted to do with myself but every choice I've made in my work and my education seems to have been leading me down that path.
My childhood was alternative and by today's standards a little bit atypical. My dad is a trained psychotherapist, and my mum is a qualified social worker in child protection. My parents divorced

when I was nine years old and by age 13 my mum remarried. My stepdad and his family accepted my three siblings and opened his heart to us all. Many of my childhood conversations revolved around 'why people behave the way they do.' On reflection, this is where my formulation skills began to develop - in my understanding of behaviours.

After school I decided to pursue topics that interested me. I studied Psychology, English Literature, and History at AS Level. I would describe myself as being intelligent but being the middle child of four I am also very outspoken. I enjoyed education but me being me, or as my dad would say, me being difficult just because I can be, meant that education was not always easy for me. I found AS-Levels difficult. They were very exam heavy, and I found it difficult to express my curiosity and felt unable to question certain theories or aspects because the examiners were looking for specific answers. Surprisingly, I failed all my AS-Levels including Psychology yet here I am: still pursuing this career path. I decided to complete a BTEC Extended Diploma, and my career developed further. I completed a three-month placement with a local authority child service. I completed risk assessments, visiting families and supervising family contacts. I learnt about safeguarding, risk, and childhood development.
I was not sure what I wanted to do after college. I worked three part-time jobs whilst studying and had an active social life. I was enjoying being young, so I decided to choose a topic that interested me and very last minute pursued Forensic Psychology at Leeds Trinity University.

My university experience was an interesting one. I had the most amazing education experience. I was part of a small cohort, and all my lecturers knew me personally. They were so supportive and actively encouraged my critical thinking and my ability to reflect. I was also lucky because my university required every student to complete a placement. I was fortunate to secure mine working with a charity who supported the resettlement of offenders within the community and were nearing release from prison. The placement offered me permanent employment following completion and I continued working here part-time during my studies. This is still one of my proudest achievements. I think the fact that I secured employment whilst in my first year is a good example of my work ethic; my enthusiasm and passion for a career supporting others, as well as some key people skills - my empathy, my confidence and my ability to build rapport quickly.

For many, university is the time where social lives thrive. This was an area that was particularly difficult for me. As mentioned, my alternative upbringing meant my outlook on life was different. I found it difficult to relate to my peers and this had a profound impact on my social life, and my self-esteem. I was quite badly bullied - even anonymous online bullying. I was also managing a lot of stress within my family. I was actively supporting a family member who was struggling with their own mental health as well as trying to manage my own. University was a big adjustment for me. Going from being a young, carefree 18-year-old with an active social life to being away from home with no friends whilst working and studying was difficult.

Going into my second year of university, things continued to be hard. I unfortunately lost my grandparents. They were two of the kindest people I had ever met and despite not being blood relatives they accepted me and my three siblings (bear in mind we are very outspoken and opinionated) as their own, with such open arms and hearts. My second year continued to be testing. It was a combination of stress that resulted in a continuous battle with tonsillitis so much so for the first time in my life I was hospitalised. This is when my health deteriorated significantly. My hospital stays became regular - practically every month over a year and a half. I started showing symptoms of a 'mystery illness' that baffled many consultants and doctors. The care I received and still receive from St James' University Hospital is impeccable. They did not let me suffer in anyway - they are always on the other end of a phone, always there for me at every step of my diagnosis, treatment and 10 months later, major surgery. I was diagnosed with three autoimmune conditions and suddenly my view on life altered. My life, my future and my identity had completed flipped upside down. I had lost the luxury of being able to walk pain free. I had lost the ability to eat whatever I wanted, and I was dependent on steroids to keep me functioning. This was my first ever experience of hospital, antibiotics, and medication. I was 21 years old, just lost my grandparents, battling my own mental health, hours away from home and had no support network nearby.

Despite all this, I continued to study full-time. My tutors were so supportive and provided me with many extensions and the ability to continue learning without attending. I have very vivid memories of writing my university assignments in a hospital bed with all the needles, wires, drips, and machines hooked up to me. I also continued to work part-time when I could.

Ten months after being diagnosed my conditions had deteriorated, I was steroid dependent, and I was out of other treatment options. I was admitted to hospital for life saving and life altering surgery. My large bowel needed to be removed and I now live with a permanent stoma. By this point, I was in my third year of university recovering from major surgery and completing my dissertation from my hospital bed. I had to get my head around having lost an entire organ! Nine months after my operation I was able to graduate. I didn't graduate with my cohort, but even after all I had been through, I achieved an upper second-class honours degree! Even writing this I still get tears in my eyes because of the pride I have for myself. From being told I could die to walking along that stage with a huge smile across my face and hearing my parents shouting my name from the audience is an incredible memory; one I will never forget.

My university experience completed changed my life and changed how I work as a practitioner. It influenced my ability to be empathetic and tested my resilience; preparing me for the challenges I could face in my career. I started university as a young, carefree, 20-year-old female and graduated as a disabled 23-year-old whose physical health was never going to be the same again.

Following graduation, I worked as teaching assistant, supporting children with social, emotional and mental health needs. I did not realise it at the time, but looking back, my confidence had been knocked and I felt I could never succeed in the competitive world of Psychology. I was disabled and I believed I had not learned as much as I could have or should have whilst at university. I thought I was at a disadvantage to everyone else. Following the breakdown of a relationship I decided to take the plunge and apply for my first Assistant Psychologist post in 2019. It was a role on the other side of the country, and I did not even think I would get an interview. I thought the experience of the application would have been beneficial for me...but then

I got an interview. And I thought 'oh pants! What do I do next?' So, I prepared relentlessly and thought of examples of my work for every single question they could possibly ask. I booked a hotel and travelled by myself down to Oxfordshire the night before. I went with no pressure, thinking 'what will be will be.' The interview went well and by the end of the week I had secured my first ever Assistant Psychologist post on my first ever application! This was the moment that really confirmed a career in Psychology was for me. I packed up my little one bed flat and moved in with two people I'd found online who had a spare room. I was at a point in my life where I really thought things were finally falling into place. I thought 2020 was going to be my year of good luck! However, three months after I moved – COVID-19 hit! So here I was, yet again unable to go anywhere, do anything and having to work from home. But those two strangers became my best friends. Just like the rest of the country we spent our evenings having zoom parties, eating takeaways, and definitely got stuck into DIY projects. 2020 was also the year where I met my current partner. Working within Psychology, we always place an emphasis on the importance of 'emotional safety'. I was not sure what this really meant until I met my partner. I felt very quickly at ease and noticed I was more relaxed around him. Going from someone who was quite lonely to being around people who very quickly became like family to me was so comforting. My condition, my university experiences, my childhood had all impacted upon my identity. Before I lived here, I really did feel as though I was not good enough and like there was something wrong with me. But being stuck in a house with two amazing friends and my partner I learnt what unconditional love and emotional safety really meant. I experienced true happiness here and 2020 was another life changing year. Alongside this, I was working as an Assistant

Psychologist specialising in attachment disorder and developmental trauma. I was able to learn all about outcome measures, able to complete comprehensive psychological assessments and learned a bit of Neuropsychology. My psychological skills developed further. I spent 18 months in this role and by the end I was excelling and confident in my abilities. I was delivering training, child-focused consultations and representing the clinical team in meetings. My supervisors and colleagues were also incredible (shout out to the Oxfordshire 2020 Clinical Team). The one area I was lacking in was my skills in delivering interventions. I did apply for the Clinical Psychology Doctorate in 2020/2021 but it was more of a trial run.

Clinical Psychology is always going to be my dream career path, but I don't want to put my personal life on hold to achieve that. By 2021, I was 25 years old. I wanted to find a way to become a brilliant practitioner, learn new skills and to start settling down. I decided to apply for a trainee psychological wellbeing practitioner role - this one was closer to my parents and closer to the county myself and my partner wanted to buy a house. As I am writing this it's May 2022 and I am about to start my eighth month as a trainee PWP. I have learnt the basics of cognitive behaviour therapy and delivered a variety of interventions to support those experiencing common mental health difficulties. I've developed my ability to manage distress, overcome barriers to change and increase levels of engagement. I have received excellent feedback from my supervisor and am already actively being encouraged to apply for supervisor training before high-intensity training once I am qualified.

My health continues to be rocky, and my life continues to be challenging However, my experiences have shaped me professionally and personally. I wake up every day feeling grateful for what I have and who I am. I no longer look at my disability as a disadvantage but as part of me. I have more confidence in myself and my skillset. I have somehow managed to succeed in every single career opportunity I have been given and this confirms that a career in Psychology is right for me.

Lydia Macallan
Trainee Psychological Wellbeing Practitioner

Oh Lydia!

Reading your story, when you walked across that stage on your graduation, I had a visceral reaction with some goose-bumps because it was so emotive! I welled up for you! You are an inspiration and a sensation. I feel so fortunate to be able to read more about you and I'm so sorry that the hurdles and obstacles you have had to navigate your way through and across have been such big ones. I am so excited to follow the next steps in your Psychology career and please know that you are doing great things and that your current and future clients, colleagues and friends will benefit so much from the insight, support and compassion you are able to offer.

I'm so pleased that along your way you met your incredible housemates and your partner too. Here's to your glittering future and absolutely showcasing that Stoma surgery can be viewed as life punctuation, and not the end of striving and achieving. I think you are a marvel and I know that you and your story will be an absolute compassionate inspiration for anyone going through adversity on their way to becoming a qualified Psychologist. Thank you!

Marianne, x

4

- Kirsty's Story -

Enjoying the Journey Counts for So Much

My journey from being an Aspiring Psychologist. to being offered a position on the Clinical Psychology Doctorate, has been a varied one. It also took 5 application cycles and involved a lot of tenacity. Reflecting on this, I can safely say that I always applied and chose jobs that I felt would fit my personality or interests, but most importantly gave me the chance to have a life alongside work. This is something I always advocate for when others say they are keen to know what experience might be 'relevant'. Initially, I thought that an Assistant Psychologist role was the 'gold standard' for what was required, but I learnt that enjoying varied roles meant much more than going for a role that perhaps had the title but not the experience I was looking for - I wanted to revel in the journey.

An important factor to know about my narrative is that I am from a working-class background, and I have relied upon scholarships to fund my education and paid roles to give me experience. The only volunteering I did was for the Alzheimer's Society as a befriender whilst studying my undergraduate degree during my study days. Undoubtedly this does bias my view against honorary positions that at the time were unattainable for me - but for some these may be invaluable. Another reflection is that I naturally seem to enjoy interviews (I love to talk and can be very opinionated)- and I think this has often helped with obtaining roles. I know for many of my Aspiring Psychologist peers, this route can come with varied amounts of rejections - and so I feel it is only fair to point out that for me this was limited. As an attempt to instil hope if you are finding rejections more plentiful than you'd like - I have four assistant applications which didn't result in interviews and an additional interview which didn't lead to a job offer. So please know, gaining experience is tough but absolutely doable!

My journey started early, whilst studying my BSc in Psychology. I obtained a bank healthcare assistant (HCA) role in a Private Forensic Medium and Low Secure Hospital. Forensic Psychology had always been an interest, but Clinical Psychology was my passion - and this role gave me the best of both worlds and the chance to put the theory I was learning into practice. Interestingly, this role allowed me to start to understand how inpatient services are run and gave me an indication of the sheer number of disciplines and expertise that are used to help an individual.

Although it was not something, I reflected on in my Doctorate application, one of the benefits of this role was that I was able to engage well with staff in different roles, some of which are in more 'unseen roles', and learn a variety of other skills. For example, I worked many shifts with the maintenance staff, safely escorting contractors around the hospital (becoming aware of risk) and coming up with spreadsheets and new systems (to make the work more efficient); administrative roles like completing and filling paperwork (helping me to understand GDPR); and, also working on reception (greeting people and maintaining security). These were all ways of improving my communication and having an appreciation for the various staff involved in the safe operation of a hospital. It also allowed me to appreciate the hard work of the nursing team who are on the frontline all day.

Within six months a fantastic opportunity came up to apply to be a group facilitator for a Sexual Offending Programme. This was the first time I found myself beginning to integrate into a Psychology department. Something that was also hugely important was that this role was paid. I was unable to afford a volunteer Assistant Psychologist post, so this gave me a brilliant chance to start to learn what is required of someone working therapeutically from a psychological perspective.

As most people are aware, competition for an Assistant Psychologist role is always fierce. Fortunately, my Group Facilitator and HCA role had given me a huge insight into what was required for this role when one became available in the same setting. Again, highlighting that it was hugely advantageous to have experienced different roles that I could draw upon within the interview.

During my first Assistant Psychologist role, my life veered from being heavily career focused to focusing on a very different area of my own and someone else's life: I was pregnant! Admittedly I found it hard to switch off during maternity leave and I found an opportunity to become a Research Assistant with flexible hours. This fitted well with my family and meant that I could continue to pursue my career whilst raising my daughter. This role allowed me to be autonomous but also manage my own time. I was recruiting families willing for their children to engage in cognitive testing. Maintaining the engagement of a 5-year-old, with an assessment that could take over an hour was a new challenge. I quickly realised I'd need to increase my creativity compared with the adults I'd previously worked with! I brought in some of my newfound parenting skills and added a few extras too. In case you're wondering, this is my go-to list:

- Get to know their family
- Have chats about their friends and interests
- Take lots of breaks
- Fuss over their pets
- Play with toys in between tasks
- And of course; lots of snacks!

After my maternity leave, I went back to work in the Forensic Hospital for a while but felt that my learning in the Assistant Psychologist role had plateaued. I needed new challenges and I thought it would be helpful to return to work full-time , so that I could ready myself for being a full-time Trainee Clinical Psychologist whilst also being a parent. I found a Behavioural Support Assistant job in a local Special Educational Needs School that was not only new and exciting, but also meant that I would easily be able to settle into the role of being a working mum and doing the childminder drop off. Admittedly I had played it safe in the interview, asking to work with Primary years, thinking that this was the age range I was familiar with. However, my first day proved different, as I was allocated a Secondary class with children aged 11-15. This role was challenging because I was suddenly working with children who were emotionally labile, and I was learning how to communicate with this age group for the first time. I found myself highly supported by my class teacher, who was very much focused on class wellbeing and psychological needs. I learnt many ways of adapting to the needs of the child and using visual aids and resources to help support their learning and development, including the use of Makaton.

It was during this role that I experienced the emotional rollercoaster of having my first Clinical Doctorate Interview. It was exhilarating to finally have an interview although my experience on the day was something I'd not prepared for. It quickly became apparent that at that particular stage in my career I was neither ready, nor prepared, for the role of a trainee. For the first time ever, I experienced dissociation whilst being interviewed. Despite my insight and instinct telling me I hadn't performed well enough; it was still a huge blow to receive a 'no'. I entered the 'bargaining' stage of grief and began to consider whether this was the only career that I could pursue. It was at this time that I found out about the Improving Access to Psychological Therapies (IAPT) Psychological Wellbeing Practitioner (PWP) training route. I felt that applying for this role met my desire to learn new theories and apply this to a population I had never worked with.

There is no doubt that this role was harder than I expected, and I was taken aback by the high workload and level of distress that was treated within the primary care setting. However, one of the most rewarding parts of the job was being able to work therapeutically to support mental health difficulties in people who had comorbid Long-Term Physical Health Conditions. I also have to admit that the pay was also an important factor in my decision for pursuing the IAPT route. This is because there was clear career and pay progression within an NHS setting. During this time, I worked within two trusts which had vast differences in their client group and inclusion criteria. This provided an understanding of the varying services available in different areas.

Having worked intensely within IAPT for several years an opportunity came up for an NHS Band 5 Assistant Psychologist (again in a Medium and Low Secure Forensic Hospital). Suddenly I was able to consolidate and utilise all the learning that I had built up over many years, to have greater confidence treating individuals with more complex needs. I quickly realised that times had changed within inpatient settings. Along with the Power Threat Meaning Framework, there was much more of a focus on the individual's need, as opposed to their 'diagnoses', and much more intention to build Trauma Informed services. I felt this fitted with my stance and helped me to think outside of the box and with greater autonomy. Through all the experience I had developed, I had found myself less manual bound and better able to work with what was in the room and the complexity that is present within forensic inpatient services.

In my last year of working in IAPT and my first year in my Assistant Psychologist role, I had two further unsuccessful Doctorate applications. During this time, I dedicated more time to working on myself and chose to undergo personal therapy. This was invaluable and allowed me to understand how to be more reflexive. I identified things that would trigger me, to understand and appreciate my intersectionality, and realise what it was like to be in therapy. The service I was working within had many opportunities to develop and network within the department and in the wider service. This was essential as it meant that I was able to learn from people with years of experience, understand more of what was required for the Clinical Psychology Trainee role, and focus on areas that were needed to showcase in both the application and the interviews. I was also involved with many service projects and teaching which was something that I had not drawn upon until this point, allowing me to learn about these core competencies for the Clinical Psychology role.

Personally, January 2022 began as one of the most difficult years of my life, with the breakdown of my marriage. The emotional rollercoaster of the Doctorate process felt like an added challenge to becoming a single mum and trying to learn how to co-parent. However, my luck changed when I found out that I had received a 'full house' of interviews for the four courses I had applied to. Suddenly I was having to juggle the emotions of a previous failed attempt at interviews, as well as the grieving process of a break-up and then finally the positives of being given four chances of a place on the course. Suddenly, I was having to utilise all the strategies I had learnt in therapy to help me manage these feelings. I prepared myself in ways that I had never used before, which allowed me to manage my fight or flight response and remain grounded. This included reaching out to other applicants and Psychologists I had met over the years or followed on social media, to gather some moral support and encouragement. Positively, I was told that I was on the reserve list for the first interview at the University of East Anglia (UEA), which resulted in a firm offer a few days later, and again another offer from Coventry. I withdrew from my two other interviews and decided that UEA was the course that I wanted to pursue.

My takeaway message would be that although the experience of being an Aspiring Psychologist can come with its challenges, there are many exciting opportunities out there. I would encourage you to look for those roles that stand out and sparkle; apply as your passion is only going to shine!

Dr Marianne Trent (She/Her) • 2:31 PM

Oh Kirsty! I could have eaten your story with a spoon! Well done to you for continuing to push and stretch yourself so far in your career. Episode 26 of the Aspiring Psychologist podcast is all about training whilst also being a mother and might well be worth having a listen to before September rolls around! I have so enjoyed supporting you via The Compassionate Q&A sessions on my socials and chatting with you on LinkedIn. I am thrilled you've been offered a place on training, and I hope you and your child have a lovely life by the seaside at UEA and that you adore this next training phase of your career! Do stay in touch 😊

5

- Addie's Story -

I Got Here in the End: A Tale of Two Crashes, Many Careers, and a Midlife Renaissance!

I came to Psychology later in life than most. It wasn't a career I had even considered at school. In fact, when I was studying for my GCSEs and then my 'A' levels, I had no clear idea what I wanted to do. Many of my friends knew their desired path but I was unsure. I can remember how we all had to complete careers aptitude tests using a special pencil so the computer could "read" the results, but when the results came back, I wasn't enamoured with the recommendation that I should be a teacher or a police officer. My parents and teachers suggested that I continue studying subjects like maths and science because I was good at them and so I did. But as I got nearer and nearer to my exams, I knew it wasn't the right path for me. Two days after my last 'A level' exam I moved out of home and into a full-time job in a hotel, having turned down the offer of a place to study civil engineering at university.

One year later, after surviving a serious car crash that meant I could not work for a while, it was again suggested that I try university – this time to study hotel management. Looking back now, I can see that I really wasn't prepared for university life, or for academic studies. I had no idea how to write a formal essay and to be honest, I didn't even enter the library until halfway through the second term! I had over 30 hours of timetabled lectures and tutorials each week which left me little free time to meet assignment deadlines, especially as I had to take up a part-time job because even with a student loan money was very tight. Despite this, I embraced the social side of being a student and definitely 'partied hard' in my first year. It won't surprise anyone when I say that the stresses got too much for me, and I dropped out mid-way through my second year.

It wasn't all bad though – I had made some catering contacts through university placements and my part-time job and was able to get a full-time job quickly. More importantly, I made some great friends, and even better than that – I met my boyfriend (now my husband)!

Fast forward a few more years, and I had moved on from catering and spent time working in customer service and customer complaints roles, before finding myself in a call centre working as a telephone debt collector (yes, that is a job!) A few promotions later and I was running a department, but again something didn't feel right: I was not happy with where I was and what I was doing. After doing another aptitude test[17] I decided to retrain as a mortgage advisor. This seemed like a

---

[17] Aptitude tests e.g., https://beta.nationalcareers.service.gov.uk/ or
https://www.pearson.com/uk/career-choices/PearsonUKQuizzes/General/index.html

great idea because I am good with numbers and chatting to people, and I already had a lot of the qualifications needed.

Unfortunately, I had got my timing spectacularly wrong. You might remember the banking sector crash of 2007-2008, and the long snaking lines of customers queuing up outside Northern Rock to try to cash-in their savings[18]... Yes, you've guessed it, I was working for Northern Rock at the time! I did manage to get another job working for a bigger bank, but I found that being targeted to make sales rather than help people buy their dream homes was not for me. When I was offered voluntary redundancy, I was relieved.

I've always been able to adapt to most situations, and so being out of work didn't worry me too much (luckily my husband has always been incredibly supportive). I signed up with a temping agency and was soon offered a part-time job working in a Community Learning Disability service:

"It's just for 2-3 months, is that okay?"

I filled the rest of my time going to college to study horticulture, something that has been a lifelong interest of mine, and is so beneficial for my mental health.

I didn't realise it at the time, but that temporary contract would change everything for me. I loved working in the team, and I was fascinated with all the different careers and roles. I particularly enjoyed working with the Consultant Psychiatrist

---

[18] Northern Rock https://www.bbc.co.uk/news/business-41229513

and Consultant Nurse (now a dear friend) in the weekly psychiatry clinic, learning about all aspects of mental health. I was offered a permanent role with the team and stayed there until the clinic was merged with another service. When an opportunity came up in a forensic inpatient service, I was encouraged to apply. Working in the unit brought me into close contact with the Psychology team. It was thanks to the wonderful Psychologists there (qualifieds, trainees, and assistants) that I learnt about the psychologist role. Finally, after years of uncertainty, I had a real sense of what I wanted to do.

I continued to work full-time as a secretary in the unit whilst I completed my undergraduate degree with The Open University. I was supported along the way by my fantastic husband (of course), and by my friends and family. I was also encouraged by my Psychology colleagues who knew what I was trying to achieve and were only too happy to talk me through therapeutic models and formulations, or to proof-read my reports. I was so surprised but extremely pleased to graduate with a first-class degree. I was a bit sad that the pandemic meant I couldn't have a graduation ceremony though. I decided to keep the momentum going by starting a master's whilst also applying for Assistant Psychologist roles.

Not long after starting my master's, I was told of a new Psychology role that has been developed here in NW England – (Trainee) Associate Psychological Practitioner[19]. Having not been successful in any Assistant Psychologist applications, I did not hold out much hope, but happily, I was successful. I spent my training year working in three GP surgeries within a Primary Care Network in South Cumbria as well as attending university

---

[19] https://www.innovationagencynwc.nhs.uk/case-studies/study/30

73

(virtually) to complete the Postgraduate Diploma needed for qualification[2021]. I wouldn't recommend taking on two qualifications at the same time, however I was able to make it work by using evenings, weekends, and annual leave so I could continue my master's (this time the pandemic helped!)

I'm now a qualified Associate Psychological Practitioner. I've really loved working in this role and being part of something new. It's been challenging at times but definitely worth it. I feel like I have grown and learnt so much in just a year – from really lacking in confidence at the start and being oh, so, so nervous to take on my first patient, to giving presentations about the role to clinical teams, running therapeutic group interventions, and speaking in trust-wide engage events. I have even attended university as a guest lecturer to talk to the new cohort of trainees about the role.

I have relished the opportunity to work holistically with people from age 11 to 90, and for a whole range of needs. I can draw from a 'toolkit' of interventions and therapeutic models such as cognitive-behavioural approaches, brief solution focussed theory, acceptance and commitment skills, and compassion-based work. I've also been able to develop skills in other areas such as motivational interviewing, stress management, mindfulness, and grounding techniques. I've become known for advocating and promoting the 'Five Ways to Wellbeing' – even creating a short TikTok-style video for social media!

---

[20] https://www.uclan.ac.uk/news/uclan-works-with-nhs-to-address-shortage-of-psychologists

[21] https://www.uclan.ac.uk/news/first-students-from pioneering-training-programme-receive-completion-certificates

I feel that I have finally found a career that will allow me to grow and thrive. At 46 years old, I know that I am not the typical applicant to the Doctoral programme[22], however after a practice run in 2021/22, I hope that in the next year or two I will get onto the programme and achieve my aim of becoming 'Dr Addie'!

Addie Beckwith
Associate Psychological Practitioner

Addie,

Wow! I adore that through various twists and turns your calling found you. I do indeed recall the mortgage catastrophe because my partner at the time had a Northern Rock Mortgage! Oops! You clearly have tenacity, determination and perseverance in spades and I'm excited to follow your journey to find out what happens next! Wishing you all the very best with your upcoming application and beyond!

Thank You! Marianne

---

[22] https://shop.bps.org.uk/the-alternative-handbook-2022-a-trainee%E2%80%99s-guide-to-postgraduate-clinical-Psychology-courses

6

- Jess' Story -

My Winding Journey so Far

Strap yourself in, get comfy and grab a drink of choice ready for the transparent and reflective tale of a thirty-something mother of 4 navigating the world of Clinical Psychology and obtaining those magical Assistant Psychologist posts.

I guess my story starts sitting at a desk writing an assignment about how brilliant Cognitive Behavioural Therapy (CBT) is. I'll admit I was disillusioned at the prospect of staying on at college to finish my 'A' levels. I'd just been offered a part-time job and sat procrastinating about life with money and freedom to spend it, something that I'd never experienced growing up "lower working class". Sitting in the lonely little library room I decided that studying wasn't for me anymore and left for the world of gainful employment at a clothing retailer.

Two wonderful years passed, I became full-time quickly, learned how to put away a rail of clothing in 2 minutes, made some friends, had some fun and enjoyed my late teens. But something was missing, some little spark in me. I had wonderful opportunities to work with an amazing bunch of people and progressed quickly into leading the shop floor, something which I loved, but I didn't feel fulfilled.

In my early twenties I was offered an entry level post working with my cousin in life assurance. This involved lots of organisation, meeting targets and liaising with our customers. Over the course of the next six years, I worked in various roles in the financial advice area. I eventually progressed to senior level and started earning all the financial perks that come with it. In one respect I was happy, I loved solving the problems I'd inherited and making other people's day a bit easier along the way. But I still wasn't fulfilled. Since I was a child, I made my siblings sit at little desks whilst making them do sums. Seeing other people learn had always been a passion of mine. Maybe that was my calling? Maybe teaching was for me instead?

My goal was to become a primary school teacher, but I couldn't give up on all this new money just yet and still survive, so I started a part-time degree with the Open University. When picking my subject, I thought about how I'd enjoyed the topic of Psychology at 'A' level and I figured I couldn't go wrong with learning how to understand people, so I chose a degree in Psychology. Life may have had other ideas for me because a month into my studies, I discovered that I was pregnant! A scary prospect and a journey I'd be making on my own. My contract at work ended shortly after this so suddenly I was jobless with a child on the way. To add a cherry on top, there was no room at the family home for a baby, so sourcing housing became far more important than finishing my degree.

The pregnancy seemed to progress quickly, thankfully at eight months, I found a place to live, albeit isolated from my support network. Now I bet you're reading this thinking about how all of these systemic difficulties sound like a recipe for disaster. You're right. After the birth of my child my mental health unfortunately deteriorated, and I was diagnosed with Post Natal Depression. At the time I welcomed the diagnosis, as a form of reason as to why I didn't get the famous rush of love new parents talk about and a tangible explanation as to why I felt so utterly rubbish. Now this is a personal preference and a great reminder that we are all individuals. Some people don't like labels or diagnoses, some do. During my career so far, I've worked with both ends of that spectrum; and all that matters is that a person's experiences and feelings are taken into account and validated, despite my personal feelings on psychiatric diagnoses. The label was a bridge to my identity at that time and acceptance that I'm not perfect, and that's ok.

I was treated in the community by a Perinatal team which was where I was first exposed to Clinical Psychology. The compassion and care I received was completely new to me and made me feel hopeful, not just that I could feel better but also that I could recover well and have a happy relationship with my child. The medication also helped support me, but what really made a difference was the talking therapy. I knew therapy existed, but first-hand experience of it has guided me through all the dark times, providing me with strategies that work for me and that I can count on, even now when stress or low mood rears its unwanted head. As I talked to my friends and family about my experiences, I realised that this was my spark, I felt empowered, hopeful, and wanted to help other people feel this. I delved straight in to researching the career pathways out there and Clinical Psychology popped up. The more I read the more I fell in love. I sound utterly uncool, but I enjoyed research at undergraduate level and wanted to continue this but felt the pull of helping people. Clinical Psychology sounded like it would be the perfect solution, a mix of both as a scientist-practitioner.

Along the journey of recovery from Post Natal Depression, I reconnected with my childhood sweetheart who also had a child from a previous relationship, making two the magic number. I quickly fell pregnant again, leaving an 18-month gap between the two youngest children. I was extremely nervous that my mental health would begin to deteriorate again, but the support I received got me through. I was able to use the coping strategies I'd learned during therapy and thankfully had a much more positive experience with my second pregnancy. Even now, I'm acutely aware that many people do not have the positive experience I had with services and use this knowledge to help focus my passion and help to make that hope more accessible for others.

Throughout all of this I remained enrolled on my Bachelor's degree and after five long years I completed it with a 2:1. I'd worked so hard to finish my degree. Two kids and a complete career path change later, my goal of being a Clinical Psychologist was finally more obtainable. Consequently, my undergraduate degree ceremony was absolutely one of my life highlights so far. The only trouble was that now I genuinely had no idea where to go from there.

I know, I'll do a master's! "What's another student loan to add to the list?" I naively thought, until of course it was deducted from my pay every month! I was accepted on to a distance learning MSc in the Clinical Applications of Psychology I could do part-time whilst being a mum, perfect. Now it's just the clinical experience part.

In a panic I searched for "mental health" on NHS Jobs, and as luck would have it an advert for a voluntary support worker appeared two miles from my home. I applied and was fortunate enough to be offered the post. I would be working in a community team dealing with people experiencing their first episode of Psychosis. I was pleased but I didn't know what to expect. Are people with Schizophrenia like the media says? I know now that for the most part they aren't, but at the time it brought up some very real emotions, the fear and anxiety of the unknown and about the sort of thing I would experience working with people who are acutely unwell. As a volunteer, I helped the support workers with the running of the services' social drop-in, and it was simply wonderful. This place was so full of hope, in a group of people that could be so easily written off as *"impossible to engage,"* we were making a difference! I felt like I'd hit the jackpot!

From the beginning, I was open about my ultimate career aspirations and as a result I was supported to be involved in psychological focused work. This started with helping to plan and facilitate psychoeducational groups under supervision from the team's Clinical Psychologist. About six months into my role, the Honorary Assistant Psychologist in the team left for a paid position. A promotion was on the cards, and I successfully moved to the Honorary role and continued to build on the work I started as a Volunteer Support Worker. I started receiving clinical supervision (not that I knew what that was at the time) and developed some snazzy new literature (leaflets and workbooks) for the service all under the banner of "service development."

Now that I had some form of clinical experience, the natural next step was the Doctorate Application process. I decided to apply for the first time in 2019 for 2020 entry. I told myself it was a 'dummy run' and went into it expecting nothing, although secretly hoping that 'miracles do happen,' and I'd get four interviews and offers! It was (understandably) not to be; my first blanket rejection came through. No matter, it was a practice.

Around this time, I remember attending a seminar by an apparently coveted and knowledgeable Clinical Psychologist, one that could easily have put me off if I'm honest. I remember this person sharing their "insight." I remember them stating that unless you were willing to give up your life and relocate for a DClinPsy course you may as well give up because it wouldn't happen for you unless you lived and breathed Clinical Psychology. I remember it so clearly because it sticks with me like a thorn in my side: how could I, as a mother of three uproot my whole life so selfishly? The feeling of anger at his words inspired me to prove him wrong, but it's his voice I hear every time I'm struggling to balance being an Assistant Psychologist with being a mum.

Life as an Honorary Assistant Psychologist continued and before I knew it the applications were open again, this time 2020 for 2021 entry. This year was more serious. I thought really hard about my application and had some guidance from my supervisor who was a Clinical Psychologist. Reading my form back now makes me cringe, it reads like someone else wrote it.

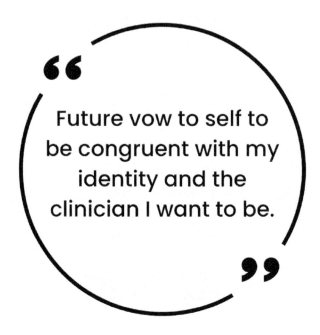

> **Future vow to self to be congruent with my identity and the clinician I want to be.**

Alas, more blanket rejections. No matter, I was still relatively inexperienced.

2020 was a big year. I was a year and a half into my role as an Honorary Assistant Psychologist and just finishing up my MSc when the COVID-19 pandemic hit. Suddenly, everything changed. A global pandemic at the same time as completing a dissertation remotely is enough to contend with, but it also coincided with finding out that I was having *another* baby. I felt that I sat somewhere outside keyworker status, I was a valued member of the team, but it wasn't essential to be in the office, so I moved to working from home from early on in my pregnancy. I guess this brought up a lot for me. I was lonely due to lack of adult interactions and upon reflection, guilty that I wasn't in the trenches with my colleagues.

To make things more complicated, a permanent, paid Assistant Psychologist post in the service was advertised which I interviewed for at eight months pregnant. The interview took place remotely, and I was so huge I couldn't fit my tummy under the desk. Despite my waffling I secured the job and started a full-time post when my child was five months old. Now, when I share this part of my journey people are mixed. You can see some judgemental looks along the way (*"woah that was fast"*), some call me superwoman. For context, my partner was made redundant because of the pandemic, and it made sense for us to do a role-swap of sorts. If I'm brutally honest with myself I felt this sense of pressure to progress, this pressure to work as if Psychology *was* the most important thing in my life.

I sit writing this in May 2022 and I have so far spent a year in the post. I am contemplating what the future holds but also reflecting on how different this year has been. Nothing could have prepared me for working full-time in the NHS in the midst of a pandemic and having four children around! I always keep in mind that I'm doing this for my children as much as myself, I want to show them that mommies can work too! I'd also like to challenge the narrative around working parents. It's tricky, yes, but being a parent really shouldn't deter us from reaching our goals. Transitioning from an honorary to a paid post was harder than I thought, and it took me some time to get used to the role: what was expected of me and everything that comes with the first paid assistant role. Eventually I became more confident in my abilities and the year flew by in the blink of an eye.

The service supported me to become more autonomous, seeing people on my own and having flexibility in the day to day of my role. I gained experience with individual, structured interventions and enhanced my group intervention skills. I led on a service evaluation, submitted it for peer review, and actively evaluated every little project I could along the way. The most useful skill I have developed is how to use supervision well. My supervisor and I decided together that we would work with the Inskipp and Proctor model of clinical supervision[23] meaning that there was time in each session to develop my skills, monitor my progress and keep an eye on my wellbeing along the way.

Another round of applications opened in 2021 ready to start the DClin in 2022. Third lot of blanket rejections. This one stung. Three years of obsessive refreshing of the Clearing House website, three years of:

"I am sorry, but you have not been successful on this occasion."

All very wearing. What do I need to do? I've kept my promise of being more congruent with myself, I've had feedback about

---

[23] If you're interested in more models, Kumund Titmarsh wrote an amazing summary that is readily available on ResearchGate!

my form from **two** *qualified Clinical Psychologists, I've reflected on how my experience has prepared me for the role, where do I go now?*

Rationally, I understand I've actually only had one clinical role in one specialised area, I do need more experience before I'm ready. Accepting that is tricky, I keep reminding myself that I'm not a failure for not being there yet, it takes lots of really good people a really long time to get on the Doctorate; I'm normal, if anything.

I realise whilst writing that my inner bully is still at it, I feel myself trying to justify why I'm not there yet. My family and friends are always hopeful (who hasn't been told *"you're amazing at your job, they would be silly to say no"* in that not-so-helpful but well-meaning tone?). But the reality is, this year was the hardest of them all. Unfortunately, I also experienced a bereavement during the application season - my wonderful grandmother. She was one of the most important people in the world to me. My shining light and never relenting cheerleader. I returned to work on the day that I sat my selection test for one course, telling myself that I should still sit it. In hindsight I should have withdrawn and saved myself the extra stress at a time where self-compassion is paramount, but the pressure I felt to just be on the course already was too overwhelming on top of my grief.

After the application season was over and I could congratulate all my wonderful colleagues who had been successful (secretly noting down how they did it), it was time for my yearly appraisal, which meant it was time to think of some goals. The imposter syndrome crept in once again... "Am I really any good?" I decided I'd be proactive and asked my colleagues for feedback on my performance. EEK. As scary as this was it really helped frame my goals for the next year. One comment was around working *"within my comfort zone,"* and that got me thinking. Four years and three job roles later, I *was* in my comfort zone. I loved this service, and I knew my job well, but staying comfy at my desk won't get me on the Doctorate.

After lots and lots of reflective diary entries I decided to bite the bullet: I needed to start applying for new assistant posts. Not just to leave my comfort zone but learning more about different areas and expanding my knowledge sounded really exciting to me! I was full of hope and lofty ideas about what I'd say in an interview to get this coveted experience elsewhere. Two Assistant Psychologist posts popped up that looked interesting, and I applied for both. I tailored my statement to each post, stating why I wanted to work there, triple checked it with my supervisor and sent them off with hope in my heart. Two weeks of refreshing the update website later and hooray! An interview! On the one hand I was excited, I have potential! But then the doubt crept in, and I realised how much I waffle during interviews. I was able to share with my supervisor that I had an interview and they supported me with preparation and practice. The day of the interview arrived and by then I'd read what felt like every resource I could find about working psychologically in an acute inpatient unit. I arrived early and sat in the reception internally rehearsing the answers to the questions I thought they'd ask. As it turned out the questions were really focused, and I didn't actually ask about anything I'd read! *Note to self: you can definitely over-prepare.* Later that day I received a call to say I was close but unsuccessful. My feedback was also focused and helpful and although I was grateful for the experience of an interview, the rejection still stung for a while.

In case you are wondering, I didn't get shortlisted for the second job either. Or for two more that followed. It's disheartening and it's hard. It's totally normal to question why you put yourself through so much rejection. For one role, I asked the recruiting Psychologist for some feedback and was naively surprised that there were over 100 applications which had to be whittled down to 8 for interviews. It made me feel better knowing that it's not that *I'm* unshortlistable, it's just that others are more shortlistable. Always ask for feedback, the worst they can say is no and you're really in no different position if they do.

Despite so many rejections in such a short and difficult period I remain hopeful that one day it will happen for me. It is easy to become jaded in this process and those days where I sit at my desk contemplating taking a job at the local supermarket and saving myself the pain of not feeling good enough, I remember the good. I remember the positive parts of my job and focus on those. Although I'm not a qualified Clinical Psychologist (yet), I'm still helping people and I'm still achieving in that sense. I'll keep this with me when I apply for more posts in the coming months.

There it is - my winding journey so far. I have carried two super important lessons with me throughout my journey, the first being that life happens. We can't control everything, life events may derail you in the short term and it's OK for things to take time, it's not a reflection on you or any perceived failings. This journey takes resilience, some days you'll be the perfect assistant, other days being just about good enough is all we can muster, we are only human. The second, and most important, is that other things matter too. I want to be a Clinical Psychologist yes, but I also love being an assistant. Sometimes it's so easy to focus on the end rather than enjoy the journey, so if you take one thing from reading my story, take that.

Enjoy the journey. Enjoy the learning, enjoy the path, and remember that even when you feel like it will never happen for you, it is a marathon not a race.

Jessica Lee
Assistant Psychologist

OH JESS!

I really enjoyed your 'story so far.' Thank you so much for taking the time to write it. There certainly have been some twists and turns along the way but you sound pretty brilliant at making hay whilst the sun shines and learning to dance in the rain. I am feeling hopeful that your time will come when it is right for you and for your family too. I'd like to wish you all the very best for your AP applications and for this DClinPsy application season too. Do keep me posted, won't you? Be kind to yourself and don't forget to enjoy the smell of your kid's heads when they are still young and super cute. They grow up so quick!

———————————

WITH MY BEST WISHES, MARIANNE

Jun 2022

DEAR MARIANNE!

Thank you! I wanted to share an update
with you all! I interviewed for another
AP post and am pleased to share I was
successful! I write awaiting a start date
for my second Assistant Psychologist
post and wanted to share the hope and
optimism I'm currently feeling!

———————

THANKS, JESS

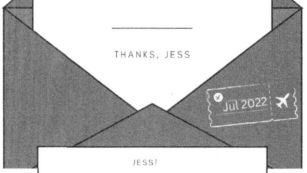

JESS!

Oh, my days! What wonderful news! So many
congratulations to you! Thanks so much for your
update! I can practically see the happy dance you
and your kids must have done when you found
out! Hope it goes so well for you when you start
and pays rich dividends for your blossoming
career 😊

Thanks so much for updating us!

———————

WITH MY BEST WISHES, MARIANNE

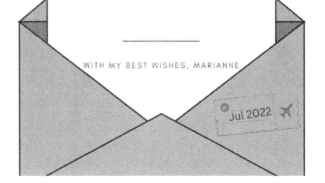

7

- Jo's story -

One Day You'll Look Back and Be Able to Join Up the Dots...

While at school, I had no idea what I wanted to do for a career. From aged 14 I had part-time jobs in hospitality and retail and while I learnt a lot, I also knew I wanted to study for as long as possible. I enjoyed learning new things and I enjoyed stories. I began learning Spanish at an early age and liked my Spanish teacher at school so felt happy with the idea of going to university to continue journeying into the language. My dad wanted me to study Business and on telling my Head of 6th form (who was also my English Literature teacher) this, she told me I should "not lose my soul". I opted to move to London to study for a combined honours degree in Spanish and History of Art; a perhaps unlikely combination for a teenager who'd grown up in a village in Northwest England and attended a state school.

I completed my degree which included a year living in Argentina, and after a series of jobs waitressing while simultaneously volunteering in art galleries, I completed a teaching certificate enabling me to teach English as a second language. Before securing a teaching job in Ecuador and then Argentina, I worked temporarily in a Lancashire College as a Learning Support Assistant. In this work, I taught people of all ages from young children to older adults. I loved connecting with my students but was less enthusiastic about the constant lesson planning and homework marking. All the while I pondered the possibility of one day training as a therapist. I've always been interested in what it means to be human and how people come to live a meaningful life despite the challenges they face. In part, this is likely a way of trying to better understand my dad who faced adversity while growing up. It is likely also a reflection of my own journey and transitioning through what at times could be quite crippling social anxiety as a child and teen. I also find the concept of how we grow and develop in connection with others fascinating and soul-shaking.

When back in the UK, I spent the next few years working as a teaching assistant in a specialist school. The children I worked with had a range of emotional, behavioural, and learning difficulties. Many of the children I worked with were care experienced and I witnessed first-hand the challenges for these young people as they grappled with attachment difficulties and learning how to regulate big emotions. I found this work immensely challenging: I now realise that my lack of formal supervision meant I didn't have a space to properly debrief and explore what was coming up for me and how it impacted my work. I burnt out, enrolled on a horticulture course, and became a self-employed gardener before working in a variety of private and public gardens. It was joyous and really helped nurture my own mental health. But then I realised I didn't want to sit on a ride-on mower for the next thirty years. I also really missed being present for and supporting other people- as beautiful as the plants were.

This time was crucial for me. I learnt that I have limitations when it comes to how much of my Self I can give. Sometimes I need time away to recharge and that's okay. It taught me that I need to work at a steady pace and find some balance. I'm still on a journey to accept and embody this, but I'm learning to recognise when I need to step away, say 'no' to work or ramp up the self-care.

Over the years, I'd always gone around in circles researching various psychotherapy training qualifications. I was torn about which therapy modality to specialise in and I was anxious about doing another course that may not lead to secure employment. After researching many pathways, I realised that Clinical Psychology appealed, not only because of the job opportunities at the other end, but also because of the unique combination of clinical work coupled with an emphasis on research. I found the idea of having a foundation of psychological knowledge energising.

I applied for a part-time distance learning MSc Psychology conversion degree that awarded the British Psychological Society's accreditation. I left a full-time gardening job and secured my first role within the NHS as a Support, Time and Recovery Worker for a drug and alcohol recovery service. I facilitated support groups with peer mentors. This was emotive, humbling, and inspiring work. I will never forget the resilience of those accessing that service. We worked in a damp, tiny and quite miserable building and we were an eccentric but lovable team with big hearts. Alongside this work I continued to complete my MSc. It was hard to juggle, and I felt like a flaky friend/relative at times. Then the Pandemic hit, and we were thrust into lockdowns. I was extremely grateful to have my head stuck in books and assignments to complete. A year and a half into my job as a support worker, the contract for the drug and alcohol recovery service went out for tender and my job security suddenly felt precarious. I also felt anxious about the potential of no longer working for the NHS, so I applied for a role as an Assistant Practitioner in a CAMHS team and fortunately, was successful.

Working therapeutically with children and young people as well as their parents is fraught with complexity and many a heartfelt moment. It's the kind of work that stays with you and can seep into your 'you' time as thoughts pop into your mind about who you're working with and what's going to be most helpful for them. I love the honesty and dynamism of young people. Their bravery is colossal. Being part of a CAMHS team is particularly hard in the current climate. Referrals have tripled and there are huge waitlists. You do as much as you can, and somehow feel like it's never quite enough. It's important work and I've learnt so much.

A few months after starting in CAMHS, I finished my MSc and a month later was able to apply for the DClinPsy. I thought I would complete my first application as a practice run, knowing I likely didn't have enough of the right experience but also thinking it was worth a shot given two of the Universities I was applying to use mental ability testing as part of their commitment to diversifying the workforce. Writing the application was a struggle. I didn't have a reference from a Clinical Psychologist but did have a friend in adult mental health services who put me in touch with her supervisor, a psychologist who kindly read and ripped apart my application form. I was struck with major self-doubt that week and then within a couple of days, as if by magic, an email dropped into my inbox to tell me I'd won an hour's coaching with Marianne as a thank you for reviewing her book The Clinical Psychologist Collective on Amazon. Marianne gave me honest and compassionate feedback and helped build me up in a way that the first psychologist's read through had not. I found my voice and felt re-energised. I practised what I could for the mental ability tests and found them hard! I got four NO's from the universities I applied to. It was not a surprise, but it still stung.

For a while after I felt that I might slow down with the idea of getting onto the training. I'm in my early thirties and I've also been grappling with the thought of motherhood and the decision about whether to try to start a family. Getting on to the DClinPsy is relayed as a very difficult goal to obtain. It sometimes feels like you must keep pushing yourself relentlessly. Given my path, I've felt like a bit of an imposter, as if I have a lot of catching up to do and this has felt like an impossible task. The experience has since encouraged me to really think about what I need and want to live life in a way that brings me meaning, balance and joy.

I began to feel a little overwhelmed by my work in CAMHS. I got shingles, immediately followed by COVID, and felt extremely low physically and mentally. I began therapy to try and keep my head above the water. I was worried about getting to the point where I'd need to ask to be signed off from work. It took me a few therapy sessions to adjust to being on the other side of the therapeutic alliance. It's felt very different to clinical supervision, and I think this is important, so I can bring this experience and empathy into future work with others. The process is enabling me to accept different parts of myself that I don't particularly like and find some inner calm.

I've felt extremely loyal to CAMHS from the outset and yet began to think I needed to step away for a while. I also couldn't get experience as an Assistant Psychologist or supervision with a Clinical Psychologist easily within my team. Although my experience as an Assistant Practitioner and the supervision I received has been invaluable, it still felt as though securing work as an Assistant Psychologist was an important preliminary step to accessing the DClinPsy.

I applied for an Assistant Psychologist post in a community older adults mental health service but wasn't offered the post. The feedback was helpful and spurred me on. Another post came up that piqued my interest, working as an Assistant Psychologist in the research team of a different NHS Trust. I applied, thinking it would be good interview experience and was offered the job. I was shocked and happy. While listening to the feedback of the Clinical Psychologist who interviewed me, I thought, 'aha maybe I can do this, after all,' a feeling I hadn't felt for a while. The work will be so different to what I've been doing for the last few years, and I will no doubt miss clinical work at times. However, I'm so excited to expand my skills in research and support recruitment to clinical studies in the NHS.

I will likely apply for the DClinPsy at the next application round, but I haven't wholly made up my mind. I want to ensure that when I do apply next, I've filled some more of the gaps where I feel I was lacking experience. I absolutely want to qualify as a Clinical Psychologist one day, and at the same time, as a 33-year-old, I might think about becoming a parent first, or continuing to accrue more varied experience as an Assistant Psychologist. I'm not currently able to move anywhere in the UK to train so there are factors to consider but I feel somehow surer that I will one day begin training, and less anxious about exactly when that needs to be. If ever there was a career that should value life experience and years on earth, it's surely got to be this one!

In the meantime, you'll find me avidly reading Tanya Byron's *The Skeleton Cupboard*, James Randall's *Surviving Clinical Psychology* and re-reading Marianne and co-authors' *The Clinical Psychologist Collective*. Current favourite podcasts accompanying me on drives to work: Marianne's *The Aspiring Psychologist*, Tanya Byron's *How did we get here?* Sue Marriott and Ann Kelley's *Therapist Uncensored* and David Nutt's *Drug Science*. I also balance this with fiction and trashy TV. As well as my work, CrossFit, yoga, the Lake District, family, and friends keep me keeping on J.

Wishing you well on your journey: *to thine own self be true* (Shakespeare's *Hamlet*).

Joanna Bathgate
Assistant Psychologist

Dr Marianne Trent (She/Her) • 8:47 PM

Hey Jo!
Oh. I adored your story. Thanks so much for writing it.
I felt like I was cheering you on all the way through
and I'll admit to wanting to hop on the back of your
mower for a bit too!
I recall one lunch break in my first qualified job
watching a chap blow a load of leaves around with a
vacuum and it looked pretty appealing! But likely after
half an hour or so I'd have been wanting to get back
to the therapy room!

I love the idea that you're giving yourself room to
grow over this next year or so and that when the time
is ready you'll have new strength and reach.

Sending you so many good wishes and do stay kind
to you. Thanks for being part of my world 🌍 😊

Marianne

> **Joanna Bathgate**   ••• 🔲
> Assistant Practitioner
>
> **Joanna Bathgate** (She/Her) • 9:21 PM
>
> Oh yes leaf blowing is fun (but not after doing it for
> several hours hehe). I liked hedge trimming at the
> time. In one of my jobs we had to do cloud shapes
> and it was weirdly satisfying making all these curvy
> lines :) Generally I preferred the non-power tool jobs
> though!
>
> Now I garden for fun when I want to on my somewhat
> abandoned allotment. I'm much better suited to the
> work I do now but there will always be a gardener in
> me :) Sue Stuart-Smith writes about gardening and
> the mind beautifully in 'The Well Gardened Mind'-
> well worth a read.
>
> Thanks for all your support and help along the way
> and for the opportunity to write.
>
> Take care, Jo

8

- Fauzia's Story -

Unfulfilling a Self-fulfilling Prophecy

Putting pen to paper to write my story feels like an extremely daunting task, and seems to be bringing up a host of mixed emotions for me – both positive and negative. You see, until very recently I saw my story and journey into Psychology as one full of deficits and weaknesses. What I now realise, is that it was in fact challenges and barriers that I experienced – that I had no control over – that made my journey difficult, and that was through no fault of my own. In fact, my story isn't one of deficits, rather it is one of strengths; fighting against the odds, overcoming adversity and unfulfilling self-fulfilling prophecies. Being an ethnically minoritised Muslim female from an underprivileged background and stepping into the world of Psychology has been no easy feat, but I'm living to tell the tale. And I'm sharing my story in the hope that if you have some common lived experiences to me, that my journey inspires you to not let the obstacles in your life prevent you from achieving your dreams. Or if you're working with Aspiring Psychologists, who identify as being from a minoritised background, I hope that my story encourages you to explore their social graces with them. I hope it allows you and them to reflect on the privileges that both advantage and disadvantage, and the ways that you can work towards sharing power. Things need to change within Psychology; you and I are that change, and I hope my story brings about some change too. So here goes...

At fifteen years of age, if someone had told me that I would one day be pursing Psychology as a career path, I would have laughed in their face, because at the time, that would have been such a far-fetched dream. I grew up in a very deprived area and attended an under-resourced school. Through the course of the five-year period that I was there, we went through four different headteachers – some of them acting, one that was brought in from a nearby school in the hope to turn things around, and another that ended up staying for the long haul. After-school fights were a regular occurrence and we were often met with police community support officers, and sometimes even police at the school gates at home time. Unfortunately, learning was at the bottom of the priority list and managing challenging and disruptive behaviour was at the top during our lessons. Sadly, the dream of academia was almost non-existent for the student majority. Looking back now, I think that if we had been given adequate support and resources, then more students could have been able to perform better and reach their full potential.

One memory that still haunts me to this day was when I approached one of the English teachers during a half-term revision class. I remember asking her how I could try and achieve a B in my GCSE, and her response of *"if I were you, I'd try and just scrape a pass"*, could not have been anymore discouraging. At the time, I didn't quite grasp the enormity of that statement, but this encounter later went onto change my life. At the time, however, I didn't think to question her, and I carried on as I was. I had unconsciously taken on a label that she had placed on me and allowed it to transpire into a self-fulfilling prophecy. It will probably come as no surprise that I didn't do too well in this subject, or any of the other core subjects either, for that matter, and therefore had to re-take my GCSEs. I had the option of pursuing a vocational course when I left school, but on Results Day, it finally dawned on me that I had been failed by the school. I firmly believed that I had the potential to do much better, and that my grades were not truly representative of my ability.

To that end, I decided to re-take my core subjects on a fast-track basis whilst also doing a BTEC in Fashion and Clothing, which was something I was interested in at the time (though I had no intention of pursing it as a vocation) and with sheer determination and hard work on my part, and support from my college tutors, I was able to turn my grades around drastically. Imagine the feeling of joy when I got an A in the same subject that I was told to just get a borderline pass in. This experience was a real turning point for me and made me not only realise the power of self-belief, but also the negative impact that labels can have, and how this can render us powerless.[24] There is

---

[24] Chrissie's editorial note: This anecdote reminds me of when my AS English Literature teacher, who made clear that she didn't like me, predicted me an E but I went on to get an A. Although this was 14 years ago, I still remember her coming to congratulate me on Results Day with

definitely a lot more that I can say about my experiences at school, but for the sake of not prolonging this chapter, I have provided a (very) abridged version of events here. During this year, I decided I wanted to do A-Levels and maybe even go to university one day. I was met with more discouragement and was dissuaded by others because A-Levels were supposedly too 'difficult' and academic for me. My applications to colleges had my predicted grades, which were promising, but my poor grades from school seemed to be casting a dark shadow over them. The fact that I had done so poorly the first time around made them doubt my ability. I remember the interviewers asking me if I was sure I wouldn't be best placed sticking with a more vocational course. I argued my case and managed to get a number of conditional places at the colleges of my choice. I achieved the grades I needed, and the following year commenced my A-Levels.

Doing my A-Levels was the most refreshing and enjoyable experience ever, and I relished it. This was the first time I had been in a classroom where I witnessed real teaching and learning taking place, without disruption, and without a supply teacher telling us to turn to a certain page in a textbook and just get on with it. This involved an active learning style and was a somewhat alien experience to me, but I loved it. I found my Psychology A-Level really intriguing, and it was then that I decided this was something I wanted to explore further, and do a degree in. I passed all my A-Levels with flying colours and

---

her tail between her legs! I'd already proved her wrong months before when, with my dad's consent, I submitted my sister's past A grade poetry essay (which conveniently was on the same topic) and she graded it an E!

excelled at university.[25] During my final year, however, life happened, and due to a change in personal circumstances, I took on some caring responsibilities. This was a really challenging and emotionally demanding time for me, but the tremendous support from the course meant that I was able to successfully complete my degree, and graduate with an excellent grade that I was immensely proud of.

Furthermore, during my time at university, my love for Psychology was ever-growing. Undertaking a placement within a rehabilitation setting for people who had experienced a Traumatic Brain Injury, as well as the voluntary work I was undertaking as a peer mentor at university and counselling with ChildLine cemented my interest even further, reinforcing my love for working with and helping people. These experiences made me realise that Psychology was my calling, and so I decided that I wanted to pursue a career as a psychologist. I was fortunate enough to secure an Applied Behavioural Analysis (ABA) Therapist post shortly after graduating and continued to actively search for Assistant Psychologist posts. These posts were the gold standard at the time (and continue to be); notorious for being really competitive and difficult to attain. I, therefore, decided to also seek out honorary opportunities after contacting numerous psychologists in my locality, who sadly didn't have anything on offer but were generous enough to give me thorough feedback on my covering letters. I then came

---

[25] Chrissie's editorial note: I did not do as amazingly in GCSEs or A Levels as you did and was very much an average undergraduate and master's student, also having to take on caring responsibilities in recent years. Despite all this though, I too have somehow managed to have enjoyed working in academic roles for almost seven years starting with my epic gap year teaching in Sri Lanka as a lowly 18-year-old!

across a consultant Clinical Psychologist, who bore some positive news and offered me a part-time honorary Assistant Psychologist post in a psychiatric hospital, which I accepted. I did this post alongside my ABA therapist post, in order to both build on my experience, and to help make ends meet. I was in a somewhat privileged position, however, in that I lived at home and this would have not been an option or even possible otherwise.

This post provided:

- My first real exposure to the world of Psychology.
- My first real insight into what the role of a psychologist entailed.
- So many invaluable opportunities to develop my skills.
- The chance to meet some incredibly inspiring people.
- And, most importantly, it allowed me to get a foot in the door.

I was also really fortunate to have an amazing supervisor who always listened to me and encouraged my 'out of the box' creative ideas, and really supported me to tap into my strengths, which made a big difference to me.

In fact, as I write this, I realise just how much of a community Psychology really is, and I am so grateful for the people that I have had the opportunity of crossing paths with through my journey – each of them have influenced, shaped and taught me something meaningful that I will forever treasure.

Following this post, I went onto secure numerous Assistant Psychologist posts in a number of different settings, namely, physical health Psychology and adult community mental health, amongst others. What really struck me during these experiences, however, was the challenges that individuals from minoritised groups and communities were experiencing when accessing these services. Some of these challenges pertained to cultural and linguistic barriers. In fact, one of my most rewarding experiences was conducting brief stabilisation work with a client who was a refugee from Afghanistan. I was able to adapt the interventions (under supervision) and conduct sessions in the client's native tongue, which I was also fluent in. This experience really highlighted the importance of adapting interventions to make them accessible, and cross-culturally valid. It is no secret that Psychology is predominantly a white middle class profession, and over the years, I have also observed the barriers and challenges that a lack of representation poses, both on a personal and professional level. There have been times where my intersectional minoritised identities have made me not only feel like a minority (sometimes even a minority within a minority!), but it has also made me question whether I belong within the profession. However, the positive impact that my presence as a minority has had in my work has also made me realise why my presence is in fact increasingly important and needed, and this has been a real motivating factor for me. I truly believe that to be able to make a difference and to bring about change, we need to be the change. I am now currently undertaking a Doctorate in counselling Psychology, which I hope will allow me to work towards bringing about change.

When I was in secondary school, if someone had told me that I would have a bachelor's degree, and would be pursuing a Doctorate, I wouldn't have believed them. But all the same, here I am. Sharing my journey for this story has been a very vulnerable experience for me, and I have connected with so many emotions in the process. I hope it helps you to realise that being from a minoritised and underprivileged background does not have to be a barrier (even though it might be twice or even a hundred times as challenging). I unfulfilled a self-fulfilling prophecy and so can you!

Fauzia Khan
Trainee Counselling Psychologist

Apr 13, 2022, 8:05 AM ✓

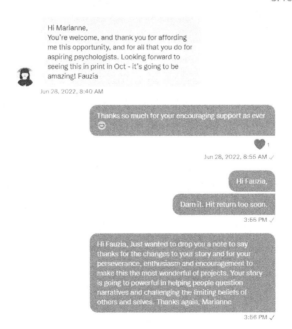

Hi Fauzia, Thank you so much for writing your story. It is going to be so wonderfully nourishing for so many. I have really enjoyed reading it and also following you on Twitter and seeing how active you are in the media too. Wishing you all the best with completing your counselling psychology doctorate and for the rest of your career. Marianne

8:46 PM ✓

Hi Marianne,
You're welcome, and thank you for affording me this opportunity, and for all that you do for aspiring psychologists. Looking forward to seeing this in print in Oct - it's going to be amazing! Fauzia

Jun 28, 2022, 8:40 AM

Thanks so much for your encouraging support as ever 😊

♥ 1

Jun 28, 2022, 8:55 AM ✓

Hi Fauzia,

Darn it. Hit return too soon.

3:56 PM ✓

Hi Fauzia, Just wanted to drop you a note to say thanks for the changes to your story and for your perseverance, enthusiasm and encouragement to make this the most wonderful of projects. Your story is going to powerful in helping people question narratives and challenging the limiting beliefs of others and selves. Thanks again, Marianne

3:56 PM ✓

9

- Nikita's Story -

I've Never Worn Cashmere

It was quite some time before I took the first step towards my dream career in Clinical Psychology. In part, I think that's because I wondered if 'someone like me' could fit the mould. The psychologists I had met during my time working in the NHS all seemed so well put together; their competency and knowledge seemed borderline magical, they radiated calmness and had an acronym for every occasion. From my observations, some even wore cashmere. In contrast, I saw myself as bit of a mess. I was a new healthcare assistant who felt more than slightly incompetent, was almost always fuelled by caffeine and radiated a constant undertone of anxiety. Couple this with the fact that the closest I had ever been to cashmere was an acrylic/cotton blend jumper, and I could quite easily convince myself that Clinical Psychology was not meant for me. If you will allow, I'd like to tell you the story of how I reconsidered.

I'm Nikita, and for as long as I can remember I had wanted a career in Musical Theatre. I danced from the age of six and was first told to go on a diet as a healthy eight-year-old; cue a strong hatred of ballet and hatred of my body that was equally as strong. There's more to it but, to simplify a long narrative, I first met a Clinical Psychologist at the age of 14 following an eating disorder diagnosis. Of course, I'm healthy and happy today, but the process of therapy led me to consider a lot about myself and the world around me. My psychologist, sensing that my whole heart was not geared towards a career in Musical Theatre, asked, "You say that you'd like a career in musical theatre, and it's what everyone expects you to do, but what is it that you'd like to do?" Of course, I drew a blank! Nobody had asked me this, and I could quickly shut down any 'careers conversations' at school because the only vocational input our school ever had was from the army, and the army don't employ actors! After a pause, I quickly read their NHS identity badge and replied, 'highly specialist applied psychologist'. Ok, that obviously wasn't a subtle move, and I realise now that it was a pretty specific job title! Although Clinical Psychology was little more than a fleeting thought at the time, it was the first time I'd thought of a career that perhaps felt a little truer to who I was.

Nevertheless, I did move to London at the age of 18 to attend one of the top three drama schools in the UK... Predictably, I didn't last long. I didn't even make it to Christmas break before dropping out on mental health grounds. After some time, I had decided it was best not to return to the world of musical theatre. I recognised how toxic it was to receive constant, harsh criticism; especially when there were some things that I just couldn't change. For example, I'm 5ft 2" and fully grown, I can't change that. However, there were some things that I wasn't willing to change, like how I valued compassion over competition and wanted to succeed alongside others, not instead of others. Once

I had hung up my tap shoes for good, my lived experience led me to consider working in mental health. Still, I didn't have the best GCSE results (because I 'didn't need GCSEs to be on the west end') and I had a BTEC Level 3 diploma in performing arts. I knew I'd have to work my way up from the bottom, but I was ready for that.

My first NHS experience was volunteering in a Child & Adolescent Mental Health Service (CAMHS) learning disability respite and I absolutely loved it. I was learning so much about the needs of others, I felt valued and developed a great ability to communicate, which still serves me now. I then secured my first paid role within a General Hospital with individuals who might need a little more support due to risk to themselves or others. I was so nervous for the majority of this role! I remember feeling so young and so incompetent a lot of the time. I was working 1:1 with people who had brain injuries, dementia or delirium, and I felt very responsible for their safety. However, I did enjoy the role once the nerves had settled. I developed my own working style, planned activities and built real therapeutic relationships. Equally, I was honoured to hear clients' stories and share in their lives. When things were difficult, I took pride in making things that little bit more comfortable for clients. Heck, I even spent one shift singing Judy Garland on repeat to help someone feel that little bit more relaxed. The role was a huge learning curve, but it taught me that connection is such a valuable thing. When I think back to this first paid role, I'm so proud. I literally started my journey on a Band 1 minus 25% apprenticeship (a band that doesn't even exist anymore!). It feels quite symbolic; just as I've progressed through pay bands, so too have I progressed personally and professionally.

I also remember feeling nervous when I secured my first healthcare assistant role, working on a Psychiatric Intensive Care Unit. I wish I could forget the fact that I was 'shadowing' a member of staff who had worked on the ward for longer, and I almost shadowed them to the toilet as I was following their every move! However, I gained so much confidence in this role; I matured in age as well as ability. I became much more serious about a career in mental health around this time, but I couldn't quite work out where I'd fit. I successfully applied for mental health nursing three times, but it didn't feel completely 'me'. I wanted to spend time with clients and teams and work in a different way. However, it was around this time that I was asked to sit in on a meeting between a client and Clinical Psychologist due to the need for two staff members to be in the room. I studied the psychologist's every move and was so impressed by how they used their knowledge. They took time to talk to me after the appointment and explained their thoughts. Without knowing it, this was the first time I had actually reflected on my own thought process too. I considered how easy it was to misjudge someone's behaviour when you're unaware of how cognitive processes can impact upon things. I wanted to be able to understand and rationalise things like that someday.

Then came the battle of Clinical Psychology versus Psychiatry. I considered medical school, because if I didn't gel with psychiatry, I could always choose surgery. After picking the brains of a psychiatrist, we received a call that some bloods needed to be taken. I was one sign off away from being competent to do them alone, and the Psychiatrist offered to observe and sign. I instantly regretted discussing medical school and was so nervous to take bloods in front of them! Long story short, I took the bloods perfectly but was a sweaty mess. Once the client had left the room, the psychiatrist looked me dead in the eyes and said, "please tell me you don't want a career in surgery?!" I laughed, but the super speed cheek flush said it all.

My last NHS role to date was in Peer Support, and I credit that role with the reason why I went onto university. It was such a different way of working; I was suddenly so aware of the power dynamic that exists between professional and client. In this role, the concept of mutuality was encouraged, and it was a joint sense-making journey. My role wasn't to advise, it was purely to relate and connect. Although I can see so much value in this role, it also wasn't the right one for me. I'm very much a problem solver, I find it difficult to switch off my thought processes in order to just 'be' with someone. Sometimes, it took a whole lot of effort to refrain from asking someone if they'd tried X, Y or Z, because it seemed like that might help. I also became very aware of iatrogenic harm and systemic issues, and I wanted to work in a role that gave me some of the power needed to tackle those issues. I spoke about Clinical Psychology during supervision sessions, and my manager was always super supportive of this. They really were worth their weight in gold and are now stuck with me forever (Aspiring Psychologists – find someone like this and add them to your team!)

So, I opted to study BSc (Hons) Psychology with Clinical Psychology at Teesside University and made a career game plan. Knowing really very little about the trajectory, everything seemed so simple. I noted that I had practical experience, so all I needed now was research experience, that way I could do the Doctorate in Clinical Psychology straight after my degree and be a psychologist in six years. I soon learned that things aren't quite so linear, but I'm at peace with that now. I fell in love with

Psychology, and I'd happily spend the rest of my life learning more about it and honing my skills. I still set out to squeeze as much as I could out of the university experience, and I'd say I've achieved that goal. The experiences I've had have boosted my confidence a little more every time. I've been a research assistant on several research projects, was awarded the BPS Undergraduate Research Assistantship, became a peer assisted study sessions leader, served as chair elect of the BPS student committee, won a poster prize at a conference, wrote many blog posts and administered over 100 COVID vaccinations. University helped me to challenge everything I had once believed about myself. I am so much more resilient than I ever thought; we completed a year and a half online due to the coronavirus pandemic, I lost three family members in the space of one month in my final year, and I wanted to press pause on my studies, but I kept going. This is also where I think lived experience comes into it; there have been points in my life where I felt like I had nothing left to give, like I was done, yet I'm still here. I know that even when I think my tank is empty, it isn't.

So, in a nutshell, that's my journey so far.[26] I've finished university and am now waiting for my final grade to be ratified, which looks like it should be a First - from someone who once couldn't see a future with any promise, to now obtaining my first Assistant Psychologist post without a confirmed degree grade. Psychology has absolutely changed my life, and I feel a sense of purpose every day. I'm so proud of who I am and where I am today. I started this chapter by describing how I used to tell

---

[26] Chrissie's editorial note: Oh Nikita – I can relate to your story and admire your tenacity and dedication. Thank you so much for sharing your journey with us.

myself that Clinical Psychology wasn't for me, and I end this chapter believing that it is for me, just as it is for anyone who is also reading this. To my fellow people with lived experience: there's a place in Psychology for the deep empathy and understanding that we bring. If this is your driving force too, then let it be the reason that you take the first step towards a psychological profession. To anyone who may be thinking of a psychological career but feeling a little nervous to take that first step: I'd urge you to do it, I wish I'd have done it years ago! Good luck, everyone, you've got this!

Nikita Sheperdson
Assistant Psychologist

THANK YOU!

OH NIKITA! THANKS SO MUCH FOR YOUR STORY. I FEEL LIKE I CAN'T COMPUTE WHAT YOU HAVE CRAMMED INTO THE LAST 25 YEARS! IT'S INCREDIBLE! IT SOUNDS LIKE YOU HAVE DONE SO MUCH AND KEPT ON STRIVING. I JUST WANTED TO SEND MY CONDOLENCES FOR THE LOSS OF YOUR THREE FAMILY MEMBERS. HOPING YOU CAN TAKE A LITTLE BIT OF TIME OVER THE SUMMER TO HAVE A BIT OF A CHILL AND ALSO TO WILDLY CELEBRATE YOUR LIKELY 1ST CLASS DEGREE! WISHING YOU SO MUCH SUCCESS AND DO KEEP ME POSTED ON HOW YOU GET ON! I DO CONFESS TO OWNING ONE CASHMERE JUMPER, BUT I BOUGHT IT FROM NEW LOOK IN 2006 WHEN I GOT MY FIRST ASSISTANT POST. SO, YOU KNOW, MAYBE CHECK OUT THE CASHMERE OPTIONS IN FUTURE TOO, YOU'RE TOTALLY GONNA ROCK IT AND BE AS INCREDIBLY PUT TOGETHER AS THOSE WHO HAVE GONE BEFORE YOU ☺

P.S. I THINK WE MUST HAVE GONE TO SIMILAR SCHOOLS AS I WENT TO AN ARMY CAREERS DAY ONCE AND AFTER CUTTING MY BUM ON SOME BARBED WIRE DECIDED IT DEFINITELY WASN'T FOR ME!

MARIANNE

10

- Elizabeth's Story -

Plan A

Within Psychology forums there is much debate about the barriers to getting onto Clinical Psychology or for that matter, any Psychology doctoral training scheme. Age it seems (on the surface) isn't a barrier as it is protected under the Equality Act (2010). In this chapter, I intend to discuss this along with other potential barriers to becoming a psychologist and provide 'food for thought' as I reflect upon my own journey.

Hi. I'm Elizabeth. I'm 43 and I'm an Aspiring Psychologist. Initially, post-graduation, 'my plan A' had always been to pursue the DClinPsy. However, my journey to working in our beloved NHS and finally finding my path towards the Doctorate has been a long road, full of bumps, humps, curves, multiple knock backs, as well as many HIGHS which we call - 'lived experiences'. All of which have allowed for growth and shaped me into the person and professional I am both today and will also be when I FINALLY get on a course! WARNING - I will

114

probably talk more about the challenges and difficulties I have overcome because I think these have been most impactful. So, back to the beginning...

I proudly come from a working-class background, and I was the first in my family to complete a degree. I grew up in a multicultural area in Sheffield, yes, I'm a 'Sheffield Lass'; and attended a 'failing' primary school (which closed when I completed Y6). I was then thrown into what seemed to primarily be a 'middle-class secondary' and realised how much I didn't know. I scraped through my GCSEs believing that I just wasn't that bright. It has really taken years for me to understand that a strong foundation in academia – laid in primary, is important and that, I am quite bright (whatever that means!) I guess I have carried that narrative, and if bright means intelligent, in the academic sense – I still don't identify with that label. I prefer; hard-working, determined, resilient and perhaps if you pushed me - emotionally intelligent. I say the latter because, I have always been interested in people, whilst holding a sensitive and 'socially shy' personality, I have been fascinated by people's reactions to situations, what drives them and noticing very slight shifts in non-verbal cues. I'm interested in what has happened to people and what has brought them to their current situations. This, along with the desire to help others mange difficult situations, is I guess what brings me to Psychology.

So, back to topic 😊 , after very average GCSE grades I went on to 6ᵗʰ Form and that's where I discovered Psychology. It felt instinctual to me. I understood the content, knew how to write in 'that way' and felt 'at home'. My interest was well and truly sparked, I had a lovely teacher (heads up to Mr Morton), and I flourished in my coursework. My exam anxieties created by many a failed assessment and difficult experiences leading up to GCSE meant that my A-Level results were two C's and a D; at least Psychology was one of the Cs! I was thoroughly disappointed and attribute the results to anxiety in pressured exam situations. P.S. Who knew that some DClin courses look at A-Level results through the short-listing process? Not me! (Something I plan to explain in the other section of the application form). Nevertheless, my results allowed me to go on to study Psychology at degree level, so off I went...

I studied at Nottingham Trent University and gained a 2:1 in Social Sciences (Psychology) an accredited degree that I am oh so grateful that I did[27]*. It taught me how much I loved Psychology and allowed me to gain work experience as a Behaviour Therapist - delivering Applied Behaviour Analysis (ASD) interventions for a young person with Autism. So, after getting my solid 2:1, which was an amazing achievement for me[28], I went off to find a job.

---

[27] Also, who knew that some courses require you to note your exact grade? I confess I did and worked hard to get this from my university, but guess what? My degree is so old, no longer exists and there is no one at the university who can remember how the scores were weighted so I cannot get one. Hmmm, maybe age is a barrier? Also, application 2023 update; a course that I was interested in are changing their criteria so that weighted scores are no longer an issue, but they require a 64% average across the last 2 years of undergraduate degree – mine is 54%. Sadly, despite emails back and forth, the university will not budge and will not account for grade inflation (though they recognise it) – so this university is no longer an option for me. It seems that age is a discriminatory factor and any master's degrees are not taken into account; I do understand this as everyone cannot afford a master's (I couldn't have without it being subsidised). It does beg the question, why have a percentage at all?

[28] A great achievement in that I worked hard and finally got a grade I was capable of – the course suited me well, having very few, if any exams (I can't remember having one); hmmm, maybe exam anxiety is a thing?!

So, after completing my degree, I went back to Sheffield, thinking that I would love to work for the NHS and get an Assistant Psychologist (AP) role, after all, I wanted to become a psychologist! At the same time, I wanted to find out more about Autism and ABA. And so, mainly because my Mum worked there and so it was easy to get a job (thanks Mum!), I began working as an admin assistant in the multi-cultural area that I grew up in. This role really meant a lot to me and was a blessing in the way it has shaped me; I was responsible for planning and developing community projects, which I believe is really valuable work. Finding out about projects in this community gave me some insight to inequalities and made sense of some of my social experiences attending school in a multi-cultural area.

I applied for numerous Assistant roles but never made interview. Whilst being a part-time, self-employed Behaviour Therapist I continued with my admin assistant role and with learning about community projects. I also took initiative and started carving out my own experiences! It was in this role that I started being supervised by Clinical Psychologists and daunting as it was from time to time, I absolutely loved the experiences. I remember organising a meeting with an NHS psychologist; the discussion topics questions on my hit list were:

1. Tips for career progression
2. Ideas to work towards an AP role
3. How to ultimately progress to the Doctorate one day.

Her advice was:

"Go out get some relevant experience and come back to applying at a later stage!"

I certainly did this[29]; I was so curious about Autism and ABA so I worked more hours, for next to nothing in wages (especially after travel time). Eventually I was able to secure an internship, working in the California office of an international company delivering quality and progressive services to families. Spoiler alert: I eventually ended working for this company for almost 20 years. During this time, I was supervised by Clinical Psychologists – something I have since learned needs to be explicit in my future applications (because apparently private practice can be viewed differently by courses/Clinical Psychologists here); another barrier perhaps? The jury is out on this one for me. What do you guys think?

---

[29] I see questions about relevant experiences on social media forums now, there are lots of different/alternative roles out there that are relevant! Go get them!

My experiences with my employers, both in the US (where I had an absolute blast and made friends for life), and especially in the UK, fluctuated and were very much influenced by the 'management' and their management style. As a result of this, I experienced what I viewed to be some pretty horrendous 'set-backs'. For example, prior to coming home to work in the UK for the said company, my progress was discussed publicly. It was decided, publicly, which was news to me, that I was not going to be a supervisor on returning to the U.K. This conversation was witnessed by me, my peers and supervisors/management and came as an almighty blow! I have likened it to DClin course rejections, but instead of the generic email coming to your inbox, it goes to everyone's! Hell, they might as well have thrown it out on Twitter! I felt completely screwed over! There was only one person in the room who recognised this as it was happening. She was so kind to me and supported me on my return to the U.K. and beyond. I honestly wouldn't have hung around and put up with the shit I did without her! The next blow didn't come till I was back home. You see, whilst being on my internship, I was allowed to flourish within the role, to conduct assessments (under supervision), make decisions during intervention and then reflect in supervision. In the U.K., management of the micro kind, let me know that I needed to do what was prescribed by supervisors and check before I did any of the above! This meeting was heart-breaking for me, and so I thought, should I leave? Should I leave after giving almost 2 years to work for this? I felt so conflicted because I had developed so much and had so much to give, so...I stayed. This experience and many more like this resulted in a confidence collapse which stuck with me for years afterwards, supervision wasn't as I had experienced or expected. So, I relied on my support network (not just family but my colleague and friend 😊), and this, along with my stubbornness to prove I am worthy and that I could work through the ranks and become a valued member of the team led to my sticking with it for so much longer than perhaps I should have.

REFLECTIVE Q&A

Q How long is too long with regards to sticking with the DClin?

Unknown A

For me, it feels it is what I am supposed to do, but am aware that, given my age, it may not happen for me. I am not yet ready to embark on yet another Plan B.

I would say that I didn't really feel valued by management until 2013, when a new manager came in and provided support. This was a game changer for me, supervision that challenged and yet supported, with reflection and room to find my own way! So yes, 9 years without feeling valued, and I hear you ask? Why not get out and come back to AP stuff? The truth is, I was kind of stuck...though whilst it sounds awful, it wasn't all bad, I learnt loads and it wasn't until recent reflection that I have in fact, as a result of 'sticking with the shit', met many competencies necessary for becoming a Clinical Psychologist. I just have to make this clear on paper for next application round!

I was rooted to the spot because I had bought a house and thought that this showed commitment to the company and to a career. So, financially, this left me in a bit of a pickle because I now had a mortgage, was earning well minus travel expenses and couldn't really afford to step back into the role of an AP or similar – so I felt that the path/plan to becoming a psychologist was getting further and further away.

This work meant significant travel – working all over the North of England. At one point I was leaving home at 5:30am and getting home at 9pm! I was in my early 20's and to quote a Sheffield phrase, 'reyt tired!' The nature of work meant that this couldn't change, despite trying. I knew at some point I would have to move on because despite loving the job (I did love it for a time), the travel was not sustainable and there was a definite sense my wellbeing or the wellbeing of others wouldn't be considered in business decisions.

Between then and now, I have been married, am raising two beautiful children and one adorable puppy. I live in a lovely house and am very grateful for what we have. Whilst these are all wonderful experiences, they have come with different challenges which impacted my ability to get back on track. Financially, I was still stuck: my second statutory paid maternity leave left us in a bit of debt and then there was the personal challenges which meant a move wasn't a wise option...

After getting married (best day ever!), my Grandma died. My Dad died when my son was 8 months old (and being in private practice, I needed to negotiate a week of paid leave to recover from this). My Mum in law died, when my son was 2. I miscarried between my son and my daughter; my daughter's pregnancy was high risk, so I had a procedure to see whether she was affected – the most agonising 48 hour wait known. Then when my daughter was about 18 months, we went on holiday to the U.S. for a wedding and after this, I began to have serious concerns about my daughter's development, a penny seemed to drop which sent me and my family into turmoil. I worried in a big and clinically significant way about her potentially having ASC and having worked with many parents who constantly have to fight the system, I broke. I accessed services for both me and my daughter, whilst trying to remain present for my son and husband. So, without going too much into this, I have lived experience as a service user and have overcome personal challenges as well as professional ones. Also, not wanting the picture to seem too bleak, I accessed IAPT services which I was discharged from following a low-intensity intervention. I believe these experiences have aided my journey and experiences. I think about these times when in the room with families/individuals and work hard to address power imbalances; I understand the difficulties of uncertainties and recognise the need to be clinically sensitive when discussing diagnosis for example. Also, I wanted to spend time with my children whilst they were at home and was adamant that I wouldn't make a change for me until they were settled in school. In these periods, it is not that I hadn't made efforts to find a new role, I tried further study (whilst off on maternity leave with my first born) – what was I thinking; oh, I know?! I will have a baby, be up all night, it's okay, I can study when he is sleeping, HA! Also, newsflash, some babies don't sleep that long and being up in the night meant that I needed to find time to rest, or clean, or cook or have conversations with other humans to keep myself sane. I applied for positive behaviour support assistant roles, not knowing how the hell I would pay my mortgage. Turns out – I sucked at interviews and especially interviews in the NHS. You have to be able to talk public sector language and truth be told, I think you have to be immersed in the system to truly understand it and I was not. I found that the language in my private practice was very different, and this is something I am looking at for this application round – what experiences I have had to date, how do they relate to Clinical Psychology in the NHS and how does that relate to training...

So, I waited, and I did work through the ranks, first as a 1:1 staff, then as a supervisor and then as a behaviour consultant (the latter two, following the completion of my MSc in Behaviour Analysis (Distinction equivalent) in 2008 – another massive achievement for me). In the last 10years +, aside from the difficulties mentioned above, I was aware of a 'niggle', a sense of being or *becoming unhappy in the role. This was because I knew I wanted to broaden my knowledge and work within different models and in an integrated way (which was happening to an extent, but this was off my own back rather than being guided in supervision), I also became very aware that because of the nature of funding, we tended to work with middle-class families who could afford to pay privately. I found this difficult to sit with and there was always the sense of not feeling valued as a person and ongoing resentment stemmed from earlier difficulties, that for me, couldn't be resolved. The unhappiness[30] I was feeling was highlighted when my friend, Helen Barley[31], left and as an ABA person, you are definitely an outsider and treated as such (another thing that was difficult about the role as Behavioural Consultant – I talk more about this later).

My roles as supervisor and consultant have meant that I have experience working systemically and a lot with schools and families too. I had previously considered Educational Psychology but had thought not sure I could do that! I had a very dated and skewed view because I only really saw them at review meetings or tribunal when they were sat on the side of the Local Authority presenting evidence against ABA. On our side I did meet a few nice ones, especially the private ones! So, when Helen said I should look at it, I toddled along to the open day and came out with a spark! It was a, thought bubble that looked like this:

---

[30] I say unhappy in the role because, again, it wasn't all bad, but like most things, it came in waves. On reflection this was because Helen was also my peer mentor, and I valued her input in my development so much.

[31] Helen has consented to her real name being included here.

Therefore, for the following 3 years, I applied to the Ed Psych Doctorate – without interviews (recognising that many Ed Psychs don't like and dare I say it, perhaps don't understand ABA and how flexibly/fluidly it can be applied). I recognised at some point, and I don't know when that perhaps the Doctorate wouldn't come until I had experiences in other jobs in the systems, I actually wanted to work in.

In 2020, when lockdown hit, I spent 6 weeks working every day and trying to home school my two little ones as my husband was out as frontline staff. I recognised this was too difficult for me to balance my family's needs and what work required. Therefore, I put my family first and fought to be furloughed. As things became a little easier – I began applying for AP positions (involving a massive pay cut) and finally (after 5 interviews) I secured my current role as an AP in Child & Adolescent Mental

Health Services (CAMHS) and I absolutely love it! I feel more confident, valued and happy! It took this to realise that I had definitely been feeling unhappy, and it is here that I have found my path and feel able to work towards my Plan A once more. I began to realise, especially after starting as a Clinical AP that the EP path isn't perhaps the right one? The jury is still out here! I love working in schools but am scared of being limited to Education and being in a service that doesn't do much hands on with young people, but instead writes EHCPs (been there and done that). I am aware that this is an assumption based on what I've learned from time on Twitter and from chatting to EPs. I have picked up the vibe that EPs don't necessarily love my background and I have experienced being an outsider before.

I was surrounded by lovely people who recognised my good work. I got the message that I would get on to the Clinical Doctorate first time! So, finally feeling, back on track and valued in the service, in 2021/22 I applied to the Clinical Doctorate. I got zero interviews. To say I was crushed was an understatement because I had really, really focussed on the application. I recognise the difficulties for someone like me in the system, with my location being somewhat limited (especially with one Uni not allowing for grade inflation); the average age of trainees being around 27, I am much, much older, my research and academic experience is 'dated', let's say (though I am working on changing this)[32]. However, I have a lot of lived experience. I believe being a parent has enhanced my clinical skills, especially in terms of clinical sensitivity and that my resilience in the trickier periods (recognising the need for self-care) is an asset. I believe that my ABA experience has taught

---

[32] I have been offered a Research Assistant post and am currently trying to agree on a secondment. I have started a research project in my service too!

me to adapt interventions, work in an integrative way and has developed my confidence 'in the room' individually and when working with systems. I believe my working-class background has prepared me for the pitfalls and as a result I hold a strong work ethic – all of which, I believe, should be celebrated and seen as a positive. Therefore, for next round, I have decided to own my unique selling points; which are my age (experience) and my 'alternative route'; with the recognition that it may take a little longer but that what I have to offer is valuable and worthy of a place. I am also shifting my mindset (I'm working on it!), instead of preparing for the application and putting everything into it, I am preparing for training in the hope it will be recognised when I am ready. Lastly, I am lucky to have a supportive family (especially my hubby) who also has to live with the rollercoaster journey that is the DClinPsy!

So, my advice and promises to people in similar situations:

- Take the pay cut and just do it (when the time is right for you) – you will manage!
- I promise to mentor an older applicant when I finally get on.
- Outliers like me do get on. Don't they?
- Have kids when you feel ready for them but don't let the Doctorate stop you.
- Spend time out of Psychology, with people you love and support you (for me this is my Hubby, Anthony; my kiddies H & F; My Mum and Sis & co. and our fur babies L & W – love them!)

Questions I ask myself:

- How long is too long to keep going?

- Will every year be harder and harder with more barriers?
- Will all Universities one day apply these new rules which will rule me out?
- Am I good enough?
- Is it impossible to get through the bottle neck?

Elizabeth Veeren
Assistant Psychologist

Hi Elizabeth,

Thanks so much for your story, there really have been many twists and turns along the way. I love how much you have been able to embrace yourself and learn and reflect on the experiences you have been through. I can concur that grief whilst trying to parent children of any age, let along super young ones, really sucks! I do hope you were well supported at this time. I am wishing you so well for the application season 2022/23! Please do keep me posted on how you get on and thanks for all of the advice you have offered our readers!

Marianne, x

11

- Priya's Story -

My Timeline

The biggest lesson I've learnt as an aspiring Clinical Psychologist is to enjoy the journey; I wish I had told myself this sooner. For many, like myself, gaining a place on the Doctorate is the ultimate *end goal* and it is often accompanied by enormous amounts of pressure and self-doubt. I spent the start of my journey thinking I should be doing more and achieving more. Everything I focused on related to the Doctorate. Some may view this as determination; however, I regularly questioned if I deserved time off or any enjoyment in life as I had not reached my *end goal*. I now see that the *end goal* is not the Doctorate; there is *no end goal*, and you should not put your life on hold for one course. It's important to take a step back, live in the movement and reflect on personal and professional experiences that shape our values to be the best version of ourselves and a good Clinical Psychologist.

I always knew I wanted to go to university, and growing up in an Indian family, I was only ever exposed to the 'gold standard' degree choices of Medicine, Dentistry and Pharmacy. I was destined for a career in healthcare. As I look back on my journey, this was not something I wanted to do, and I had no real reason to pursue any of the above careers. When I picked my A-Levels, I chose subjects based on other people's expectations of me studying a course that would lead to practising a profession.

Sixth Form was challenging, and I did not enjoy it. I was expected to know the answers to all problems; if not, I was told to solve them independently. This was a steep learning curve. Teachers soon began to say that university was not for me, but that there was 'no harm in applying' but I should find an 'easy' degree or consider an alternative option to higher education. I finished my first year of Sixth Form with the grades E, E, U. It won't surprise you that it's below the grades required for any course including an 'easy' one! I was disappointed in myself, but in a last-minute attempt to improve my grades and prove my self-worth to both family and teachers, I continued to work hard in my final year. I gave up on applying for a 'gold standard' degree and was pushed into applying for Geography. I enjoyed the subject but not enough to study it for the next three years.

Unfortunately, my best was not good enough, and I was met with repeated negative comments and constant comparisons to others more academically gifted than me. As no surprise, on results day, I left Sixth Form with DEU and no university offers. The panic set in almost immediately. What was I going to do with my life? What would I tell my family? Would I ever get to university? I opted to take a gap year, it was never my intention, but this is where I like to think my journey to becoming a Clinical Psychologist started.

Most students who decide to take a gap year do something enjoyable, not me. Whilst attempting to obtain better grades in my re-sits I worked in my local Marks and Spencer café! At this point, I had set my sights on becoming a Clinical Psychologist; there was something about the profession that interested me. I liked how varied the role could be in terms of whom you could work with but also that I would be using my knowledge to support the most vulnerable members of society. It's strange because I found A-Level Psychology boring, the teacher dictated, and we listened – nothing was exciting about the subject. My opinion on Psychology changed when I began to revisit topics ready for my re-sits, and I found learning about different models and theories interesting. For the first time, I was excited to embark on my journey as it felt like I was making the right decision for *me*. Fast track to results day (again), my grades weren't much better, but I did manage to secure a C in Psychology. Yet again, I had no offers and spent hours on the clearing house website desperately trying to find a Psychology course that would accept me. I called every university that had spaces on the course and was rejected by all of them. Sometimes I even called them more than once a day to see if they would offer me a place based on my resilience! It worked; I was offered a place at Birmingham City University.

During my time at university, despite most lectures informing the entire cohort how difficult it was to gain a place on the Doctorate, I firmly had my sights set on becoming a Clinical Psychologist! I finished university with a 2:1 and secured a place at the University of Manchester to complete the MRes in Psychology.

At this point, I remember thinking how hard can it be to become a Clinical Psychologist? Hindsight has shown me......How naïve was I?

The Master's was challenging, nothing like undergraduate; deadlines were tighter, and expectations were higher. What made it difficult was balancing a part-time job in retail, assignments and finding that ever elusive 'clinically relevant experience!' There were times when I wanted to give up, but after a very long year, I graduated with a Merit.

During the second half of my master's, I had started working as a Mental Health Support Worker. I enjoyed this role as I was involved in the direct care of individuals with a range of mental health difficulties. If I thought the master's was hard then the real work started when it came to me applying for Assistant Psychologist posts. I had been in this role for around six months before I began applying for Assistant Psychology posts. I never counted how many applications I completed; I expect it was well over two dozen. I was keen to become an assistant and move on to the next step in my journey, but I soon became frustrated and disheartened as every application or interview was a rejection with the same feedback: 'It was lovely to meet you, and we think you're great, but unfortunately another applicant just had more experience than you'. Just as I was about to give up and apply for a graduate scheme unrelated to Psychology, I came across an Assistant Psychologist post in Malvern working with adults with Autism. Given my track record, I was reluctant to apply but decided I would give it one last go. I certainly didn't even expect to hear back let alone get an interview.

September 2019:
Shock! I got the job! I was one step closer to the Doctorate.
In all honesty, although I was excited and eager to get started, I felt nervous and anxious. I questioned whether I had the skills to provide the support service users needed as prior to this role I had limited experience working with clinical populations. In addition to these feelings, I was overwhelmed with the pressure to impress my supervisor so that she would view me as a 'good assistant' and not the fraud I felt like.

The first few weeks in post were intense as I navigated the responsibilities of an assistant, but I soon settled in, and my confidence began to grow. My clinical supervisor, Helen, was amazing; she was incredibly supportive and knowledgeable. Helen ensured I had a varied role to develop the clinical skills I needed to succeed in my future endeavours.

November 2019
It was in this role that I applied for the clinical Doctorate for the first time. I had only been in post two months and did not think I was ready but decided I would submit a 'practice' application

to know what the process was like. Unsurprisingly I didn't get any interviews. I was disappointed, but I also knew that it was normal to have to apply a few times before getting a place. As my ability to share my thoughts and feelings grew in supervision, I was able to share my raw emotions about receiving four rejections. I found myself questioning if I was good enough and if I even had the ability to acquire the skills needed. I always embraced supervision as an opportunity to focus on my needs. I left that supervision session feeling that a weight had been lifted from my shoulders and with an important message: Make the most of your experience. It's not about quantity, but quality and what you have learnt. Unfortunately, the COVID-19 pandemic hit and remote working and limited access to the service made it difficult to continue developing my therapeutic skills.

August 2020

The time eventually came to move on and gain further experience. I assumed that having had one Assistant post, I would be able to find other assistant jobs more easily; this was not the case. I was again repeatedly told that I did not have enough experience. This was beyond frustrating. Helen kindly recommended me to a friend who had just moved to a children's service as the head of the therapeutic team. At the time, the service was recruiting two new assistants. I applied and was lucky enough to be offered a position.

October 2020

I left my first post after 14 months and was sad to go, but I knew it was the right thing to do if I wanted to continue developing my skills. I left the service with better insight into critical areas such as the importance of good clinical governance and being a responsive practitioner rather than a reactive practitioner. I also learned to thrive on new challenges rather than being intimidated by unfamiliar models and techniques.

November 2020

My second post involved working with looked-after children, and as with any new assistant role comes a new supervisory relationship. This can be daunting at the best of times but forming a new relationship with your supervisor during a pandemic is strange. The usual in-person introductions no longer existed, and you were expected to operate entirely remotely.

I found this role challenging for a few reasons, but what I found most challenging was my supervision. Due to unforeseen circumstances, my allocated supervisor went on emergency maternity leave on my second day, which was not ideal but also not something that could be helped. This made my first week difficult as I didn't know who to ask for help or what I should be doing.

Emma, the head of the therapeutic service (also Helen's friend), kindly stepped in as my temporary supervisor. Emma was great; she understood the challenges of working with others, especially in highly emotive circumstances. Emma encouraged me to understand that working clinically is rarely working with one individual and how this can impact therapeutic engagement and the overall outcomes of our work.

I was also lucky to work alongside a brilliant Trainee Clinical Psychologist, Emily. I learnt a lot from Emily in terms of understanding the importance of a well-written formulation. Emily also introduced me to new models and techniques that I could consider when working with looked-after children. I thoroughly enjoyed working with Emily and found her support in developing my clinical skills helpful, as well as providing interesting discussion points for my reflective practice and personal development.

January 2021

Sadly, Emma left to take on another role, and for me, the service never felt the same after she'd gone. The role became increasingly challenging and my supervision was shared by five qualified psychologists. Each psychologist worked differently and seemingly had differing expectations of me. I was used to having one supervisor but being supervised by so many different psychologists left me feeling lost; there was no *real* supervisory relationship which made all aspects of the role difficult. Unfortunately, Emily left soon after Emma and further challenges arose.

Autumn 2020

At the start of my second assistant post, I applied for the Doctorate for the second time. I thought this was the year I would secure an interview at least; I met the minimum criteria for every course, and my application was much better than last year. In my eyes, there was no reason why I wouldn't get an interview. It's fair to say I underestimated how difficult getting an interview and a place on the Doctorate. Come springtime 2021, within the space of 48 hours, I received another four rejections.

I took each of those rejections personally, which led me down a dark path of sadness. I didn't want to speak to anyone about the Doctorate, and I did not want to see people post about receiving interviews. On reflection, I don't think it was just the rejections that made me feel sad and incredibly low it was also because I wasn't really enjoying my current role anymore.

I searched high and low for another job, with no luck. I desperately wanted an NHS job as I thought this would help me with my future applications for the Doctorate, but at each interview, I was again told that I didn't have enough experience. I gave up on applying and just plodded along in my current post.

June 2021

Out of the blue, I received a LinkedIn message from a senior recruitment consultant asking if I would be interested in an NHS role, they had available as they thought I had the skillset. Initially, I didn't think it was a real role, but regardless of my doubts, I sent over my CV as requested. I never expected to hear back, and a few weeks passed, and I still hadn't had any further communications from the agency. At this point, I was sure it was a 'fake' role until I received a call inviting me to an interview the following day. I jumped at the opportunity and began preparing for all possible interview questions. I wanted to showcase all my skills to illustrate that I had enough experience.

On the day of the interview, I felt unprepared given the short notice but despite my nerves, the interview went well. I was told it would be a few weeks before I would hear back, and given my previous track record with NHS Jobs, I didn't hold out much hope.

The next day I got a call from the recruitment consultant offering me the position. I was beyond shocked.

July 2021

I started my first NHS post working in the neurodevelopmental service. I didn't feel the usual first-day nerves, and for the first time, I felt proud of how far I had come in my journey to becoming a Clinical Psychologist.

I was able to draw upon all the skills I had learnt from my previous roles to support me. I used my knowledge of attachment theory when working with individuals who may have had difficult early life experiences. Having also worked with adults with Autism, I could draw upon the therapeutic strategies I had learnt when supporting families awaiting a neurodevelopmental assessment.

October 2021

I had only been working in the Neurodevelopmental service for four months when I was offered a post working in a category C prison for young offenders. I spent several weeks deliberating if I should take the job or not. I was happy in my current role and knew a part-time job was just not an option for me, but at the same time working in prison sounded exciting and gave me more varied clinical experience, something I knew I needed if I were to apply for the Doctorate again.

I couldn't give up on the opportunity of working with a new client group, but I also couldn't take the pay cut. I was stuck. I didn't know what to do. Eventually, I mustered up the courage to ask my line manager if it would be possible to work part-time so I could also work at the prison. Much to my surprise, she agreed.[33]

---

[33] I recognise my privilege of being able to work part-time in two different NHS roles.

November 2021

As an assistant in the prison service, I worked in the mental health and substance misuse team, an area in which I had minimal experience. I listened and learned a lot. I used my interpersonal skills to connect with others to learn about their histories and family dynamics to better inform my practice. I realised that all people could be vulnerable, and it's essential that they all feel heard and accepted regardless of their background.

Even though I had been applying for the Doctorate every year, I felt confident and ready to apply. I worked on feedback from previous applications and reflected on my experiences and how they shaped me into a 'good trainee'.

February 2022

Working in two very different posts wasn't all sunshine and rainbows; it was difficult to switch between the two, especially when you had a particularly challenging day at one. In addition, I felt the pinch of the pay cut and spent most of my monthly salary commuting to the prison.

I loved working in prison, and it was probably one of the best jobs I've had but working two part-time roles was no longer a viable option for me, and I handed in my notice.

March 2022

I started working at the neurodevelopmental service full-time. As I settled into the service, I eagerly awaited to hear from the Universities I had applied to but I received another four rejections for the third time. I started to panic about whether I would ever get onto the course.

My friends were worried about how I would take it as they all saw how hard I took the previous rejections. Coupled with having just had minor surgery on my face, I felt sorry for myself and vowed that I would never apply for the Doctorate again.

May 2022

The journey to Clinical Psychology pushes you to your limits and you go through a range of emotions from disappointment and anger to jealousy and frustration and everything else in between. I gave myself time to feel the emotions of not being offered an interview and started reflecting on my strengths and weaknesses. Through this process, I learned a lot about myself and how I feared failure, and I just wanted to be great at everything. I realised I was my own worst enemy.

I reframed my unsuccessful attempts as a 'you're not quite ready yet but keep trying' and I'm now working on the gaps in my application to apply again in November 2022.

Final reflections:

- Your life does not revolve around Clinical Psychology. Take time out for yourself to do the things you enjoy.

- Everyone's journey is so different, try not to compare yourself to others and instead use other people's experiences as a guide not a tick box.

- You don't have to be *the best*; you just need be able to let your personality shine through.

- Make the most of your experiences in your current role and ask for other opportunities.

- Most importantly believe in yourself; the journey to Clinical Psychology is a tough road and not everyone will know what you're going through but keep at it and enjoy the journey.

Priya Baden
Future Trainee Clinical Psychologist

Dr Marianne Trent (She/Her) • 6:01 PM

Oh Priya! I just adored reading your story. I am so pleased you persevered with the re-sits and I was practically whooping for you when you gained a place at Birmingham uni – got to absolutely love your tenacity in repeatedly calling them until they relented! Please do keep me posted on how you get on with this year's application cycle. I think you are absolutely right that one of the main take home points is to enjoy where you're at right now, regardless of what stage of the journey you're at. That said, right this second as I type this I am actually in the beautiful Malvern Hills. I am enjoying an afternoon of book writing and editing as I wait for my 3 friends to arrive. I really enjoyed our random Malvern synchronicity, this is my first time visiting and it's just glorious! That said.... They'll be here soon...I'd best pop another log on the hot tub!

12

- Georgie's Story -

Ride the Wave of Uncertainty

Hello to all you Aspiring Psychologists, my name is Georgie. Thank you for starting to read my story, I really hope you enjoy reading it ☺

After following Marianne for quite some time, I knew that I was very keen to contribute to this book when she announced that this was her next project. I was so pleased when she gave me the opportunity to share my story. I often see posts on social media wondering about academia and how this option could be a potential route to Clinical Psychology training. As a less conventional route, the posts I see often reflect uncertainty surrounding the option and so, I was keen to share my experiences highlighting my experience to training.

My story comes with a caveat; I am only one voice and so can only speak from my experience. I understand that I am privileged to have had positive experiences and this may not be the same for others with a similar path to myself. A large part of my journey to training was spent as a doctoral researcher but it is important to note that each PhD is unique and so everyone's experience will be different. However, I am keen to share my story to give people an insight into conducting a PhD. I believe, my experience has been invaluable in preparing me for further Psychology roles in the NHS and clinical training.

Firstly, I think it may be helpful to distinguish between a PhD and Clinical Psychology training. A PhD is a Doctorate-level qualification where an individual conducts research that makes a significant new contribution to knowledge in a particular field. Completing a PhD gives you the title of Doctor of Philosophy and allows you to conduct research, perhaps progressing onto post-Doctoral roles and Lectureships. Clinical Psychology training (DClin, ClinPsyD) is also a Doctorate-level qualification; however, it combines academic e.g., assignments, teaching, and research work with clinical placements. Completing the DClin gives you the title of Doctor of Clinical Psychology and allows you to conduct research and practice clinically.

Before going into detail about my PhD experience, it makes sense to start at the beginning. I was first introduced to Psychology when taking it for A Level. If I am honest, a big part of my choice here was due to my favourite teacher delivering the lessons (Thanks Miss Martin!) However, I did thoroughly enjoy the subject and felt that it only scratched the surface in terms of my intrigue for the subject. My next crossroad was choosing my undergraduate degree. I was conflicted here, due to thoroughly enjoying all three of my A Level subjects.

Psychology felt like a mixture of biology and sociology and so I went with that! I thoroughly enjoyed my degree and so when there was an option for me to apply to do a fourth year with a placement, I decided to apply. I didn't feel quite ready to leave university or finish learning about Psychology.

I did my placement in a research centre, aiming to improve the lives of individuals with rare genetic syndromes and their families. Whilst I had a really good experience during this placement and the team were brilliant, there were times where I wondered if I had made the right choice picking a research placement. I compared myself to others who had completed clinical placements in the NHS and worried I had set myself up to struggle to get clinical roles.

Despite this, I continued to encourage myself to be open to opportunities and made the most of my time on placement. Coming to the end of my placement, my supervisor let me know that she had an opportunity for a PhD student to join her team. I never planned to do a PhD, the opportunity just happened to arise at the right time, in the right team on the right topic. I am so glad I took the opportunity. Currently I am writing this sitting on my sofa waiting for Love Island to start. Reflecting on my journey is particularly fresh because I submitted my PhD thesis just last week - and what a journey it has been!

When applying for my PhD, I completed two interviews for potential funding, one interview was with the university where I would undertake my studies and the other was a charity that funded research focusing on individuals with learning disability (The Baily Thomas Charitable Fund). If you are interested in completing a PhD and you can apply for funding from different sources, I would encourage this as it increases your chances of being successful and also adds to your experience of doctoral interviews.

My PhD focused on improving the identification and assessment of anxiety in individuals with moderate to profound learning disability, including those with an autism diagnosis and/or rare genetic syndrome diagnosis. The experience supported my development, both personally and professionally. This included research and leadership skills, team working, clinically relevant skills e.g., psychological and risk assessment, adapting my communication and working with systems. Conducting a PhD will also likely reassure Clinical Psychology programmes that you can manage a doctoral level qualification. It is often noted that during clinical training you must juggle multiple competing demands – a PhD is absolutely that! You may have multiple research studies running at the same time, each at different stages in the research process.

From my experience, research (particularly the thought of statistics!) can be an area that is daunting to many Aspiring Psychologists. I felt exactly the same, as someone who was told by a schoolteacher that I would never get an 'A' in my Maths GCSE. It struck me how moments like this have impacted my beliefs about my ability to succeed (even though with real hard work, I managed to prove this teacher wrong!!) For me, it was the uncertainty surrounding whether I would be able to get my head round it and how I would work things out on my own; with the right support and some perseverance, I managed to get through it. My tips would be to embrace the uncertainty or fear you might feel around research. I spent my PhD riding the wave of uncertainty and fear that I wouldn't know how to successfully conduct my analyses. It's been such a learning curve and from what I understand, the learning continues during the Doctorate and post-qualification, I have learnt to embrace this continual learning, and this is one reason why I believe choosing a Clinical Psychology career is the right path for me!

When coming to the end of my studies, I was keen to get some experience within a clinical setting. I prepared myself for 'failure' and the worries came creeping in that my research background would not serve me well during NHS/clinical interviews. I did have unsuccessful applications and interviews, and I suspected that getting a clinical job in a 'new' population for me, i.e., not a job working with autistic individuals and/or individuals with learning disabilities, would be even more tricky. After a few attempts, I secured a job as an Assistant Psychologist (AP) in a CAMHS service in May 2021 and was absolutely thrilled.

Working as an AP has been such a positive experience for me. I am in a warm and supportive team of people whose main focus is improving the lives of children, young people and their families. I started the job very much feeling out of my depth because I had never delivered therapy before. This worried me, consuming a lot of my thoughts for some time. With the right support, I have been able to be honest and take clinical work at my own pace, this has been invaluable for developing my skills and confidence as a therapist.

Taking into consideration how competitive the Psychology field is, a message that was drummed into me during my undergraduate degree was that I needed to accept that if I wanted a career within Clinical Psychology, it is a long one. Also, that a lot of us probably wouldn't get onto the Doctorate because it's so competitive! Whilst it is important to manage our expectations around the profession, I would encourage you to not let it put you off if you feel Clinical Psychology is for you.

Adding to the competitiveness of the field is also the instability of roles, with often fixed-term contracts. Don't burn yourself out or overload yourself with opportunities – I did this in my AP role which in the end helped me to develop the skill of being realistic and being better able to manage my workload. However, the pressure to succeed, appear competent and get involved in as many opportunities as possible was overwhelming. You are in these roles for a reason – you have already shown colleagues your fabulous self!

I applied for clinical training in 2021 and 2022. To focus on reality and give context to my situation, I share below my application outcomes:

- 2021: four Universities, no interviews
- 2022: four Universities, one interview, one reserve place which materialised into a place.

I feel very lucky to have been offered a place, but I have already noticed that imposter syndrome creeping in, and I have caught myself noting that I got a reserve place, not a 'real' place, doubting my abilities and skills. These reflections are very new and something I am still learning to manage. I'm also aware that these feelings will probably ebb and flow throughout training and perhaps beyond.

To end with a few reflections and hopes, I hope my story shows that you don't need to be a die-hard Psychology fan right from the start, and you don't need to have your journey completely planned out. There is value in keeping your options open and seeing where opportunities take you. Everyone's journey is so different which I find often makes it easier to compare ourselves to others and worry about areas where we feel we 'fall short'. I would urge you to remind yourself that your journey is valid and important, do what makes you happy and what you feel is right for you. At different times in life, I like to believe that you are exactly where you need to be. My advice would be to ride the wave, you gain so many skills along the way, even amidst periods of great stress or sometimes without even realising it.

I am sending you all good luck and well wishes for your Psychology journey – to show dedication, determination, and passion for a profession with such a complex career route is astounding and something to be immensely proud of.

I hope you know the Psychology profession would be lucky to have you.

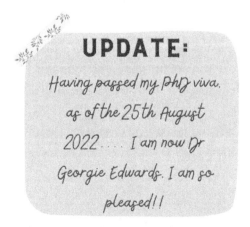

UPDATE:

Having passed my PhD viva, as of the 25th August 2022..... I am now Dr Georgie Edwards. I am so pleased!!

Dr Georgie Edwards
Twitter handle: @georgietedwards

Resources:
https://www.bailythomas.org.uk
https://www.findaphd.com
https://www.jobs.ac.uk/phd

Thank You & Congrats!

Dear Georgie,

Oh Georgie! Thank you so much for your story, you write beautifully. I just wanted to specifically thank *you* for helping *me* develop more insight into the cogs and processes involved with a PhD. I know that our readers will find this enlightening, and that you'll help instil hope and help people feel more informed about options.

I am so pleased that you have been offered a place. Embracing compassion is so important and I really like the Compassionate Mind Approach to Difficult Emotions book by Dr Chris Irons. And also, the audiobook version of Prof Paul Gilbert OBE's The Compassionate Mind.

Please do be so proud of yourself and let me know how training goes for you. I hope you are able to take some time to unwind and have some fun this summer so that you can make a mindful and excited start come September. So many congratulations to you on passing your viva and becoming a Dr! Here's to the double Dr years and beyond....!

Stay kind to you,
Marianne

13

- Cian's Story -

Finding My Feet

Hello! I'm Cian and I am 22 years old. To give a little context about who I am before I jump into my story - I was brought up by my parents with my older sister in a small town in Hampshire. I feel privileged to say that I am one of the lucky ones who completely and utterly adored their childhood. Never once do I remember waking up with dread to go to school or worrying about whether anyone would play with me in the playground. I loved my home environment, I loved the summer afternoons playing with the kids in my Close, I loved going to dance classes in the evenings. During secondary school I found a group of friends who mostly remain my friends to this day, and I continued my passion for dancing, taking part in the summer theatre production each year. Then when Sixth Form came around, I quickly found my feet and fell straight into the wonderful world of Psychology. I'll be honest - I wanted to study medicine throughout my schooling years, and it was only when I realised that maths and chemistry were not exactly my strong suit, that I reconsidered my aspirations of becoming a medical doctor.

Year 12 was the first time I'd ever studied Psychology, and I found almost everything fascinating! At my college we had the option of doing what was called an Extended Project Qualification. This was where you could choose a topic to study, research and present information on – I chose Post Traumatic Stress Disorder, (PTSD). I think my interest stemmed from when I did work experience at an army barracks, and it got me thinking about the field of trauma. Even when I wanted to become a doctor, my goal was to be an army medic, and since then I can honestly say that trauma has been on the forefront of my mind regarding the kinds of people I'd like to help.

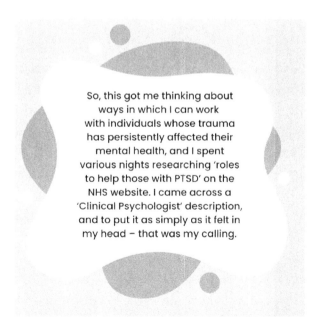

So, this got me thinking about ways in which I can work with individuals whose trauma has persistently affected their mental health, and I spent various nights researching 'roles to help those with PTSD' on the NHS website. I came across a 'Clinical Psychologist' description, and to put it as simply as it felt in my head – that was my calling.

University was an exciting idea and one which I had been looking forward to for years, whether that was Medicine or

Psychology I knew I wanted to go, so I needed to make sure I made the right choice. I visited a few – from memory these were Southampton, Cardiff, Plymouth, Royal Holloway, Surrey, and Exeter. A few were a definite no, but one was an immediate yes. Exeter was an easy decision to make for me because it felt weirdly familiar. Looking back now, I think this was partly because all of its characteristics were so similar to the place where I grew up and knew so well, and partly because three generations ago my family lived in Devon. Whether you believe all that oogly boogly stuff or not, I do think that I was drawn back to my roots for some reason. My gut was right, and I loved my time at uni – I adored Devon and still miss it so much. There is just nothing like the Devon countryside, and every day I long to be back on those moors, walking my stresses and worries away! I made incredible memories, friends, and met my long-term partner too. On my second day in university halls, a boy moved into the room next door, and as they say.... the rest was history! Whilst our homes are now miles and miles apart, we make it work and he has supported me every step of the way. On my third day of my first year, I met Jade[34]. She and I have walked hand-in-hand through every lecture, essay, and mental breakdown over these last four years and I couldn't be more grateful to have her. That support from someone going through almost exactly what you are going through is invaluable and I feel very lucky. Whilst we had similar backgrounds, we both had our own reasons for exploring Clinical Psychology.

For me, I knew for years before I started university that I wanted to be a person who helps other people. I wanted to be the person who listened to others' struggles; to empathise with their difficulties, and to help them understand what they are dealing with. This began with my first ever job at aged 16 as a playworker

---

[34] pseudonym

for both children with typical needs and children with additional needs, within a holiday club. Then during my time at university, I worked as:

- A youth enabler for special needs children in respite,
- A research assistant intern on a perinatal mental health project,
- An operational assistant for the university sports grounds,
- A healthcare assistant (HCA) on an eating disorders unit in a psychiatric hospital.

I still...

- work (voluntarily) for the perinatal project every week,
- work at the hospital most weekends.

I absolutely love it!

Whilst I have honestly adored every job, by far, I learned the most from my role as an HCA. Becoming accustomed to the ins and outs of an inpatient unit has been truly eye opening and has allowed me to grow so much as an Aspiring Psychologist. I've seen some pretty terrifying things which to be honest made my passion for the field even more intense.

My first three years at uni were your standard BSc in Psychology - broadly studying various divisions of Psychology and critiquing key research papers. I did my third-year dissertation on 'The Mediating Effect of Emotion Regulation on Intolerance of Uncertainty & Parenting'. Unfortunately, we didn't find any significant results, but I really enjoyed the process and got very engaged with it all.

My Master's year was where I started to specifically focus on Clinical Psychology, in the realm of Improving Access to Psychological Therapies, (IAPT), and I will qualify as a Psychological Well-being Practitioner (PWP) by the end. For those who are unfamiliar – as I was when I started the course – a PWP delivers low-intensity cognitive behavioural therapy-based interventions to individuals experiencing common, mild to moderate mental health problems. In the stepped care model, we fall at Step 2 and work alongside other PWPs, counsellors, peer support practitioners and CBT therapists to name a few. There are several routes you can go down to train as a PWP, but I went down the integrated master's road. I actually fell into this opportunity by chance, as I only realised in my second year at University that Exeter offered this course – so I immediately asked to interview and transfer over! The year was split in two – teaching in the first half and placement in the second. I enjoyed learning about PWP work: how to conduct assessments and treatment sessions in a person-centred way, and by the end I felt very much ready to begin training.

In the middle of April this year (2022), I took that next step in my aspiring Clinical Psychologist journey and began my 5-month placement. To be honest it felt more like a leap than a step... Whilst I did feel prepared on the academic side, I did not feel as prepared in dealing with real-life actual patients. This may sound silly, and you may be thinking 'well what did you expect'?! But the truth is, Uni can teach you how to fundamentally be a PWP, but it simply cannot teach you how to be a human helping another human struggling with the fluctuations in their mental health. Being adaptable and responsive to fluctuating needs, is part of the role and are things you learn with experience. Role-plays with peers can only help so much, and it was a huge learning curve for me when I began conducting my own assessments and treatment sessions. I don't think I necessarily had any expectations, but now I look back and I definitely thought I would have managed the transition from Uni life to real life a little more seamlessly. But it was ridiculous to put that much pressure on myself!

As I have throughout my life, I did find my feet quickly and soon started to enjoy the work as I became more and more comfortable. My schedule at the moment is:

- PWP work Monday to Thursday,
- University study days alternating Fridays,
- (Plus, HCA work on the weekends to have some income, and assisting with the perinatal project).

Whilst we are doing nuts and bolts stuff it might be helpful if I whizz over what my day as a trainee PWP looks like:

🕐 I start at 9, but usually don't have my first client until 9:30 to give myself time to set up, load clinical systems, check emails etc.

💬 I will see around 5/6 patients per day on average, but that does change depending on how many of my availability slots have been filled. For example, whilst I put out 3 assessment slots and 4 treatment slots a day, it is very rare that they will all be filled. I should mention here as well that as a PWP you manage your own diary so can choose when you see clients, provided you meet the weekly contact targets.

📋 Before each client I prepare my notes. For a treatment, I copy my notes from the previous session to remind me what we did / how they were last week, then take a look at their Minimum Data Set (MDS) scores (PHQ-9, GAD-7, WSAS and Phobia scales), and then think provisionally about what I might want to check in on.

? For an assessment – I just load up my assessment template, take a look at their referral information and check their MDS scores. A treatment session lasts around 35 minutes and an assessment around 45. After each, I do their clinical notes and risk assessment forms on the clinical system, send any outcome emails, and request supervision if needed.

✍ But, essentially my day is spent speaking to clients, writing clinical notes or emails, and any spare second doing work for uni assignments. I love all of these parts to be honest – the thrill from assessments, the rapport-building nature of treatments, summarising my notes in both lay terms and succinct clinical terms, and getting stuck into the academic side of things.

WHAT IS SUPERVISION ANYWAY? **?**

For those who don't know – case management supervision is given weekly to all clinical staff and involves presenting your caseload to a supervisor in order to discuss any risk concerns, suitability for treatment, and treatment options. It is a supportive session which really helps with building confidence in your decision-making ability and confirming that you have your clients' best interests at heart. Clinical skills supervision is a more practical based session with your peers, where you can bring questions you have about clinical practice, and generally discuss tips or suggestions for improving practice. This happens fortnightly for me.

However, I won't lie, having full-time university alongside almost full-time work, plus part-time work, is draining. At the time of writing this, I have 6 weeks left of placement and 4 ginormous assignments left. I have had several assignments to work on over the course of my placement and I've found it tricky to find the time for these. When you are so new to having real-life people relying on you for 'expert' support, you feel a huge amount of responsibility to maintain that ideal and be 100% present in every session. Because of this, there were times early on in placement where I asked to delay my Uni assignments for a week, as I just did not want to give my clients less than what I knew I was able to give them. But I am doing it, and I'm getting there. If anything, it is also giving me a taste of what I anticipate life will be like as a trainee Clinical Psychologist! I have struggled, but I do feel like I have grown a lot so far and that I still continue to grow. I could give you a whole reflective spiel of what I've learnt about PWP-ing and about myself, but you're not exactly here to read my CV!

What I will say though is that it has been hugely different to my experience as an HCA on an inpatient eating disorders unit. I love both tremendously, but they are just so stark in contrast. Whilst I knew this of course, it was never made as apparent in my mind until now – and has just highlighted even more the importance of getting a range of experience with varying needs and settings. Over the years I have networked with several Clinical Psychologists, and I haven't been afraid to ask for advice or support. I've received nothing but kindness and pure willingness to help, and I think that really just sums up the kinds of people who aspire to be Clinical Psychologists. What I've also been reflecting on the last few weeks, is that I am ready to move on again now. I'm ready to work with more complex needs and I am excited to move outside of the boundaries of IAPT. Whilst IAPT is great and I think it is a good system, I do feel constrained and as though some of my abilities are not being challenged enough. When I finish in August, I hope to get an Assistant Psychologist job. Easier said than done... But I'm ready, and I am so excited for the future. I am so excited to work with the clients I have always hoped to work with, to challenge myself and push myself out of my comfort zone as I now know I can do.

Mental health is something I'm so passionate about and something I'm learning more and more about every day, and I desperately want to put my skills into clinical training and to learn exponentially from others too. I like to believe that I'm not naive to the brutal application process, but I am also hopeful that I can convey my passion and show that I may very well be the kind of person who belongs in the role of a Clinical Psychologist. I hope that this has been at least a little helpful to at least somebody out there, or that perhaps you can resonate with something I've said.

If there is one take-home message, I'd like you to leave with then let it be this: if the prospect of helping people sparks something inside you, explore it - explore what that means to you and ask for guidance if you need it. If you've got so far as reading this book - you are already well on your way.

Best of luck, fellow Aspiring Psychologist.

Cian Hancock
Psychological Wellbeing Practitioner

MY MEMO

Dear Cian,

Your story is going to be so fantastically useful for people wanting an overview of IAPT and PWP work and will be an invaluable resource. I love that you have been able to recognise that you're now ready for a new challenge and I hope you manage to get one soon. I too believe that some of the nicest and most supportive people I have met have been in the field of Clinical Psychology. Lucky us eh? It all sounded fantastically romantic when your fella moved in next door to you! Hoping you can find a way to reduce the number of miles between you or just have really good excuses to bring on the mini breaks!

Thanks again, Marianne

14

- Rebecca's Story -

My Journey to Becoming an Associate Psychological Practitioner

To begin talking about my career in Psychology, it would be good to talk about where it all began and how I came to be one of the very first Trainee Associate Psychological Practitioners (TAPPs).

My Psychology journey started when I sat down to choose my GCSE options at the ripe old age of 14. I was very lucky that my school offered GCSE Psychology and it instantly jumped out at me. I was always fascinated by how the brain works and why people behave the way they do, which much to my parents' horror, usually presented itself as a keen interest in serial killer documentaries. So, the opportunity to gain an academic qualification in this before even leaving high school was incredibly appealing to me. I then went on to study Psychology at A-Level before gaining a place at Bangor University to study

Clinical & Health Psychology at both undergraduate and master's level.

Despite my clear enthusiasm in the subject, my high grades and my volunteer experience, leaving university and stepping into the "adult" world felt like stepping off a spaceship and into the abyss. Like a lot of Psychology graduates, I knew that I wanted to be a Clinical Psychologist one day. I spent several weeks researching the career path, emailing professionals for advice, applying for jobs, even contacting Clinical Psychologists directly and asking if I could shadow them or volunteer with them. Much to my surprise, I got absolutely nowhere. Looking back now, I can see how naïve I was in thinking it would be easy to get a job in mental health or anything remotely Psychology-related, especially with the typical "Assistant Psychologist" or "research assistant" roles being so fiercely competitive. After many failed attempts, I ended up having to claim universal credit. Now while there is absolutely no shame in this, never did I think that just one month after gaining a first-class master's degree I would end up back in my hometown at the job centre. I now felt even more motivated to get my foot in the door of the world of Psychology, so I tried to expand my search and look outside of the typical routes. I was taken on by an education recruitment agency which meant I was placed into different schools and colleges to support students on a 1-to-1 basis. These students tended to struggle with the usual classroom environment due to difficulties such as Autistic Spectrum Disorders, (ASD) and Attention Deficit Hyperactivity Disorder, (ADHD). This was probably the toughest job I have ever done, but so rewarding when I saw the change in the students.

After 6 months I decided to leave the role and move from Greater Manchester to Lancashire where I started as a support worker; a role which I would stay in for nearly two years. I supported individuals with a range of presenting issues including Down's Syndrome, dementia, alcohol dependency, schizoaffective disorder and more. I was working through the height of the Coronavirus pandemic which meant staff shortages, supporting individuals who didn't understand why they could no longer go out and do their usual activities, and generally changing our whole way of working. Whilst this job was rewarding, it was also both mentally and physically tiring, especially when I was lone-working or working night shifts. Unfortunately, this hard work and anti-social hours weren't reflected in my wage.

In November 2020, I came across the "perfect" job advert online. The 'essential criteria' were:

- An undergraduate Psychology degree, and
- an understanding of the needs of people with mental health difficulties.

This felt so right for me and didn't seem to require a whole wealth of experience that usually comes with "entry level" jobs. After spending hours perfecting my application, in time I was invited to interview, then just before Christmas, I received the call to say I had been successful and that I was part of the very first cohort of TAPPs!

I began my training with the University of Central Lancashire in January 2021, whilst also undertaking a placement in an NHS primary care setting. To pass the course and gain the postgraduate diploma we were required to meet a set of competencies which were assessed through clinical and academic reviews, reflective practices, presentations and competency records which formed a 10,000-word portfolio.

We attended several lectures (mostly virtual due to the pandemic) throughout the year, which supported us in our daily practice. For example, we completed teaching on different therapeutic interventions such as Cognitive Behavioural Therapy and Motivational Interviewing, as well as lectures on risk, working with children and their families, and inclusivity and diversity. It was great to begin learning via university teaching again, although due to the lectures being online, it was difficult to stay concentrated and motivated, especially during the weeks where we would have lectures from 9-5 Monday-Friday. Nonetheless, I managed to keep up with the teachings and apply it to clinical practice alongside the support from my clinical supervisor. I passed the course in December 2021 and have since been working as a fully qualified APP!

I have been given so many wonderful opportunities during this role and can see a clear progression for myself in the NHS. I hope to apply for the Doctorate in Clinical Psychology next year, but I am not putting any pressure on myself to be successful. I understand how stressful, difficult and competitive the process is and I am ensuring I set clear boundaries with myself beforehand to prevent myself from boiling over! Even if I do not get invited to any interviews, I will be pleased with myself for even trying for the first time.

Overall, it has been a difficult and unexpected journey thus far, but I believe that everything happens for a reason, and I am so proud to say that I have managed to become a homeowner alongside my partner (who I met at university – big up Bangor for bringing us together) and be employed in a full-time NHS position by the age of 24. I can only see bigger and better things from this point onwards and I cannot wait to see what's to come.

Rebecca Jarvis
Associate Psychological Practitioner

Thanks

Dear Rebecca, Honestly as I read your story, I felt a bit dewy eyed! I feel so proud to be able to include your story and to help you teach people about the role of TAPP and of course APP! I hope you are wearing that name badge with such pride. Thank you so much for taking the time to write your story and wishing you all the very best with the next stages of your career. I have such fond memories of living with my partner in our first home in my 20's and I hope you are managing such good work life balance and having stacks of fun along the way.

Marianne

15

- Layla's Story -

Your 'Why' will Carry You Through

At the age of 18, starting my undergraduate degree in Psychology, I had no idea the path would be this long! I pretty much thought I would walk out after graduating with a First Class Honours and be a practicing psychologist, and never need to step foot back into university again – sorry but Doctorate, WHAT?! I felt under equipped and that this gem of information could have been helpful! By the end of my undergraduate degree, I remember feeling overwhelmed and fairly lost about my next steps.

I knew whatever career path I would eventually choose I would need a lot of resilience and have to navigate some additional barriers. Due to a disability, this is at least something I am already well versed in! I use mobility aids, so I am quite resourceful and adaptable, and am very determined to overcome the limits set against me. You could say 'stubborn'?!

I think everyone has their 'why' for Psychology, and this has been mine. I see the world through a different lens and have a real desire to connect with people and their stories, and to really hear them.

After my Undergrad I managed to secure an internship at the Student Union and was incredibly lucky to get a scholarship to study a part-time master's degree at the university over two years, so I signed up for the Attachment Studies programme. This taught the assessment of parent-child and adult attachment and caregiving, based on a specialist model of understanding human attachment behaviour and functioning. Even though it was a bit of an impulsive whim for me selecting this course over the other options, it has been one of the best decisions I have ever made. It changed my outlook on people, relationships, and has been invaluable in my Aspiring Psychologist roles. I learnt from world renowned attachment theorists, alongside my cohort of social workers and psychotherapists. As a bright-eyed recent graduate in my early 20's, I was the youngest, and I really valued peer support to cope with the emotional demands of the course and the material. Studying this degree fuelled my desire to want to work with families in safeguarding and child protection services, or with adoptive families, because of the specialist assessment and intervention training. I think finally knowing my 'destination' meant I could realise the variety of career routes that could take me there - like social work, play therapy, family therapy etc., but I still felt I need to give this Clinical Psychology thing a go!

My experience so far:

My first 'proper job' was working in a supervised contact service, facilitating contact between birth parents and children in foster care.

After this, I secured part-time roles as:
- A Family Support Worker in a Local Authority adoption service
- An Honorary Assistant Psychologist in a partnership of schools to gain clinical experience under supervision.

For the past 18 months I have worked as an Assistant Psychologist (AP), in a Neuro-disability service in London. This is mostly assessment focused with some research and intervention experience.

I applied for the Doctorate in Clinical Psychology for the first time in 2021/22, and I consider myself very lucky to have been offered a place at my first-choice university!

For some time, it felt like working in Psychology was not going to 'pay off' for me, as I felt my career was not very secure and I was not sure how to manage this! Looking back, I think I put off applying for the Doctorate for a couple of years for various reasons, but my advice would be:

"Just submit an application as soon as you feel ready to and try a 'practice' run to acclimatise yourself to the process and desensitise yourself to it!"

I put a lot of pressure on myself this year as I felt ready to move on from AP roles, but the application process is such a mammoth beast to try and conquer and I am not sure if there is any rhyme or reason to how to be successful in gaining a place. I still cannot quite believe I have been successful and am sure I am being pranked! The biggest lesson I have learnt over the past few months has been how important it is to be kind and gentle to yourself! Your 'why' will carry you through your journey in Psychology – and even though it does not feel like it at the time when you are riding the waves, you will probably look back in a few years' time and your path to getting where you want to be will suddenly make sense.

Wishing you all the very best of luck with whatever brilliant things you decide to pursue, and the change you will all make!

Layla Harding
Trainee Clinical Psychologist

DEAR LAYLA,

SO MANY CONGRATULATIONS TO YOU ON SUCCESSFULLY GAINING A PLACE ON TRAINING. I CAN DEFINITELY STILL RECALL THAT SLIGHTLY DAZED, OTHER WORLDLY FEELING OF HAVING BEEN OFFERED A PLACE AND FEELING SIMULTANEOUSLY DELIGHTED BUT ALSO WORRIED THEY'D ACCIDENTALLY PUT YOUR NAME INTO THE 'WRONG' PILE, AND IT WOULD ALL BE TAKEN AWAY! DO TRY TO LEAN INTO THIS WONDERFUL TIME AND TRY TO MAKE THE MOST OF YOUR SUMMER DOING FABULOUS THINGS AND ENRICHING YOURSELF.
HOPE TRAINING GOES SO WELL FOR YOU!

MARIANNE

16

- Emily's Story -

Thinking Outside the Box

I have kept thinking about whether to start this once I have it confirmed if I have a place or if I do it now; right in the middle of this cycle of frantically checking my emails and trying to manage the anxiety that a third-place reserve offer creates.

I have thought about it hard, but actually, I feel it is worth sharing this part of the process too.

Often, we see the celebrations, but it is good sometimes to know the other bits that come before and alongside that!

So here we are.

I'm 32 and this is my first Doctorate application. I have worked for a local authority for 8 years, starting out doing admin for a children with disabilities team, then moving into commissioning then doing direct work with families. I am now working as a health and well-being coach with adults which I have been doing for 18 months.

Due to some personal mental health issues and a complex mix of all the things life throws at us, I started studying again at 24. I completed an Access to Higher Education course in Social Work as I had failed my A Levels previously. Psychology wasn't available to take part-time and I had bills to pay so reducing down from full-time work was not an option for me at the time. I ended up completing a part-time degree in Education, Culture and Childhood before completing a full-time Psychology conversion master's.

It is potentially a little backwards compared to the 'traditional route' of education – however it has been helpful during the past couple of years to read other peoples' stories who have come into Clinical Psychology through differing routes. I had thought about putting applying off but having others' stories out there helped me to view my experiences in a new light.

Working whilst studying was something I found really valuable and definitely enjoyed. I have loved gaining experience by working with children, families and adults in different environments and providing a variety of support.

What might seem particularly unusual to you as you read this is that I have neither worked in the NHS, nor have I been supervised by a Clinical Psychologist. That said, I have reached out to a couple during my career who have been really helpful and supportive.

Due to not having had such regular access to a qualified psychologist supervisor I felt I needed to push harder to make outside connections. I found and messaged trainees on Twitter and reached out to CPs. These relationships really helped me ascertain that this really was the career path I wanted.

Fast forward a few months from putting my application in and I was invited for an interview. I must admit I was very surprised and definitely celebrated as I knew it was an achievement to come this far no matter what the outcome. I worked hard for the interview, but actually, if I were to do it again, I would try and be a bit easier on myself. I spent a lot of time dismissing the experience I had gained and trying to learn what I thought I may be asked about. In the end, nerves got the better of me and I can barely remember a word I said; I just remember it feeling awful!

I was lucky to only have to wait 3 days for the outcome which surprisingly was a reserve place. I then found out I was third which actually meant I was in with a shot! I am leaving this here and will update once I know whether this has materialised into a place.

A few days after I wrote that previous section (and about 6 weeks after my reserve email), I was offered a place! I couldn't believe it and there were tears when I received the email. I feel very grateful for this opportunity to pursue the career I feel so strongly about.

I would say to others wanting to progress to the DClinPsy to not dismiss any experience you have had or are looking for. There is definitely not just one route to the course and there is a lot of incredibly valid experience to be gained in different organisations.

Emily Holmes
Trainee Clinical Psychologist

Dear Emily,

Thanks so much for your story. I loved being able to follow your process in real time. Hoping that you continue to grow and develop in your training and thanks for showcasing that NHS and direct supervision from a qualified Psychologist is not always essential to gain places on training. I know people will take comfort from this.

Thanks again, Marianne

17

- Adrian's Story -

Not all 2:2's are from Partying

My journey toward the Clinical Psychology course started over eight years ago. Upon leaving school at 16 I tried a variety of careers including hotel work, various office jobs and managing an MOT garage. I always liked the idea of working in care, and at the age of 24, was offered the opportunity. Once I started and loved this line of work, I started looking at which professions I could pursue. In secondary school, I had considered going into Clinical Psychology but never wanted to go straight to university without some experience of working in a similar role. It never made sense to me to work for years towards a career you may not even like in the end. Early into my first care job I was already sure I wanted to make this my vocation and so I found an access course in health science. The course mainly prepared people to go into nursing studies. I started it in in 2014 and by this time I'd worked as a support worker in a dementia specialist care home for over six months. It was set up as a full-time course, but I also worked full-time alongside this.

Along my route I got married to my wonderful and incredibly supportive wife. She was also studying whilst working too. She also had some extra stressors which I supported her with in my role as her husband. Her brother, my brother-in-law, has some additional needs and as a result lives in full-time care.

After about a year of working in dementia care and when I was halfway through the course, I secured another support worker job. In this role, I worked mainly with adults with physical disabilities but also worked at a project with older adults with a mixture of learning disabilities and Autism. I worked there full-time for over three years. This job role also spanned my undergraduate degree in 'Psychology with Clinical and Health Psychology' which I studied at Bangor University in North Wales. Alas, for several reasons I didn't do that well in my undergrad.

1) I had to carry on working full-time whilst also studying full-time. If you're considering the same, I wouldn't recommend it.

2) My family situation with my brother-in-law meant that my wife's mental health was affected to the extent where she had to leave her job and university course. My brother in law's care was sub-standard and over a number of years he had been moved to several inappropriate placements, one where he actually ended up having his leg broken. The family took the local council and health board to court, leading to a lengthy case that started just before my second year of university and lasted until about a year after graduating. This put a lot of pressure on us, and I didn't end up with much time to study. But at the end of the day, there are more

important things than grades and I don't regret my choices.

Almost straight after graduating, there was still a lot going on and it looked like the family situation was still going to carry on for a while. My original plan was to go straight into my master's, get a better grade, and hopefully apply to some clinical Doctorate courses. As with a 2.2, there were only two courses I could apply to[35], I applied but both used selection tests and I didn't do well enough to get an interview. However, given my circumstances, it didn't seem like a good idea to go straight back to do my master's. Instead of going back into education, I looked at the available jobs that would help me to build my experience.

I applied for some management jobs as I felt this would give me the experience of working within Multi-Disciplinary Teams (MDT) alongside Clinical Psychologists and other healthcare professionals. It also meant I would be responsible for completing and updating risk assessments, care plans, Positive Behavioural Support (PBS) plans and all sorts of essential documents. Happily, straight from graduating I got just such a job working for a nationwide learning disabilities charity. My role was to manage a respite house run on behalf of the local authority for adults with learning disabilities, Autism and some physical disabilities. This gave me the experiences I was expecting but also much more. It added to my management skills, dealing with a large staff team including an assistant manager. It allowed me to improve my budgeting and financial awareness, as the job included responsibility for a large budget. It's improved my understanding of HR practices, knowledge of legislation and required standards. And I'm sure lots of things I haven't even thought about. During my last year with the

---

[35] At the time of editing, these are Lancaster and Plymouth.

company, due to extended leave from one of my colleagues, I also managed another respite home in the neighbouring county.

After just over a year in the job and completing my level 5 Qualifications and Credit Framework (QCF), the situation with my extended family had calmed down. Due to our responsibilities we still needed to stay in the area, but I decided to study for a master's. I wanted to do this to improve my chances of getting an Assistant Psychologist role and to strengthen any future DClinPsy applications too. So, back I went to university to study for a master's in clinical and health Psychology. Of course, me being me I also did this alongside my full-time job. Thankfully this time, I had the sense to study part-time, and it was much more manageable. However, there were also further emotional times during my studies with my wife and I having conceived two pregnancies which sadly resulted in miscarriage. Although this was a difficult time for us, it wasn't the same as the constant pressure of the court case. I finished my master's with a Distinction but more importantly with a sense of pride and knowledge that I could work to the required level whilst also undertaking a full-time job.

By this point, I had been in my care management position for over three years. I felt I'd plateaued in terms of what I still had to learn and gain from it. Whilst I still enjoyed the work, I decided that putting myself in a new environment with different clinical groups would enable me to grow and develop more.
Even with a Distinction in my master's, my 2.2 undergraduate degree reduced the number of assistant jobs I could apply to. In fact, there were very few Trusts who would accept my applications. This combined with the competitiveness of these positions even when people have a higher degree classification,

I knew my chances were poor. I am aware that other competitive industries have modernised their application processes to consider contextual factors. This means mitigating circumstances and experience are also considered rather than solely relying on academic grades. I see Clinical Psychology as being behind in this area and I think it is worth highlighting as another potential diversity and equality issue within the profession.

I am realistic and know that these caveats exist in order to reduce the volume of applications received. I think that most DClinPsy programmes also do the same.

When I had finished my master's and no longer had to stay in North Wales, I was desperate to finally get my foot in the door and work in a psychological role. I applied for over 200 Assistant Psychologist and trainee PWP roles across the country. Because I was aware that my problem was getting through the initial screening process, which was likely even just an electronic process looking for a 2:1, I would be failing at the essential criteria stage and would never get to the next step where actual people view my forms. So, I had to get creative with my job applications! In order to get my experience and master's degree considered I had to get past the initial screening. The answer to this came from an unexpected place. During my time at Bangor one of the academic team asked me in passing whether I'd ever considered appealing my grade due to my extenuating circumstances. No one had ever mentioned this to me before, so I hadn't even been aware it was a possibility. So, after the completion of my master's I decided to appeal. Early on in this process, it became pretty clear that my appeal would be rejected because it turned out there's a two-week time frame for appeals post-graduation, and ultimately it was rejected. But I found the appeal procedure itself helpful as it created a Schrödinger's cat situation[36] [37], if the grade was under appeal, I could have either a 2.1 or a 2.2. Once a decision has been returned you are able to resubmit to someone higher up the chain. Done enough times it will eventually reach the desk of the university chancellor. During my repeated appeals I was able to put 2:1 as my undergraduate grade on applications. I then waited to see if I would get invited to interview. If I did, I would email the Clinical Psychologist listed as the contact and let them know that I had a 2.2, but the grade was under appeal, and I had a Distinction at master's. Considering the minimum requirements for the role, I expected instant rejections. However, that's not what happened. Surprisingly, 37 of the 40 interview invites stated that my Distinction at master's meant my undergraduate grade didn't matter. The remaining 3 asked me to withdraw my application once they'd received this information. I would have imagined the split would have been the opposite way around 3 people to have been breezy and 37 asking me to withdraw. The funniest thing was the tone of the emails I got in response. Almost all of them were surprised I thought my undergraduate degree would matter when I had a

---

[36] Marianne's little note: I'll save you a google here, I'd never heard of this expression so here is what Wikipedia had to say on it - "with its origin in quantum mechanics, Schrödinger's cat is a thought experiment that illustrates a paradox of quantum superposition. In the thought experiment, a hypothetical cat may be considered simultaneously both alive and dead as a result of its fate being linked to a random subatomic event that may or may not occur."

[37] Adrian's footnote about the footnote: This is a very fancy explanation from Wikipedia! The more basic version might make a bit more sense to everyone. The thought experiment proposed that if you put a cat in a box with a sealed vial of poison that was set up to break open at a random time. As there is no way to tell if the poison has opened, the cat can be thought of as both alive and dead. Luckily, this was just a thought experiment!

Distinction at master's. It had quickly become apparent that recruiting Clinical Psychologists didn't know their own Trust's minimum requirements for Assistant Psychologist roles!

Of the three that asked me to withdraw, I asked them to explain why they had this criterion in place when it seemed Trusts were moving to accepting 2.2 with a subsequent higher grade at master's level (albeit very slowly). Two recruiters didn't respond to the email, but one Trust did. The Clinical Psychologist in question said she couldn't explain why this was in place and didn't agree with it. She ended up having a conversation with the Trust's HR department and came back to me a few weeks later informing me that, as of September, this was being changed to allow those with a 2.2 but with a subsequent higher grade at master's to apply. I don't think that it was just my inquiry that changed the policy, it's likely they had this a few times to bring about change. But this highlighted for me how much disconnect there is between who Clinical Psychologists feel would be competent for assistant roles and those that are setting the minimum requirements.

Overall, I feel this has highlighted a big issue in the application process in the majority of Trusts and this probably applies to the majority of Doctorate courses too. I think many Trusts have got in the habit of asking for these criteria to keep the application count down and simplify the process. But given that life happens whilst we are pursuing a career in Psychology, I know that many others will also have had hardships along the way. My experience suggests that many Trusts agree if given a chance to hear the circumstances around why the grade was low, and you can demonstrate that you have worked to a 2.1 level or higher in a master's degree. I think this would apply to many clinical Doctorate courses as well.

There is a stigma around having a 2.2, where people assume you have just got caught up in the university lifestyle and didn't study enough. This isn't always the case, particularly for students with more responsibilities for example those with caring responsibilities or those who had to continue working full-time. But even if it is the case, if a person has done all they can to gain experience since then and gone back to university to demonstrate they can do better, should they be limited by an old undergraduate grade? At the end of the day, an academic grade is no guarantee of anyone being a good clinician. This is primarily learnt through experience working in various roles with client contact. This was one of the reasons for me starting my blog, which I will talk about later, but I feel this issue needs greater attention and discussion. Anyway, that's enough of my rambling!

One of my 37 interview offers resulted in me being offered an Assistant Psychologist job with the Birmingham and Solihull Mental Health Trust in a prison within a forensic personality disorder service. If they had kept to the minimum criteria listed, I shouldn't have even had this job! This was a really interesting role, and I learned a lot from my time there. But it wasn't easy for me financially and emotionally because I chose to live away from my wife for most of the week and the 7-hour round trip at weekends meant I couldn't sustain it for long. Whilst working there I applied for the DClinPsy for the second time (the 2022 intake). This time I got invited to two interviews. My experiences living away from home meant that I decided to withdraw from the one near London as, sick of the constant sacrifices in the name of Psychology, I'd realised that living apart wasn't going to be viable for me. I attended the second interview but was not successful.

Upon reflection, I feel that my undergraduate grade is still holding me back. The application process also made me realise that although I was lucky enough to get two interviews, both courses relied on selection tests. Holly from the Facebook group 'Clinical Psychology Community UK' was nice enough to give me a lot of feedback on my application. I was pretty happy with it and felt it was quite strong. But I received rejections from both courses that relied on the application form, suggesting that my 2.2 at undergraduate level or my limited AP experience may be the reason for not being considered. But as I have a fair amount of experience in other roles (4.5 years as a support worker and 3.5 years as a care manager), I feel it's more likely to be the undergraduate grade. Reading Marianne's previous book also confirmed this suspicion; one of the chapters detailed how one individual with a 2.2 and subsequent master's worked as an AP for over ten years before getting on the course.

Once I got the rejections, I thought about my options while waiting for the interviews. I was fed up with being judged by my undergraduate grade, but getting a PhD is the only way this isn't considered (at least for the courses I was interested in). Surprisingly, a PhD won't open many more courses. There are a large number of Universities that continue to judge you by your undergraduate grad, no matter the circumstances around the grade or what you have done since. I had always thought about getting a PhD, but I imagined doing this later in my career for several reasons, including being able to afford it. Also, working within a Clinical Psychology service made me realise that despite the idyllic-sounding scientific practitioner model, there is little to no research within the Clinical Psychologist role. I'm also aware that there are research assistant jobs, but these seem few and far between. I'm also not sure how much clinical work is available in these roles? I know this observation is only from minimal experience within one service and one Trust. However, from what I have heard, the pressures and understaffing are widespread and very few Clinical Psychologists have the time to publish any papers. I'm aware that people say routine tasks such as service audits are technically research, but after these are produced, nothing seems to happen with them. If you aren't comparing the results with the wider literature and/or comparing it to the effectiveness of other interventions while also publishing this to add to the knowledge base, is there any use to them? As I mentioned, I don't blame Clinical Psychologists for this, I think with the other pressures upon them they simply don't have the time. Plus, many of the tools university courses teach us to use for research (e.g. SPSS) aren't available to clinicians once they have finished their qualifications.

I've always wanted to work therapeutically with clients and add to research. I feel that only by working as a clinician will you truly understand the research needs in the area. This was always the appeal to me of the scientific practitioner model and Clinical Psychologist role. But now I feel this is far more of an ideal than a reality. Completing a PhD, and hopefully, perhaps one day working in a split post may be the only way to work in this way truly. This and the opportunity to open up a few more courses once again, so that I can limit my applications to Wales and the Northwest, meant the option of completing a PhD earlier in my career became much more appealing. Especially when I discovered that PhD studentships are tax-free and monthly income isn't too different from an Assistant Psychologist.

The only thing that I still opposed and another reason I wanted to complete a PhD later in my career, was the principle of it.

Many people don't seem aware, and many Clinical Psychologists don't seem keen, on telling anyone (I think they enjoy calling themselves Dr too much) that the DClinPsy isn't classed as a Doctorate but a taught master's. This is because you don't produce enough original research for it to be classed as a Doctorate, compared to something like a PhD. But the fact is most Clinical Psychologists don't have a PhD. The fact they can sit there with a straight face and tell others their master's isn't good enough, go and do a PhD, is quite frankly unbelievable! However, as I had plans to do this anyway, this wasn't a good enough reason not to do this and I applied for a few studentships of interest.

After six months of working in the Assistant Psychologist role, I got another assistant position with Betsi Cadwaladr NHS Trust, this time with an older adult's service. By this point, I knew I didn't have a place on the DClinPsy, but I was happy I could still build experience without having to live away from my wife. Living away was costing me a lot of money and was very emotionally challenging; Birmingham and Solihull Trust were nice enough to let me leave the position with very little notice. I had to wait a while for the pre-employment checks to be carried out and to be able to start the new one. However, during this time I had an interview for the PhD studentship that interested me most. To my surprise, I was awarded the studentship. I was hoping to continue with the assistant job on a part-time basis, to continue building experience, but they could not accommodate this.

So that brings us up to date with the story. I'm currently waiting to start the PhD. Unfortunately, I don't have an assistant job. Luckily, I kept in touch with one of the individuals I used to support. He was having trouble with staffing and when he found out I was moving back to the area asked if I could do some bank work. So, I'm currently back working in care until my PhD starts. It will also provide a flexible extra income while studying, but I will keep an eye out for part-time assistant posts. The PhD itself will build upon the work of a previous PhD student, continuing to trial and develop a resilience-based intervention for adolescents in contact with forensic services. One reason I'm particularly excited about this is my experiences in the forensic service. I feel the interventions offered were useful, but only provided to the most problematic inmates with long sentences. I feel if these were offered to adolescents on the wrong path instead of adults further down this path, they would be more successful.

I plan to do all I can to make the most of the PhD opportunity. One of the things I realised during the assistant role is that I'm still uncomfortable presenting, even in front of small groups. Although co-facilitating groups did help with this, I would like to improve this skill and intend to take part in as many teaching and presenting opportunities as possible. This is also one of the reasons I started the Aspiring Psychologist blog, to improve non-academic writing and possibly presenting skills if I ever get around to making YouTube videos. But the main reason was to build a community, share useful information for those on the same journey and hopefully sharing my experiences will be helpful to others.

So, I've made my journey towards the DClinPsy longer. If I continue applying after my PhD, I'll be into my 11th year of pursuing this. I hope sharing this story will bring some attention to the problem with minimum requirements that is clearly an issue in Assistant Psychologist roles and DClinPsy courses. Hopefully, they will eventually change to consider mitigating circumstances. But as I don't know if this will change anytime soon, one thing students should take away from this story is to make your life easier and do all you can to get a 2.1. The irony is that despite the caring nature of the role, the route to Clinical Psychology is one of the least caring and most demanding routes I have come across. So be sure you are prepared for a long and challenging journey if you go down this route.

Adrian Cross
PhD Student / Bank Worker

- To follow Adrian on Twitter: @AspiringPsy
- To Follow Adrian on Instagram head to:
  https://www.instagram.com/aspiringpsychologistuk/
- To read Adrian's blog head to:
  www.aspiringpsychologist.co.uk

MEMO

Dear Adrian,
Thanks so much for your story. I'm sorry that your appeal wasn't successful, I was rooting for you! It certainly seems a bit of a strange process that a distinction at masters doesn't alter the impact of a 2:2 undergraduate degree.
Wishing you so well in your PhD and with your social channels.

Do stay in touch!

Marianne

18

Aligned Training Places

A NOTE ON ALIGNED TRAINING PATHWAYS IN SCOTLAND

Aligned training pathways were implemented as a response to key workforce priorities within NHS Scotland, aiming to expand the workforce in high priority clinical areas. So, every year there are several places aligned to specific clinical populations in addition to the generic pathway. While most of them are national, meaning it is the same clinical specialities offering alignments across Scotland, some health boards offer additional local alignments in different specialties. If you opt in for an aligned training pathway, you will undertake your third-year specialist placements as well as your thesis with that population. You will meet all required competencies and qualify with the same qualification as trainees undertaking on the generic pathway. The clinical populations may differ every year, depending on which areas are identified as high priority. When Jacqui whom you'll meet in the following story applied, national alignments were with Child and Adolescent Mental Health Services (CAMHS), Forensic and Older Adults.

There is no expectation for applicants to opt in for these alignments if you prefer the generic pathway. You will have the opportunity to indicate your preferences clearly during the application process.

Given that you will also be asked to rate your preferences with regards to health boards when applying to the two courses in Scotland, it is recommended that you check your alignment choices in accordance with what each health board offers and vice versa. This will help you to make informed choices that are right for you. If you get to the interview stage, you will have a meeting with a local area tutor to ask any questions you may have on alignments and health boards, after which you will need to submit your final choices. These will be considered by the panels when selecting successful applicants after their interviews.

18a

- Jacqui's Story -

No, hang on. Self-Care Actually Sounds Quite Nice!

As I am writing this, I am sitting in my favourite coffee shop, quietly chuckling to myself. Not because anything particularly entertaining happened, but because reflecting on my journey so far made me recognise some rather unhelpful behaviours and thinking patterns. And now I am attempting to share the little wisdom I have. Feels a bit hypocritical to be completely honest. I often prioritised advancing my career aspirations before my own wellbeing, which contributed significantly to my struggles with physical and mental health. I am still exploring why self-compassion does not come naturally to me because I'm happy to give unconditional support to literally anyone else. At this point I could probably make some educated guesses. If I have learned anything over the last couple of years, it is that self-care is an essential component to reaching your goals. Getting on THE course is not everything. Life away from Psychology continues to happen, so please don't exclude yourself from living it and do prioritise your wellbeing.

So, let's wind back a bit. I grew up in a working-class family in a really rural part of Germany. Nobody in my family had pursued higher education, so when six-year-old me announced I would be a psychologist it raised quite a few eyebrows. I cannot say for certain why I knew that's what I wanted to do. My upbringing probably influenced this decision, albeit subconsciously for a long time. I witnessed severe mental health problems in immediate relatives, navigated my way through complicated family dynamics, and ticked quite a few of the Adverse Childhood Experiences (ACEs) for reasons I won't disclose here.

Throughout these times, my grandparents were a constant source of love and unconditional support, even when I packed up my bags at 18 to move to Edinburgh to work as an Au Pair with a young girl on the autism spectrum with severe learning disability. In Germany, the grade requirements to study Psychology are on a par with Medicine and with my high school grades being pretty average, I didn't meet the entry criteria to study in my birth country. So, working and studying in the U.K. made sense as my grades were considered good enough here. And happily, Scotland just felt like home, so I decided to stay. I had not long started my job as a Support Worker when I was accepted to a local university. Being from a working-class background, there was not much financial support from home, and I was not eligible for SAAS[38] at the time. It meant that

---

[38] This is the Student Award Agency Scotland who support 'young' students under the age of 25 and 'independent' students post 25. They

money would be tight for the next couple of years. Especially since most of my family, except my grandparents, did not approve of me pursuing a degree.

Working and studying full-time was intense. I missed out on a lot of the fun of being an undergraduate student. I also took on quite a few extra activities such as student ambassador, class representative and vice-president of the university's Psychology society. I felt doing as much as possible would make me a more desirable candidate for when I would apply to the DClinPsy. Not only for the panels, but also to prove to my family I was able to achieve this goal. Thankfully, my support worker job enabled me to learn outside of the lecture theatre. The service users and their families were my best teachers, and I am still humbled they allowed me to support them through some of the most challenging times of their lives. I cannot stress enough how valuable support worker roles are as they offer so much learning and the privilege of meaningfully connecting with people we support. However, it is also one of the most challenging jobs and can become overwhelming if we are not mindful of our own wellbeing. And I certainly did not look after myself very well.

Towards the third year of Uni, I really struggled juggling all my commitments. Eventually, I was signed off sick from work due to poor mental health and a chronic health condition that started to develop around that time. However, I had to finance my studies somehow and in true working-class fashion, I took on more hours to make up for time off sick. You can imagine how the next year went. At the time, I didn't ask for help. I was raised

---

offer funding, loans, bursaries and more for people resident in Scotland. Check out https://www.saas.gov.uk/ for more info.

to just get on with it and it took me a long time to detach myself from that way of thinking. It's ironic how we treat others with such compassion, but when it comes to ourselves – Well, it's often a case of "take my advice, I don't use it anyway."

In 2019, I graduated with a 1st class degree, but I was mentally and physically exhausted. Instead of taking a break to recuperate, I pressed on and applied for both Clinical Associate in Applied Psychology (CAAP) and DClinPsy courses. I failed miserably. Sometime later when I read my applications back, it became apparent to me that I was just not ready. I realised I was just listing everything I had done, there was no substance to it. It really is the quality of our reflections on what we did, not the quantity of experiences that are important. I continued working as support worker for some time, feeling a little lost and defeated. I struggled to accept that I was not ready for the DClinPsy because I had put in so much work over the years at the expense of my wellbeing. I wondered whether it had been worth it.

After some time, I started a voluntary Research Assistant (RA) position a few hours per week with the University of Stirling. It helped me feel proactive and less lost in self-doubt. Again, I am laughing a little bit here because what I really needed was a holiday, not assisting on an MRC-funded research project on top of a 50h work week. It seems that lifelong habits are difficult to break!

For me, it was just as well that COVID-19 hit and brought the world to a near standstill. I know for many people this was the source of anxiety, stress and often trauma. So, it may sound strange that I personally experienced the pandemic as a time of healing. Everything slowed down, forcing me to hit the brakes, too; although it did take time and a few gins for me to appreciate this. I still thought about what was next regarding my career aspirations, but without subscribing to the pressure of having to do everything all the time. I stopped feeling like I had something to prove and was finally breathing again.

Eventually, I applied for some Assistant Psychologist (AP) jobs and to my surprise, secured a position fairly quickly. Following a brief stint as AP with a community mental health team and a computerised Cognitive Behavioural Therapy (cCBT) service, I left for a permanent AP position in adult mental health. I noticed most of my peers had master's' degrees, some even a PhD! Again, I started to feel pressure to keep up and enrolled in an MSc Health Psychology course. I had developed a keen interest in the field through my work as RA and my own experiences of living with a chronic health condition. Also, I felt gaining a better understanding of the relationship between physical and mental health would enable me to work with service users more meaningfully and holistically. With the help of my RA supervisor, I secured a full scholarship to fund my MSc. I would not have been able to take my education further otherwise as I did not have the funds to support myself and pay for the MSc. Thank you, P!

So, there I was. Working and studying again. Notice a pattern here? I still struggled with my mental health and painful flare-ups as that chronic condition decided to accompany me for the long run. This time, however, I felt ready to ask for help.
During most of my MSc I worked with a mental health mentor, which was arranged through the university's student support services. Our sessions together encouraged me to accept that

choosing a career in Psychology didn't mean I was not allowed to struggle with mental health myself and that it was okay to access the support available. Despite all the great work that is being done, there still is a lot of stigma surrounding psychologists who experience mental ill-health, which I think is quite ironic because no one bats an eyelid at a GP being prescribed medication or a surgeon requiring surgery.

I no longer saw living with mental and physical ill-health as a weakness in myself, but as a strength that enabled me to connect deeply and meaningfully with people I work with. Additionally, my working-class background and living in the UK post-Brexit (yep, that was a bit of a bummer!) enabled me to have a wider perspective on critical issues such as social inequalities, lack of diversity and the impact of deprivation on accessing healthcare. I reached out to other Aspiring Psychologists and discovered that these experiences were common, but generally not openly talked about. In an attempt to contribute to change, I started peer mentoring by reading AP applications and facilitating reflective sessions. Through sharing my journey and what I learnt along the way with others, I became aware of what I had achieved and the value of my experiences. I was getting to know who I was as an Aspiring Psychologist and felt ready to give the DClinPsy application process another go.

Out of the four Universities I applied to that year, I received three interviews. I will be forever grateful to my friend, Cat[39], who supported me through interview preparations. She collated over a hundred interview questions and took the time to listen to my rambled answers on WhatsApp every day. I cannot wait to return the favour! My advice on preparing for interviews is to

---

[39] Cat has absolutely consented to me name checking her here.

identify key aspects in documents such as NICE guidelines, the NHS long-term plan or current mental health strategies that are relevant to your experiences. Remember, the purpose of the DClinPsy is to learn, you do not have to know everything. Rather, it is about how you make sense of your experiences and reflect on your learning. How your experiences shape who you are and who you aspire to be. Yes, it is important to be able to apply psychological knowledge to this. But focus on a few selected models or theories that really add to your experiences rather than trying to memorise it all. Although that big folder full of notes and annotated journal articles felt comforting at the time, I now realise I definitely over prepared which contributed to nagging self-doubt and constant worry about not being able to remember it all. And of course, I didn't remember everything in my interviews. And that is okay.

My first interview went as well as it could have with me being a nervous wreck. Somehow, I still managed to secure a reserve place, which gave me a much-needed confidence boost. But as we know, life continues to happen whilst you are busy with the DClinPsy process. A few days before my next interview, I tested positive for COVID. And despite having had all of the vaccinations, I got it bad. After a minor existential crisis and tearful, socially distanced conversations with my partner, I decided to be transparent with the interview panel. They were all incredibly supportive and kind, which surprised me. I heard many stories of panels being very intimidating and uncaring. But from my experiences, they want you to do well and will support you however they can. I accepted I would do the interview for experience only, which took away the pressure of needing to perform. It enabled me to be myself and I genuinely enjoyed chatting with the panel as people not assessors. To my surprise,

I got an offer. The day I was nearly hospitalised due to COVID ended up being the day I got on the DClinPsy. Well, kind of. I still decided to take the next interview, as that course offered an aligned training place[40] within physical rehabilitation unique to a local health board. Due to my background in health Psychology, I was extremely interested in this alignment. I didn't feel too nervous on that day because I was still significantly struggling with post-COVID symptoms. I could only do my best and see where it got me. Of course, having the safety of an alternative offer did help, too. Doing the interview turned out to be the right decision, as I got an offer for that perfect alignment with the health board of my choice. Waiting for the Clearing House website to update so I could accept the offer were the longest three days of my life so far (okay, maybe I am being a little dramatic here).

Looking back, I wish I had allowed myself to recognise that even being in the position to apply to the DClinPsy is already an incredible achievement! So much work goes into getting to this point in our careers, so give yourself credit where it is more than due. Amidst the stress and anxiety invoked by the application process, it can be easy to lose sight of that. I wish I had been more open to seeing it as the amazing learning opportunity it was. That might have helped balancing the demands of the application with looking after my wellbeing and life outside of Psychology. I learnt so much about myself over the last years as I had to challenge the deep-rooted beliefs and unhelpful values I held for a long time. I had to learn to ask for help and appreciate my weaknesses as well as my strengths as they contribute to who I am as an Aspiring Psychologist. I am very

---

[40] For further information on aligned training places please check out page 187 just before this story

excited to start the DClinPsy in September, but also nervous as my body still hasn't quite recovered from COVID and my chronic condition worsened as a result. I find it difficult to take things at a slower pace and accept this may be my new normal. However, this time round, I will be compassionate and kind towards myself. Selfcare is just as important in achieving our goals as hard work. It's about getting the balance right.

Jacqueline Ackerman
Trainee Clinical Psychologist

MEMO

Dear Jacqui,

Danke für deine Geschichte!

Well done to you on your achievements and so many congratulations to you on achieving your place on the doctorate! You'll also have helped make someone else experience that 'cloud 9' feeling by declining that first offer too!

Compassion is absolutely something that I wish I had learned about and embraced earlier in my life too and I'm so pleased you have now been able to do the same.

Wishing you every success in your training and in your recovery from COVID of course.

Stay Kind to you, Marianne

DR MARIANNE TRENT
www.goodthinkingpsychology.co.uk

19

- Lucy's Story -

The Process of Perseverance

Up until I was 16 I had no idea what I wanted to do, but was adamant that university wasn't for me - the furthest my career plans ever got was my dream to be a hairdresser when I was about 7 years old. In 2012, after my GCSEs, I committed to doing A-Levels since it seemed the next logical step. I also I wasn't really sure what else to do, so I chose to do four AS-Levels:

- One subject I loved (Art)
- One I was good at (English Language)
- One so I'd continue to keep healthy (PE)
- And one new one (Psychology)

I remember sitting down in my first ever Psychology lesson at the age of 16, thinking that if nothing else, at least Psychology sounded interesting. My teacher, Miss Chutter, "paper-bombed" us with module breakdowns, model exam answers, past exam papers, and a checklist of all the homework assignments and essay questions she'd be setting us over the next two years. I fell in love with Psychology within the first week, and recall going to my Aunt and Uncle's house in Essex and telling them that I'd had a total turn-around, and that I was going to go to university to study Psychology, and then do the Clinical Psychology Doctorate and I'd be a Clinical Psychologist. Simple! Right?

I began looking at universities that offered Psychology courses, and when it came to choosing my first-choice university, and my insurance choice, I found myself stuck between two Universities with the same entry requirements: University of Reading (UoR), and University of Southampton. It made no sense to put them both as they had the same entry requirements, so if I didn't get into one, I definitely wouldn't get into the other. As someone who has lived in Reading their whole life, and despite it having a great reputation for Psychology, I wanted to have a change of scenery. I debated for a long time before my then-boyfriend suggested I stay in Reading so we could stay together, which I agreed to. As it turned out, in the week leading up to 'A-Level Results Day,' I decided to end the relationship. I then dreaded the day in case I'd have to stay in Reading. I'd never hoped to have failed an exam so much in my life because I was really hoping to be able to get into my insurance choice and move away! But no, it was a very strange sensation when I read that I'd achieved my As and Bs and had got into my first choice - University of Reading - I'd never been more disappointed with doing well!

But I went to UoR and had the best time at university – the course was great, the nightlife was great, I even bumped into the local nightclub photographer that I used to go to school with, who ended up being my boyfriend a few years down the line! At the end of my first year, I received my results whilst on holiday in Corfu, and received my highest result in the Clinical Psychology module. For me this confirmed that I was aiming for the right career. During the summer between my first and second years, I did some voluntary work one day per week. I was an Honorary Drama Therapy Assistant within a local Autism Spectrum Condition (ASC) organisation. This also contributed to my placement module in my second year. In order to increase my placement hours, I also reached out to a local secondary school Psychology department and was able to volunteer one day a week helping out by creating revision resources and classroom displays for the Psychology A-Level students. At the end of my second year, I contacted the local research unit at UoR, which was also connected to the local CAMHS anxiety and depression pathway. They offered me a placement for the summer; transcribing data and making certificates for the young people that had taken part in the research that was taking place. It was there that another girl I worked with mentioned she'd been offered a role as a Healthcare Assistant (HCA) in an inpatient hospital nearby, but she'd declined because she'd also been accepted onto another university course. She told me that the vacancy had been advertised on the NHS Jobs website again and suggested I apply and supported me in the application process. I was shocked when I got an interview, and so nervous to attend an interview for my first paid role in mental health services, and even more shocked when they called me a few days later to offer me the job!

I worked full-time as a Band 3 HCA in the adolescent inpatient service alongside studying for the final year of my BSc in Psychology. Because the shifts were three 12.5 hour shifts a week, for the most part, I managed to work it around my studying. That is until it got to the March of my final year, exams were ramping up, and my dissertation was due in. I became overwhelmed with working full-time as well as studying full-time, and one of the lovely nurses I worked with suggested I go and visit my GP to discuss my stress levels. I was surprised to be signed off of work for a month with stress, but also very relieved to have the time to focus on my dissertation and revising for exams. When I returned to work, I was refreshed, more motivated, and definitely more focused as I wasn't constantly thinking about university. Out of all the roles I've had in mental health services, I really do feel that this one was the most valuable as it taught me how to interact with teenagers as an adult (which was a challenge because, as a 20-year-old, I definitely didn't feel like an adult compared to the 17-year-olds I was working with!) It also gave me all the amazing skills required to work in a mental health setting, such as empathy, active listening skills, patience, and the ability to act in high pressure and highly emotive situations. After a while I was invited to co-facilitate some of the Psychology groups for the young people – we used The Decider (Ayres & Vivyan, 2019) to help teach the young people Dialectical Behaviour Therapy skills.

In 2017, I graduated from UoR with a 2.1, and continued to work as a HCA until late 2018. As I now had my degree and a year of relevant experience under my belt so I thought I'd see what the application process was like for the DClinPsy. I applied to Bath, Birmingham, Surrey, and Royal Holloway. I was invited to sit the selection tests for Birmingham and Surrey, although this was far as it went that year. It was a great experience to sit the selection tests, and definitely prepared me for how brutal the process can be! After this, I applied for *a lot* of Assistant

Psychologist (AP) roles, and like everyone else, I struggled to actually obtain one. I experienced the disheartening, frustrating process of being told by interviewers that I definitely should be looking to progress onto an AP role, but that they wouldn't be offering me one. In the autumn of 2018, the inpatient hospital I was working at mentioned that they'd be looking for an AP, and I was lucky enough to get an interview, and became that hospital's first ever AP in the December of 2018! This role was very much focused on routine outcome measures (ROMs) and group work, and I also had the opportunity to do my first pieces of one-to-one therapeutic work which involved activity planning for a young person with low mood, and graded exposure for a young person with social anxiety. In the autumn of 2018, I also applied for the DClinPsy for the second time to start in the autumn of 2019, this time applying to Royal Holloway, Surrey, Bath, and King's College London. Since the first application I'd worked for another year as an HCA. I was once again invited to the selection test for Surrey, although didn't get any further than this. Around this time, I also began my master's in Clinical Psychology at Royal Holloway, University of London, which I completed alongside working as an AP at the adolescent inpatient ward. I also did a placement as an Honorary AP with the local Primary CAMHS services as part of my MSc. Paying homage to my experiences of being signed off sick with stress, my dissertation focused on student wellbeing. Happily, when I graduated in December 2019 it was with a First in my dissertation, and a Pass with Distinction in my MSc Clinical Psychology.

Towards the end of my MSc in the autumn of 2019, I applied for the DClinPsy for the third time. This would have been to start in the autumn of 2020. This time I applied to Royal

Holloway, Surrey, Oxford, and Southampton. Since the last application I had worked as an AP for almost a year, an Honorary AP for a few months, and had also completed an MSc in Clinical Psychology, passing with Distinction. I was yet again, invited to the selection test for Surrey, but got no further than this. Around this time, I decided it was time for a change of scenery and began my role as an AP for a private hospital. This saw me working across an eating disorder unit and a general adolescent unit. I ran mindfulness groups, coping skills groups, and also did one-to-one DBT-informed work as well as anxiety work. As much as I valued the experience I gained from working here, I decided that the NHS was the place for me as well as wanting to gain some experience in adult mental health services, and managed to secure a role as a Band 5 Senior AP in adult services. I worked across a Ministry of Defence (MoD) ward, an acute ward, a PICU, and the crisis team.

During this role I:

- Helped run 'The comprehend, cope, connect' group programme designed by Isabel Clarke.
- Did short term one-to-one work, mostly centred around creating emotion focused formulations, before the service users I worked with were transferred back to their community mental health team (CMHT). The formulation would inform the work they'd then do with their CMHT, or with us if they were open to us long-term.

I was in this role when the COVID-19 pandemic hit, and we had to facilitate all groups via Zoom, and only do phone calls to those under the crisis team. It taught me a whole new way of working and delivering therapeutic intervention, but it showed me how quickly I (and the rest of the world) could adapt when needed.

I absolutely loved my job as a Senior AP, but everyone I worked with would comment on how my face would just light up when I spoke about working with children and teens. I was speaking with my colleague (a fellow Senior AP), who mentioned a High-intensity Cognitive Behavioural Therapy (HiCBT) course that she was thinking of applying to. I'd seen these roles advertised but was under the impression you had to have a core profession (e.g. in nursing, social work, teaching) in order to apply. Harriet told me about the BABCP's Knowledge Skills and Attitude (KSA) route. This is where you write a big portfolio explaining that you're as experienced and suitable for the course even without this core profession. I found a few job adverts that were specifically for children and young people and had a go at applying. To my surprise I was offered a role! The role was a "recruit-to-train" role, where I'd be paid as a Band 6 Senior Mental Health Practitioner in a community CAMHS team and would study for a Postgraduate Diploma in Evidence-Based Psychological Therapies for Children and Young People at the University of Reading for a year. This was a huge opportunity to me, as I thought that until I got on the DClinPsy, I'd be capped at Band 5 role and unable to provide therapy in a qualified capacity. I was offered the role and a place on the course the day before my birthday (which is 1ˢᵗ October) in 2020 - a great start to turning 25! I decided not to apply for the DClinPsy that year, as I would be around nine months into my CBT course at this point. I worked with some amazing young people during my training, who had difficulties such as:

- Anxiety,
- Depression,

- Post-Traumatic Stress Disorder, (PTSD);
- And specific phobias such as emetophobia.

It was so much fun to learn how CBT could help those with these difficulties, and it was amazing to watch these young people's situations improve!

Towards the end of my course, in the autumn of 2021, I knew that I'd be finishing my course in January 2022. I wasn't really sure what I'd be doing beyond this, so I applied for the DClinPsy for a fourth time to start in the autumn of 2022. Since my last application I'd expanded my experience considerably by:

- Adding work as an AP in a private hospital across an eating disorder unit and a general adolescent unit.
- Working as a Band 5 Senior AP with adults in a range of areas (crisis team, acute ward, PICU and MoD).
- Acquiring nine months working as a Band 6 senior mental health practitioner.
- Being nine months into a postgraduate diploma course.

I applied for Salomon's (Canterbury Christchurch University), Southampton, Royal Holloway, and Oxford. I was shocked to be offered an interview at Salomon's, which was then followed by an invite to interview at Southampton. I was so excited, but extremely nervous as the realisation set in that I had to actually do the interviews now! I was put on the reserve list for an interview at Royal Holloway (8th position on the reserves list) and didn't receive an invite to interview with Oxford. I was eventually invited to interview at Royal Holloway, and this felt like a huge deal because I had interviews for three out of four of my chosen Universities! My first interview was with Salomon's, and it felt very formal, the interviewers really gave nothing away! I felt like

I gave quite weak responses and came away quite disheartened, feeling as though I hadn't done well at all. However, I was offered a place on the reserve list, although I was 46th on the reserve which pretty much meant that I wasn't going to actually get an offer. I then had my Southampton interview which I felt went a lot better than the Salomon's one, the interviewers were really friendly, and I felt that I was really able to showcase my best self. However, the dreaded email came a week or so later to say that I'd been unsuccessful. I cried. A lot. Southampton had been my first choice, particularly as I felt I'd missed out by choosing to go to the University of Reading for my undergraduate degree. I felt that, because of my disappointment with the result from Southampton, I lost motivation and totally bombed at my interview for Royal Holloway and found out within days that I hadn't got a place on that course either. Initially I just felt so disheartened, and soon realised that I had been particularly disappointed with not getting on this year because this was the last year that I could have got on the course and graduated before turning 30. Even if I get on the course later, I will be in my 30s when I graduate, and that felt quite scary. I cried and droned on to my boyfriend, Jordan[41] (the nightclub photographer you met earlier in the story), as well as my parents, and anyone who would listen really, and they gave me all the encouragement and positivity. They reminded me of the fact that I'm only 26, I'm a qualified High-intensity CBT Therapist working at a Band 7, so I'd have to take a pay-cut if I had got on the course, as well as the comment from Jordan that "there are no doctors in their 20s, you can be a doctor when you're old".

Jokes aside, I've come to the realisation that getting onto the DClinPsy would be amazing one day, but there's no rush.

---

[41] He's happy for me to use his real name here.

There's no age limit for becoming a Clinical Psychologist, and not getting on this year has given me the opportunity to focus on my current role as a CBT Therapist. This is a process that can be 100% disappointing and disheartening, but in order to deal with these feelings I've found it helpful to write down all of the things I can do over the next year knowing that I don't have the commitments and limitations of being on the Doctorate.

I can:

- Go on holiday for mine and my boyfriend's birthdays (29th Sept and 1st Oct) as the majority of the DClinPsy courses start around this time.
- Complete my CBT accreditation year.
- Go through the house-buying process without additional stress and commitment that might come with the DClinPsy.
- Focus on Continuing Professional Development (CPD) and gaining more experience in my current role.

Additionally, I made a list of things I can work on for future potential applications for the DClinPsy:

- Working on my research abilities (the last research I did was for my MSc three years ago, and honestly, I ditched that knowledge the moment I handed my dissertation in!)
- Broadening my focus to other forms of therapy so I'm not 100% in CBT mode for future applications and potential interviews,
- as well as looking into areas of Clinical Psychology that I've not yet ventured into, such as perinatal mental health!

To you, dear reader, I say, although it can be a really brutal and disheartening process, it's so important to focus on current achievements, and also think about gaps in experience or knowledge, and progressing in your current role (or progressing onto other roles) that could benefit future applications to the DClinPsy and of course your future roles as a Trainee Clinical Psychologist...... I hope to see you there!

Lucy Gray
CBT Therapist

Hi Lucy,

Thanks so much for your story, it is fair to say that my heart was in my mouth as I read. I so thought that after all your incredible growth and change that you were going to get a place to train in 2022. I am so sorry to learn that it didn't work out for you.

Thanks so much for sharing your wisdom and guidance with our readers.

Please know that as you have been offered a reserve place you are most definitely doctoral calibre and I am excited for what these next years bring for you.

We can often stand in our own way with beliefs whch aren't really grounded in any reality and you will make a brilliant Clinical Psychologist regardless of the age you qualify at. And when it's time for that, with Jordan on your team it's fair to say you stand a great chance of getting a truly brilliant graduation photo of you in the funny hat and robes for the DClinPsy! Stay kind to you,

Marianne, x

20

- Jessica's Story -

The Healing Roads to Psychology

My name is Jess, I am 26. Whilst I'm originally from Sutton Coldfield in Birmingham, I currently live in Poole, Dorset and have previously lived in Southampton too. You see, in pursuit of The DClinPsy, I've moved around a fair bit and in a few weeks' time I am also moving again. This time to West Sussex for a new Assistant Psychologist post.

I am an aspiring Clinical Psychologist, and my journey towards the Doctorate has been slightly twisty and turny. Ever since being a small child I wanted to work in a role that involved helping people, and originally, I wanted to be a police officer (or a princess, if that didn't work out). When it came to my A-Levels and applying to university, in a bit of a panic I decided to apply for Midwifery. I ended up getting 4 rejections and withdrew from my last choice as I assumed it would also be a rejection. I then went back to my original goal of policing and got a place on BSc Criminology and Psychology at University of

Southampton and so I was off to university! Luckily, my Sixth Form boyfriend also got a place at the same Uni and ten years later we are still together! Happily, he tolerates a lot of moving about because he is very supportive of my career goals.

I thoroughly enjoyed my undergraduate degree, where I had the opportunity to learn about Criminological Psychology, policing and the prison service, including a visit to HMP Winchester. Many of you might expect the course to cover juicy true crime like serial killers, mass murderers and sex offenders. But sorry to disappoint, much of my course was theory based and covered the theoretical aspects of crime. However, one module called 'Violent and Sexual Offenders' allowed me to postulate why people commit such heinous offences which is of course the real reason why many people are interested in crime.

Being a joint honours student meant I was able to experience two different subjects that linked reasonably well together. Psychology had always been an interest of mine but because my 6th form hadn't offered it at A-Level this was my first experience of the subject. It's fair to say that my modules, which included three stats ones and two empirical research ones, meant I was disappointed with the content of the course. Although I now realise the importance of developmental and cognitive theories, learning and memory and neuroscience from my working life, at the time I wanted to learn about why people did things, and I couldn't see the relevance of the modules I was studying. Therefore, by my final year I had resigned myself to either joining the police or probation service. However, by the time I got to the end of my degree the idea of joining the workplace made me panic. By this stage I hadn't actually applied for any graduate schemes, because, as you might have observed, I struggle to make big life decisions! So, I applied for and was accepted on a Forensic Psychology MSc at University of Winchester.

Whilst studying there I stayed in Southampton with my boyfriend, and this was a real turning point in my academic career. I LOVED my MSc; I was able to learn about Investigative Psychology, such as the impact of alcohol on eyewitness testimony, how the court system worked and some higher-level statistics[42]. The most enjoyable modules I completed were writing mock treatment plans and case reports for offenders. Finally, an opportunity to put my undergrad theory into practice, or at least pretend practice!

At the time I was doing a voluntary role for a charity supporting recently released sexual offenders in the community. This work was to guide their rehabilitation and reintegration into society. Given that I had access to a population of volunteers ready and available for research and with like any master's there was a dissertation element to complete, I decided to make this my area of focus.

Summary of my research processes:

- I completed a qualitative analysis of the experiences of volunteers working with sexual offenders in the community.
- I conducted and transcribed hour-long interviews with volunteers.
- I then learned a whole new type of analysis - interpretative phenomenological analysis (IPA); which is

---

[42] If I'm honest, I still didn't enjoy that module, but it was helpful to learn with a smaller group of people.

experiential in terms of understanding the whole experience for a person.

TOP TIP:

If you ever have the opportunity to get something published, definitely do it – it was a learning curve into the real world of academia but it was such a valuable learning experience and looks great on the CV!

It was my master's' dissertation which made me realise how much I enjoyed the process of conducting research. I really enjoyed the whole process including working with my supervisor, whom I still keep in touch with today. Ultimately, I enjoyed the course so much I got a Distinction and as I write this am waiting on my dissertation research to be published.

Following my master's, I had committed myself to Psychology as a career path, although initially I had decided Forensic Psychology was going to be the direction I wanted to go in. I got a job as a band 2 Healthcare Support Worker working with young people[43]. This commenced my journey working in Children and Adolescent Mental Health Services (CAMHS), where, 4 years later, I still work today. My support worker job was in a medium secure forensic inpatient unit. The unit served two populations:

1) Young people who had either been convicted of criminal offences but needed additional support with their mental health, or

---

[43] I had been a student ambassador all through Uni and felt like I preferred working with this demographic.

2) Those who presented with violence and aggression towards staff and/or other patients in previous inpatient units, so had been escalated up to medium secure.

About Adolescent Medium Secure Units

1 What is it?

Medium secure is the highest level of security in the country for adolescents, and there are only three of these units in the UK. In forensic secure units; there are multiple locked doors preventing patients from leaving of their own accord.

2 What is it like?

Staff carry keys, radios and alarms and are trained in restraint. Cutlery is counted in and out and patients have restricted access to 'risk items', which are usually electronics and anything that could potentially be used as a weapon including sports equipment or CD's/DVD's.

3 Do patients stay there all the time?

In order to leave the unit, patients have to be signed out by a nurse who will have closely observed and assessed their mental state. Initially clients usually start off on leave supervised by staff and work their way up to unescorted leave. Due to their age, patients also have compulsory education on site. They attend the school building which supports them to complete formal qualifications. They also have access to occupational therapy, psychology, family therapy and psychiatry.

4 Who is there & for how long?

Many young people in units such as these have themselves experienced significant abuse and neglect. It is therefore not uncommon for them to be self-harming and demonstrating extreme emotional dysregulation. It is common to need to work with young people for around two years until whichever comes first: they are either ready for community discharge or they turn 18 and are therefore transferred to an adult unit.

Although now you've read the infographic you might think that working in medium secure sounds daunting and slightly scary; I absolutely loved it. Whilst it was really challenging at times - I have been verbally abused, physically attacked by patients and unfortunately involved in multiple restraints - it was so rewarding to see a change in patients and to be able to support them to build secure and healthy attachments with the staff members in the unit. As a support worker, I was not directly involved in delivering therapy, but I was able to help young people by taking them out on leave and getting them involved in activities, maintaining the safety of the ward, supporting the nurses with their tasks, and having lots of training on attachment and trauma and non-violent resistance (NVR) as a way of understanding and responding appropriately to the young people's behaviours. I worked 13.5-hour shifts, 3 times a week. I also did nights, so for 18 months I was absolutely exhausted, but I feel like I learned so much. However, due to the stress and pressure of the unit, this was where my difficulties with anxiety and mental health began to emerge. Don't worry, I'll come back to that.

When a role in community CAMHS came up in Dorset, I jumped at the chance to deliver therapy to young people. I was apprehensive about moving away from forensics but having had conversations with colleagues and researched potential job roles, I felt like I would like to try out a clinical role and see whether this was something I might prefer over forensics. I joined a team in Bournemouth as a Trainee Children's Wellbeing Practitioner[44]. As part of this, I completed a PGCert at University of Reading which taught me low-intensity CBT skills which I then delivered to young people on my non-Uni days. The role was based around cognitive and developmental

[44] Similar to a Psychological Wellbeing Practitioner but working with children.

theory, so this is where I realised that my degree was actually useful! I would work with young people struggling with mild-moderate anxiety and/or depression presenting with low risk to self and offer 6-8 sessions of cognitive behavioural therapy to give them skills to improve their mental health and wellbeing. All was going well...but then the pandemic hit. All interventions were paused while the NHS Trust I was working at tried to work out whether we could deliver the same quality of treatment online. As a result, my course suffered. There were a number of requirements I had to meet to be able to pass it. These included clinical hours and a set number on my caseload. But as time progressed, meeting those requirements began to look less and less likely. My team weren't the most supportive as they previously hadn't had trainees for a long time, and so my colleague and I were left by the wayside with little support. This was when my recently recovered anxiety spiralled, and a lovely layer of depression was added on top. I couldn't cope with the job or course and very much contemplated dropping out, feeling like I wasn't good enough and I couldn't do anything right. However, I also couldn't cope with the idea of failing something, so I pushed through and was eventually able to pass the course, although I needed a two-month extension to my training due to the impact of COVID-19.

Despite trying to convince myself that once the course finished, I would be leaving mental health altogether, I took a qualified role on the opposite side of the county. Turns out it's hard to say no to a permanent, full-time band 5 role when it's offered! Thankfully this was to become the most supportive team I've ever worked in. It allowed me to develop personally and professionally and to mend my mental health crisis. I worked with lots of young people and was able to discharge many of them from CAMHS as they did so well with the low-intensity

CBT work. I gained a lot of job satisfaction from this, and this is where I decided I wanted to do Clinical Psychology rather than Forensic Psychology; I had opportunities to initiate real change in my clients and loved being involved in lots of different projects. I had also joined the social media team too, which allowed me to create resources and posts to raise awareness of mental health and mental health services. It was within this role that I applied for the Doctorate for the first time and based on this experience I received one reserve list offer (ultimately unsuccessful) and two reserve list interviews which didn't materialise. For my first go and considering I hadn't had an Assistant Psychologist role yet, I was really pleased, and this gave me a massive boost in terms of my self-esteem and belief in myself.

> ### N O T E   A B O U T   M E
>
> Volunteering is something I am very much passionate about, for example, I was the volunteering officer at Uni. I think it is so valuable for your own personal development. I think it is also important to mention that throughout all of these jobs and Uni experiences, I also volunteered. Volunteering has been invaluable and definitely helped me along the way in securing the various paid posts I've had.
>
> 1) I first volunteered as an Independent Custody Visitor, who entered custody suites across Hampshire unannounced to inspect facilities and interview detainees to check their rights were being adhered to under the relevant legislation.
>
> 2) As mentioned before, I also volunteered with recently released sexual offenders to help them reintegrate into the community.
>
> 3) I also had the opportunity this summer (2022) to volunteer at the Commonwealth Games in my hometown of Birmingham, which was an amazing opportunity and has given me some awesome lifelong memories.

Finally, I was able to secure the elusive Assistant Psychologist post, also in CAMHS in Dorset. This was pivotal in my understanding of being reflective and learning about myself and my triggers. My supervisor was very nurturing and wanted me to have the best experience possible, so I had the opportunity to:

- Observe and help score neuropsychological tests.
- Conduct Autism and ADHD screening.
- To offer sessions based around dialectical behavioural therapy (DBT) for emotional regulation.
- Complete multiple service evaluations into staff wellbeing.
- Complete an audit into the use of routine outcome measures, giving me valuable experience of completing research within a healthcare setting.
- Be supported to take time to think about clients and hold them in mind – something which I didn't really have time for before because of the high-speed and high-volume nature of delivering low-intensity CBT.

This is where I really started to heal myself and reflect on my mental health journey. I have alluded to it throughout, but I have always struggled with my mental health, although I wasn't necessarily aware of it until recently. As a child, I was bullied for my weight and bullied for being clever – I was the only one from my socially-deprived primary school to secure a place at the local grammar school and pass the 11+ exam, and for this I was constantly berated. The grammar school I went to was single sex, so I was surrounded by girls constantly. This fostered a comparative atmosphere where if we weren't competing in terms of grades, we were competing in terms of how we look or how many boys we had relationships with. As a shy, chubby teenager, this led me to develop an opinion of myself where I wasn't good enough, I couldn't do things right and the only way for people to like me is for me to put them and their needs above my own. This followed me throughout university, but it really came to a head while I worked as a support worker. There was an incident where I left an observation torch unattended, and a young person brought it to staff having removed the batteries. Thankfully they had not used the batteries to harm themselves, but I was (rightly) given a stern talking to by the nurse in charge and this triggered a constant and absolute fear of doing things wrong. Working in such a volatile environment where young people were looking for ways to hurt themselves, or other people, meant we had to be vigilant, but I became hypervigilant and couldn't cope with the idea that I might do something wrong. I would constantly catastrophise and worry about a young person getting hurt because I missed something.

Ultimately, I realised this couldn't go on like this anymore and decided to seek help for myself. I attended a worry management group through my local IAPT service. This offered me ways to cope with my anxiety, and although at the time I wasn't too impressed with it, I can reflect that actually I wasn't willing to put in the effort to practice the CBT skills. Regardless, my anxiety improved until I was in my trainee role and the pandemic hit. I felt so dissatisfied with my job and course, and on top of feeling constantly anxious I then started to feel depressed. I lost all motivation and interest in life, and this was compounded by the uncertainty around the pandemic and changing expectations of my course at the time. Christmas 2020 was a particularly difficult time, and one where I expressed to my boyfriend that I was feeling suicidal and couldn't go on like this anymore. My self-esteem was at an all-time low. I felt like I was awful at everything

I did and had no confidence in my ability as a clinician, or a person at that point. I reluctantly decided to go on antidepressants – these helped me to stop feeling suicidal but numbed all of my emotions. I still felt very unmotivated to do anything and ended up putting on a lot of weight from comfort eating. I decided another IAPT spell was in order, so I was able to go onto a high-intensity CBT waitlist. Unfortunately, the clinician-patient pairing wasn't great; I felt completely invalidated because I worked in mental health, and despite me expressing that I wanted cognitive restructuring work to address my chronic negative thinking, I was told that because I was depressed, I would be receiving behavioural activation, and this would be best for me. I felt so ignored, that ultimately, I decided to drop out of treatment. I wish at the time I had been able to address this with the therapist, but this felt too difficult. Despite this, I continued on antidepressants and moving to a new and more supportive team allowed me to heal myself and actually feel satisfied in my role. This time gave me a boost and allowed me to feel confident enough in myself to take the next step and take my chances in applying for the Doctorate.

This summer, I have come off antidepressants and feel so much better in terms of my negative thinking, depression and anxiety. I genuinely think my time as an Assistant Psychologist has helped this, as I've learned to be more reflective and to be willing to challenge my own thoughts, which has in turn helped me to improve my mood and have more belief in myself. Joining the Doctorate rat-race is really challenging and did trigger a lot of my previous difficulties of comparing myself negatively against others, so this time I am making sure to be more kind to myself and take some pressure off through self-care and distraction, so I'm not constantly focused on the

Doctorate. I think it is important to remember as well that we don't all follow the same path. I've spent my whole academic and career journey worrying I'm doing the wrong thing and everything I do has to meet my end goal as quickly as possible, but all experience is valuable, and I think it makes you a more well-rounded person to have wider experiences that aren't just limited to Psychology. My best piece of advice would be not to compare yourself to others. Everyone has different experiences and backgrounds and knowledge, so even if someone has had a similar background to you it doesn't mean one of you is more likely to get onto the Doctorate than the other. Take the time to be kind to yourself, take opportunities as they come and be reflective of what you need. It's not a race, you are the most important person in all of this so make sure you put yourself first.

Jessica Parkes
Assistant Psychologist

THANK YOU!

DEAR JESSICA,

THANKS SO MUCH FOR YOUR INCREDIBLE ACCOUNT. THE THOUGHT AND TIME YOU HAVE GIVEN TO IT IS CLEARLY TESTAMENT TO YOUR DESIRE TO SUPPORT AND GUIDE OTHERS COMPASSIONATELY TOO.

I'M SO PLEASED TO HEAR THAT YOU'RE ALSO THRIVING PERSONALLY AS WELL AS PROFESSIONALLY TOO.

PERSONALLY, I FOUND THAT HAVING BOTH OF MY PAID ASSISTANT ROLES IN SECURE SETTINGS TAUGHT ME SO MUCH AND I'M GLAD YOU ENJOYED IT TOO. SINCE TRAINING AND BEING QUALIFIED HOWEVER I HAVE REALLY ENJOYED HAVING MY KNOWLEDGE AND INSIGHT INTO THESE AREAS BUT WORKING WITH PEOPLE IN THE COMMUNITY.

WISHING YOU SO WELL FOR THIS NEXT STAGE OF YOUR CAREER,

MARIANNE

21

- Shereen's Story -

A Little Bit of Faith

his account is a reflection of my journey into Clinical Psychology. In writing it, I aim to provide a balanced and Trealistic reflection of the high, lows, and potential barriers into this profession. However, I'd like to preface this story by acknowledging that, of course, not everyone's experiences are— or will be— the same. Still, there may be parts of my story that resonate with you, and in this way, I hope that you can take something useful from this.

Before I begin, I'd like to invite you to read a short poem I wrote, which provides a true snapshot of my thoughts and feelings at the start of my journey. Please hold

'I'm not good enough'
And there's no point in ever thinking
That I am skilled and worthy of being a Clinical Psychologist
Because I know
I'll never make it
So I won't fool myself into thinking
The journey takes time, perseverance and passion
Because you're right when you say
My efforts are never good enough
And I was wrong to think
All I need is a little bit of faith.

· · · ·

this in mind as you read my story.

You might wonder where I developed this idea about myself from. Perhaps the words of my A-Level Maths teacher might shed some light for you:

"Don't bother revising for your Maths exam; it's unlikely you'll do well at this point."

For maximum shame-making this was of course said candidly, in front of several others.
I smirked in embarrassment, seemingly shrugging it off as I walked away.
But it's forever etched in my memory.

The thing is, I wasn't even *bad* at Maths. I achieved the equivalent of an A* at AS level, and only dropped down two grades during my mid-term test as I was struggling with parts of the content. However, at the time of this comment, I couldn't see the wood for the trees to be able to 'examine the facts' (classic Cognitive Behavioural Therapy (CBT!)) In fact, upon hearing this comment, I took it as a message to "*try harder*". At that moment, I certainly hadn't processed how much of a pivotal moment this was for me in igniting a longstanding battle with my inner critic...
In many ways, I was very privileged to attend a private school. I had access to some of the best teachers, and always had the resources I needed to succeed. Yet, even in writing this, I couldn't help but feel guilty for my head and heart misaligning... for *knowing* I was privileged but not actually *feeling* as though I was. I guess in many ways, society (including my parents) told me that I *should* feel privileged to have this quality of education.

223

What I found most interesting about this setting was the stark contrast between how peers and teachers at school saw me compared to how others outside of school saw me. My contemporaries outside of school never failed to praise me for my intelligence and ability to articulate myself well beyond my years. Yet, within the school environment, I was considered to be performing at a 'below-average' standard. That was one of the reasons I was 'allowed' to study a 'soft-subject' like Psychology at A-Level, alongside a small pool of six others. Despite being able to study a subject I grew to love; you can imagine I already felt unaccomplished at this point. This was only exacerbated by my own cultural and familial narratives that "Psychology isn't a *real* subject". I distinctly remember the day my parents were having a conversation with me about my A-Levels and had already insinuated the subjects they felt I should be taking. Much to their surprise, I decided to pick Psychology as one of my options. They, of course, completely disagreed with this... at least initially. I fought hard; there were many arguments and a river of tears. Their approval meant so much to me. I did eventually succeed but this only complicated the picture for me, as I then felt I *had* to prove it was all worth it by being the best at what I had chosen.

Despite a rocky start, I did well in my A-Levels, attaining ABB in Psychology, Maths and English Language respectively. However, in comparison to my peers at school, my grades were 'below average', so for the longest while, I struggled to appreciate how well I had performed, in spite of the immense pressure and backhanded comments I received from various teachers at school.

For various reasons my performance in the mock A-Level examinations was not as I had hoped, which meant my predicted grades were relatively low to apply for the Universities that I wanted. As a result, I went through the adjustment process to find a suitable university to continue my Psychology studies. The university I found wasn't exactly my first choice, and for years I was preoccupied with unhelpful comparisons to my peers and wishing I could re-write time and do better. Needless to say, I experienced some of the best teaching I have ever received and had access to some of the best work experience opportunities.

I attained a high 2.1 in my undergraduate degree. I wish I could say I was pleased with my classification, but at the time I felt deeply unhappy with the result. Not only did I feel I had fallen short of my own expectations, I also believed that with this grade a career as a Clinical Psychologist would be unattainable. My ideas about the high standards required for the profession were mostly due to constant messages from my university that Clinical Psychology is "very competitive" and that a First Class classification would be desirable. I decided to test this out and apply for various Assistant Psychologist roles around the country, which I was continually rejected from one by one. Eager for actionable critique, I contacted recruiters for feedback on my application, I was constantly tuned away and subsequently left in a state of limbo. With my never-ending list of cold shoulders and plummeting low self-esteem, I decided to complete a master's programme in Social Cognitive Research and Applications. I obtained a Distinction. Hooray! Finally, the grade I was looking for!

Chuffed that I had somehow re-written a history of poor grades and disempowerment by others, I decided to gain some more practical experience for the Doctorate. Initially, I assumed paid roles as a Support Worker and Healthcare Assistant as well as a voluntary position as an Assistant Psychologist. These were all extremely invaluable in exposing me to range of clinical populations across the lifespan and developing both my hard and soft skills relevant to Clinical Psychology. Yet, within my professional circle, it was often implied that gaining a *paid* Assistant Psychologist role was the 'golden ticket' to getting onto clinical training. *Just* as I thought I was sorted! So, with this in mind, I applied and networked, and eventually secured myself a part-time, paid position. By this point I had been working in my existing roles for a year and decided to gain another year's worth of paid experience before my first attempt at applying to the Doctorate programme.

As such, I had four roles:
1. A Support Worker
2. A Healthcare Assistant
3. A voluntary Assistant Psychologist
4. A paid Assistant Psychologist

Anxious about 'missing out' on valuable experience and gaining enough experience to apply for the Doctorate, I decided to stay in all four of these roles, which unfortunately meant working 60-hour weeks at the minimum. Seven days a week. No breaks. Crazy, right? Well, I was actually *encouraged* to work this hard, both by my family and some people within my professional circle.

So, I continued. Certainly, it didn't take long for this lifestyle to catch up with me, and before long I found myself feeling physically, mentally and emotionally drained. I was burnt out and felt sad, hopeless and isolated. At this point, I wanted to resign from my voluntary Assistant Psychologist. Determined, I organised a meeting with my supervisor and explained my reasons for wanting to resign. In response, and without hesitation, I was candidly told to stomach the fact that I was working for free and to "continue grafting" because "the hard work will pay off", and that if I continued for a few months longer, I would be "granted" a CBT case I could work with as a "repayment". This was followed by a comprehensive explanation as to why I should be grateful to work for free in the service. I was assured that many others would bend over backwards for my position. I was told that I should continue pursuing this role as an Assistant Psychologist as it was the "golden ticket" to getting onto clinical training. Without question, and adamant to gain a place on the Doctorate with my first application, I agreed to stay. For months I continued ploughing through dire admin duties, for the sake of this "golden ticket" and *one* CBT case I could gain therapeutic experience with. With every ounce of my being, I believed that this was the "right" advice. So totally blindsided, I also decided to retain my other, paid Assistant Psychologist role. The paid Assistant Psychologist role was very similar to my voluntary one: totally consumed with tedious admin duties, such as trawling through every client's record system in the borough and inputting all the appointments clinicians had missed. But that wasn't the worst of it. In fact, the monotony of the job role and misuse of my time did not come close to the fear I felt each time I entered the workplace, where I was constantly belittled and criticised by my manager.

My manager usually fell behind her workload and was often questioned by *her* manager during our weekly meetings. Typically, she'd turn to her manager and explain that she had allocated the task in question to my colleague 'Tom'[45] and I, but

---

[45] The name here is a pseudonym.

that we hadn't followed her instructions. Of course, this was not true, but Tom and I frequently took the blame for her shortcomings and were scrutinised further behind closed doors. This would happen all too often, that it came to a point where Tom and I actually began to question our own sanity and proceeded to trawl through our emails and meeting minutes to doublecheck that we hadn't missed anything. To say my manager was gaslighting us, is to put things very lightly. Debilitated with anxiety and low-self-esteem, Tom decided to seek psychological therapy and I decided to speak to the service manager to report my experiences. Long story short, nothing was done. In all honesty, the fact that the service manager brushed my feelings under the carpet was not surprising, given that she was very good friends with my manger. What surprised me the most was the fact that my manager was actually a Freedom to Speak Up Champion, which is essentially an advocate for staff members experiencing abuse and discrimination within the workplace. I was astounded – and quite frankly, repulsed – at the irony of the situation. But nonetheless I persisted and was fortunate to have a strong support network of friends with whom I could share my experiences. It was during this year, in 2020, that I applied to the Doctorate for the first time and right off the bat received four rejections. And then it clicked...

None of my roles were offering me what I wanted or in fact needed to pursue a career as a Clinical Psychologist. None of them were facilitating the experience I needed and had politely asked for on countless occasions. None of my them offered a reciprocal relationship where they were also invested in my personal or professional development. It goes without saying that within all four of them there was not an *ounce* of support or nurturance. No one was supporting me to develop a balanced and realistic understanding of what the role of a Clinical Psychologist entailed. And I suddenly thought to myself:

'If I apply to the Doctorate again and get rejected, then I'll have 2 years' worth of rejections and I'd have suffered many more years' worth of unhappiness and burnout'.

The cost to my sanity and peace of mind was too high. So, I re-evaluated my choices — this time, without consulting others. Just focussing on what *I* truly deserved and wanted.

As such, I started looking for full-time Research Assistant and Assistant Psychologist roles. This time round I paid closer attention to the job descriptions to ensure that:

1. There was a balance of clinical and administration duties.
2. I would be supervised by a Clinical Psychologist.
3. I would be offered training opportunities.
4. I would be offered a reasonable salary that reflected my qualifications and skillset at that point in time.

Eventually, I landed an interview for full-time, paid Assistant Psychologist role within a Neurodevelopmental Service. In interviewing this time round, I took it upon myself to think about what I really wanted to know about this role, and to ask my interviewers about all of the things I had previously compromised or missed out on:

- Training
- Support networks for Aspiring Psychologists
- Supervision
- The admin versus clinical work split, to name but a few

This was the first interview I experienced where the panellists were *genuinely* attentive to what I was saying. They thanked me for my time and for attending my interview. They smiled when I said something impressive to let me know I was doing well. They lent in when I spoke about my personal experiences to show they were interested and listening. The interview experience was all in all a positive one, and for once, I finally felt as though I wasn't settling. I had no doubts about this role and it turned out to be everything I expected and more. I finally felt nourished, supported and treated with respect. I finally felt I had knowledge and expertise to offer in my role, and that people appreciated this. I finally felt happy. I loved each and every day I went into work. It was during this role that I applied for the Doctorate again and was eventually offered three interviews and two places.

Becoming a Clinical Psychologist is more than just a job for me; it's my passion. It represents the peaks and troughs of my journey, and the strength and resilience I have gained as a result. It beautifully allows me to represent my culture and to model an alternative narrative for those who fear the stigma of help-seeking. It draws upon my strengths and everything I love doing and wraps this all up together in one. It allows me a platform to elevate and advocate for minority voices. My experiences have only strengthened my ardour and dedication to this profession. But truth be told, Clinical Psychology training is tough... and at times emotionally draining. In experiencing this, I now understand why people often say:

"It's just not your time yet... You'll get on when the time is right."

And they were right. Because had I attained a place on the Doctorate a year earlier, I wouldn't have had the emotional or mental capacity to engage in the work I do, and to create a safe and contained space for my clients. The realisation that the stability of my emotional and mental health is just as important for my clients as it is for me, was a big one, and was a key factor in reducing my comparisons with others who happened to get onto clinical training before I did.

After struggling profoundly in my earlier roles, I eventually learnt to slow the pace down a bit; focus less on ticking the boxes and more on the journey. This came with the realisation that this methodical autopilot approach was only leading me into situations and job roles that left me very unhappy and with diminishing self-esteem. In other instances, I'd tick the box or attain a specific goal I'd set for myself, and *still* end up unhappy, because I'd respond by setting the bar even higher for myself the next time round. This way of thinking helped me to decentre the Doctorate for a while and focus in on:

1. What I *genuinely* wanted to do next
2. Where I wanted to work
3. And what I wanted from that role.

In turn, this helped me to foster a healthier work-life balance. This way of repositioning myself led me to a role that had as much to offer me as I had to offer them. It's perhaps unsurprising then, that during this role I gained two offers for the Doctorate.

Since getting onto clinical training, I have learnt that there is no magic formula or role that extends you the "golden ticket". I have met many people with varying pathways, lengths and types of experience, each unique and valuable in their own right. I have learnt that what's most important is your belief in yourself, your value, and your ability.

In repositioning myself and representing this change within me, I now invite you to read my poem once again, this time starting at the bottom and working your way to the top:

'I'm not good enough'
And there's no point in ever thinking
That I am skilled and worthy of being a Clinical Psychologist
Because I know
I'll never make it
So I won't fool myself into thinking
The journey takes time, perseverance and passion
Because you're right when you say
My efforts are never good enough
And I was wrong to think
All I need is a little bit of faith.

* * * *

Shereen Charles, Trainee Clinical Psychologist

P.S. Lastly, I asked a range of people in the field to write a small message including any advice they would give to their younger self or others pursuing a career in this field. I hope you can find comfort and hope in reading these messages and that you find it helpful J

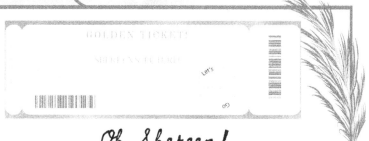

Oh Shereen!

I adored your story and your wonderfully
beautiful incredibly clever poem.
I'll admit I almost shed a tear at that point!

Well done to you for your perseverance and also
for your personal growth along your journey. I'm
so sorry to learn of the awfulness you
experienced along the way.

Your determination to support, guide and
nurture others totally shines through in your
words.
I feel that you do merit a golden ticket and do
hope the destination features an abundance of
self compassion too!

Thanks again, Marianne

P.s. Thanks also for your hard work and kindness
over the next pages.

21a

Shereen's Buddies:
Advice from my Network

Anitta, Trainee Clinical Psychologist

"

I would definitely tell myself to not be confined to applying to only Assistant Psychologist or Research Assistant roles. A lot of emphasis is placed on these roles particularly when it comes to applying for the DClin, however they're not the only avenues you can take. I wish I did more support worker roles or even possibly explored a PWP/CWP course as I know it would've helped improve my CBT skills. I think work experience is very important whether that's paid or unpaid. It's a great way of tasting different areas of psychology and discovering paths you never knew existed! Finally, I would definitely tell my younger self and encourage her to keep going despite the hurdles that might come along the way. It's easy to have your confidence knocked when you don't get accepted to a job, don't get into the DClin, or face the never-ending challenges faced with being the one person in your Asian family studying psychology. Not everyone's paths are the same and I would definitely tell my younger self to stop comparing my journey to that of others or the expectations they have of me.

"

Ashley, Assistant Psychologist & Incoming CBT Trainee

My advice would be to acknowledge that this journey is going to be tough and the route to where you want to be is not necessarily going to be straight-forward. I think sometimes we put a lot of pressure on ourselves, thinking 'this is where I've got to be by 25, 27, 30 etc.' Maybe acknowledge that the route to clinical psychology may not be able to offer a lot of certainty and ask yourself whether you will be able to tolerate that. I know it's said very often "enjoy the journey" but this can be so hard when you are starting from nowhere and the roles that you want (e.g. assistant psychologist or research assistant etc.) seem so out of reach and unobtainable. Just remember that every bit of work you are doing is going to add something to the type of clinician you are going to be. Learn to be patient and also learn to be kind to yourself. Because you will hit rough patches and you will need to find a way to get through it. Don't think too much about what you HAVE to do or what you SHOULD be doing, because ultimately the route you take is going to make you the unique clinician and person that you are. Furthermore don't let your passion and ambition allow you to feel like being exploited or taken advantage by others is ok, because ultimately, if something is making you unhappy, it needs to go as nothing is worth that.

Megan, Clinical Psychologist

Don't compare yourself to others! It's hard not to when you feel that everybody else is doing things 'better' or 'faster' than you, but everyone is on their own unique journey, and you'll get onto the course/enter the profession at a time that's right for you. Go at your own pace and try to make the most of each new adventure as it comes along, whether that be psychology related or just general life experiences!

Anne, Trainee Clinical Psychologist

"

I wish I'd known from the start of my journey that every professional and personal experience inside and outside of 'traditional' psychology would and will contribute to me becoming a more wholesome, rounded, authentic and relatable (I don't like the word 'better') psychologist and, ultimately, person. I wish I could've seen from the start that working in areas that don't immediately strike one as psychological, going through varied personal life experiences (e.g., becoming a parent, moving to a new country), being a 'mature' trainee, and not speaking English as my first language, are not 'undesirable' criteria for the DClin, but rather make me a stronger candidate, trainee and person in the end. I also wish I'd known that I can work on myself as a psychologist by living a rich life outside of the DClin, and I can learn from the DClin how to work on myself as a person.

Annie, Clinical Psychologist

Everyone else will tell you you're ready for the doctorate but being ready for the doctorate isn't about what jobs you've done or your academic record, it's about your resilience and the lessons you've learnt from life. It's about knowing who you are, what you stand for, how to fail and how to pick yourself back up and those are not things that can be taught.

Kirsty, Clinical Psychologist

" You don't have to follow what you think the tick boxes are or what you think the courses are looking for, follow your heart & gut and do jobs that fulfil you. In fact, the more 'creative' and 'outside the box' roles are the roles that will come to serve you the best. Learn who you are, what values guide you and why you are heading for this path - what motivates you, what are the non-negotiables in how you want to show up in the world, and by that, the kind of Psychologist you want to become: this is who you want to shine through on your application and in (hopefully) any interviews. Know there are many other options, not everything has to ride on DClin, explore your possibilities and invest in options B and C too: ironically, you're more likely to gain a place the less pressure you put on the process. "

Shah, Clinical Psychologist

Think about your own values, the reasons why you want to become a Psychologist and what your hopes would be from getting onto training. I've heard so many stories of people being discouraged to apply, due to not being 'good enough'. Keep going as anything is possible! Network and see who else is around you to support you in your career goals. I did not think that myself, someone from Tower Hamlets, being the first in my family to get a first-class degree from University and a doctorate would be able to become a Psychologist! If you are willing to work hard and enjoy the journey of building up skills and learning along the way, it will be worth it. It has not been easy, and the profession has much that still needs to change, such as having more representation of people from racially minoritized communities, who must be supported in the profession. I appreciate the position I am in and opportunities I have had, remembering the core of why I am doing this; wanting to support people from all communities, motivating me to do the best I can.

22

- Meg's Story -

Navigating the Clinical Psychology world with lived experience

My journey into Clinical Psychology has been a bit of a rocky road. There have even been times when I've doubted whether it was the right career path for me.

Throughout my school years I was always seen as the 'shy, quiet one.' I found it difficult to put my hand up in class and being in groups made me anxious. I remember worrying a lot about getting the wrong answer or that I'd embarrass myself. My school reports described me as a passive learner, they suggested I should do more to participate lessons otherwise I would struggle to do well academically.

Funnily enough, I ended up leaving school with a bunch of As and A*s. Apparently being vocal doesn't equate to academic achievement, who knew? Joking aside, mental health really wasn't spoken about during my school experience. Unless you had a problem that presented itself physically, there wasn't really a lot of talk about mental health or wellbeing.

Starting college was a bit of a turning point for me. I decided to study Psychology, Biology and ICT at A-Level and went somewhere that I barely knew anyone, which forced me to come out of my shell. I wasn't happy with being 'shy, quiet Meg' anymore and decided to try and be more sociable. A goal which looking back now, probably put too much pressure on myself to achieve. While it was fun being invited to parties and making new friends, I realise now how much I was using unhealthy coping mechanisms to manage my anxiety, especially around social situations. The reality of this set back in when it was time to apply to university. All my friends were applying for prestigious Universities, but I'd struggled with my exams so didn't get the predicted grades I wanted. This limited my choice in terms of Universities, and I wasn't sure what I wanted to do. I knew that the brain and human behaviour was something that interested me, so I decided to apply for a mixture of Psychology and neuroscience courses.

When results day came, I'd gotten the grades to get into my choices but was having second thoughts as to whether they were right for me. I came to the decision to take a year out to re-sit some exams then reapply the following year. By this time, however, I was really struggling with anxiety and low mood. My friends had moved to different areas of the country, and I was still at home. I was getting fed up with how I was feeling and angry at myself for feeling somewhat 'different' to other people. This is when I decided to speak to my GP. I think by this stage I'd only met them once or twice before and I'd never spoken to a professional about how I was feeling before. I felt worried about what they would say but thankfully they were understanding and for the first time in a while I felt listened to. This was also the first time that someone had spoken to me about anxiety disorders and depression. Not long after this, I started counselling which gave me an opportunity to speak about my life experiences. I'd realised that I'd been experiencing social and generalised anxiety for a large part of my life. It felt very validating to know that there wasn't something 'wrong' with me and these feelings weren't just part of my personality; they were the result of childhood experiences. Receiving this help confirmed for me that I was interested in working in Clinical Psychology. I wanted to support others who had also struggled with their mental health.

Come September I started my BSc in Psychology that September at the University of Manchester. Being able to utilise my new toolbox of skills to manage my mental health meant that I graduated with a 2.1. Don't get me wrong, I still struggled with anxiety at times, especially around assignment deadlines and exams but over time it became easier to challenge my negative thought patterns. I was also referred to the Disability Support Office (DSO) who provided me with a mental health mentor who I saw each week as well as

TOP TIP:

If you find yourself in this position in future, I would highly recommend contacting the Disability Support Office at your university as I don't think I would have finished my degree without them!

support around exams and deadline extensions.

While studying I also volunteered for several mental health and learning disability charities. This provided me with the invaluable experience of being able to put theory into practice.

My roles were:

- Supporting children and young people with learning disabilities which involved co-facilitating weekly activity clubs and trips out.
- Volunteering with Mind.
- An honorary placement with Anxiety UK which gave me an opportunity to use my experience to help others.

I absolutely loved these experiences volunteering and found them so rewarding. I'd highly encourage those thinking of a career in Clinical Psychology to try and gain some experience of supporting people with mental health needs while at university. I found this particularly useful as I was able to speak about my voluntary experience when applying for my first paid job in mental health post-graduation.

This first position was as a healthcare assistant on a child and adolescent mental health ward in a private hospital. This was my first experience of seeing an inpatient ward and I struggled a lot in this job, it made me doubt whether pursuing a career in Clinical Psychology was right for me. I remember going home at the end of one shift and thinking to myself that maybe I was 'too emotional' and 'needed thicker skin.' I wasn't in this job for very long, and feeling disheartened, decided to go for a completely different job working in admin. I think for me it gave me time to reflect on what I wanted to do as a career. I felt torn as I was still passionate about wanting to be a Clinical Psychologist but doubted whether I was the 'right' sort of person for the job.

I'd been pondering for a while whether studying a postgraduate degree might offer me the time to consider whether I did still want to pursue Clinical Psychology. I looked at various courses before deciding on a master's in Clinical and Health Psychology. However, given that I had received a low 2:1 overall and a 2:2 in my research modules, my heart sank when I saw that I didn't meet the entry requirements. Despite this, I was determined to see if there was a way! So, I emailed the programme directors and discussed my situation and my eagerness to take the course. I was very fortunate that they got back to me with a statistics task which I needed to complete to meet the requirements.

TOP TIP:

If you don't meet entry requirements for a course, you'd really like to study I'd really recommend getting in touch with them directly. It won't always guarantee that you'll gain a place but demonstrating your eagerness and motivation can only go in your favour

I was over the moon when I received the email telling me I had been accepted.

My master's covered a mixture of taught and research modules and I really enjoyed learning about the different theories and interventions relating to Clinical Psychology. I also gained experience in conducting my own research project. Although I don't think that everyone needs to do a postgraduate degree, I personally felt that having a 'low 2.1' as my undergraduate grade would hold me back for future job applications. However, there are also certain factors to consider such as financial and living situation and whether going back to university is right for you. I was fortunate that I was able to apply for a disability grant which along with the postgraduate loan which covered the tuition fees, helped with living costs. Despite this, I could only afford to study the degree part-time, while also working part-time doing content writing for a digital health company. It involved a lot of juggling and if I'm honest there were times when I considered dropping out. However, I stuck it out and ended up graduating with a Merit.

After my master's I was made redundant and decided this was an opportunity to give working in mental health another go. I applied for a job in the NHS as a nursing assistant on an acute inpatient ward and was successful. On my first day I was so nervous, I remember thinking that this was my 'last go' working in mental health and that if I didn't enjoy this job then I'd need to consider a plan B. Thankfully, I joined an amazing team who were so incredibly supportive and gave my confidence a boost. My favourite part of the job was meeting the patients and hearing about their life stories. When some patients would become hostile or aggressive, I did struggle but my team had my back and over time I learned to be more assertive. Working on an acute ward also gave me such rich experience of working clinically with people with various mental health problems, learning skills that can't be taught from a textbook. I also met the Clinical Psychologists who worked on the ward and gained some experience of creating psychologically informed self-help resources.

After being in this job for 18 months I got an email advertising a vacancy for a secondment as an Assistant Psychologist for another acute ward in the Trust. Knowing how competitive the positions were, I didn't really think I stood a chance, but decided to go for it anyway. I thought if nothing else it would be good experience of writing an application. I still remember the feeling when I received the email inviting me to interview. I didn't want to get my hopes up, but I remember thinking 'maybe just maybe, I could do this.' On the day, I was a nervous wreck. I was being interviewed by a consultant Clinical Psychologist and the Clinical Psychologist who would be supervising me. Imposter syndrome was kicking my arse, but I practiced some thought challenging and told myself that I had done everything I could to prepare and reminded myself that I was doing my best. The interview was on a Wednesday, and I had to wait until the following week to hear the outcome. I've realised that uncertainty is a trigger for my anxiety, so I was obsessively checking my phone all of Monday to see if they had responded. When I finally got the call to say I was successful I burst into tears. Not only was this a foot in the door to my career in Clinical Psychology, but I also felt that it was confirmation that I *was* good enough and that I gave myself too much of a hard time.

At the time of writing this in August 2022 I've been working as an Assistant Psychologist in adult secondary care for about 9 months now. I can honestly say I'm so happy that I stuck it out. I'm currently preparing to make my first application for the Clinical Psychology Doctorate and while I know that there'll be more challenges to come, I'm certain this is the right career path for me. A few things I've learned along the way is that no one enters this field as a clean slate free from problems. I've met so many people who also struggle with their mental health, it's just often not spoken about enough in this profession. Looking back, I reflect on how I could have been more compassionate and accepting towards myself instead of thinking there was something 'different' or 'flawed' with me. I focus on the positives my experiences provide me: my patience, listening skills and ability to attune to what someone else is feeling. As cliché as it sounds, our differences make us unique, and I am confident that this will be highly valued on our journeys to being Clinical Psychologists.

Megan Knight
Assistant Psychologist

MEMO

Dear Meg,

Thanks so much for your story and for your wonderful top tips. I'd not heard of the DSO before so I know this will be really useful information for our readers.

I'm so pleased you have been well supported and continue to be.

I hope you continue to learn and grow in your AP role and that your experiences bloom for you come spring 2023 or beyond with DClinPsy interviews and course offers!

Thanks again, Marianne

DR MARIANNE TRENT
www.goodthinkingpsychology.co.uk

248

23

- Lizzy's Story -

Lessons in Empathy

At the age of twelve I watched Dr Tanya Byron on House of Tiny Tearaways and couldn't get my head around the way she took all the information from her observations and made a plan to help the families. A few years later I had the opportunity to study Psychology as one of my A-Levels and loved learning about different presentations and treatment approaches. Although at this point, I didn't have a full appreciation of the role of a Clinical Psychologist, I knew that I would love taking on a detective-type role and trying to understand the nuances of clinical presentations.

After this, I went to study for a BSc in Psychology at the University of Birmingham and learned more about the use of research to support practice. I loved studying theories on attachment and understanding how an individual's history could shape their difficulties in the present. During my studies I also had the opportunity to support a research project investigating unhealthy eating behaviours. This helped me to understand how using an artificial environment to gather data could later become information useful to clinicians working with service users. One of my clearest memories is a talk from a senior lecturer about the Clinical Psychology Doctorate course offered at the university. They told us how competitive it was, and that the majority of the group should try something different. Well sorry to whoever that was but if anything, that made me even more determined!

With that goal in mind, after my graduation I applied to a couple of Assistant Psychologist posts but, unsurprisingly, didn't hear back. Instead, I secured a place at Coventry University on their Applied Psychology with Professional Experience MSc. As well as specific modules on Clinical and Counselling Psychology, the course offered a placement opportunity. I was lucky to acquire an Honorary Assistant Psychologist role in a Chronic Pain and Fatigue Management Service. Now don't be confused by the "honorary" bit of the title because it definitely makes it sound like a better version of an Assistant Psychologist post but all it means was that I did the work for free.

As I wasn't getting paid and the job was in Buckinghamshire, but my course and part-time job were in the Midlands, I got to know the M40 very well. My weeks invariably involved three days on placement, one full day studying, half a day volunteering for Childline, and up to 30 hours over the weekend waitressing to pay for living expenses. Don't get me wrong, I was exhausted by the end of the six months, but I don't regret this by any means. I learned so much from the multi-disciplinary team – made up of Clinical Psychologists, Physiotherapists, Occupational Therapists, and a fabulous Assistant Psychologist. I had the opportunity to sit in on triage meetings and treatment sessions, as well as support the organisation and delivery of their acceptance and commitment therapy (ACT) and cognitive behavioural therapy (CBT) groups. It was also an interesting role because I grew up with a number of family members living with long-term health conditions. This meant I could appreciate how much of the rest of life happens in the other 167 hours of the week outside therapy - and inevitably involves the individual's family.

All this knowledge put me in a good position to apply and secure a paid (yay!) Assistant Psychologist position in the same service once I had completed my dissertation. I worked for a year in this service and gained so much experience of the ins and outs of a secondary care team, particularly the importance of service user outcomes and feedback to shape service development.

I then felt that I needed to gain more experience in an adult mental health setting, but with less of a focus on physical health, so applied to an Assistant Psychologist role in an Improving Access to Psychological Therapies (IAPT) service. Although I was unsuccessful following interview, I was offered an Assistant Psychologist post in their partner Step 4 service for individuals with severe and enduring mental health presentations. This role permitted less clinical work, but I was responsible for supporting the multidisciplinary team in their triage process. I worked closely with psychiatrists, Clinical Psychologists, counsellors, CBT therapists, and other clinicians with expertise in a range of therapeutic modalities. Hearing the rationale for offering assessment and treatment for particular presentations has shaped my understanding of the formulation process for each.

During my time in this role, I applied for the first time to the Clinical Psychology Doctorate but received flat out rejections from all four courses. The feedback stated that I needed more clinical contact and re-reading my application I realised I was not very adept at reflecting! It just so happened that the COVID-19 pandemic was starting, and I was reassigned to work on our Trust's mental health support line which was integrated with the local IAPT team. By meeting their clinicians, I learned more about how IAPT functions and was then lucky to secure a place on their Psychological Wellbeing Practitioner (PWP) training. The course itself was stressful as it was the first apprenticeship course, meaning we were essentially 'guinea pigs', and working through the pandemic only added to this. However, I was speaking to service users on a daily basis from pretty early on, gained a solid understanding of low-intensity CBT, and practiced how to reflect on my experiences!

Sadly, during my training year, we lost my grandmother (at the grand old age of ninety-nine!) and I spent much of my time in the months before her death providing care and support. This definitely shaped me as a person and meant I could empathise with clients who were themselves taking on more of a caring role. There have, however, been occasions when client contacts have brought this to the surface. I know that as clinicians we all have that one area that really gets to us, but I remember sobbing in the toilets after hearing a carer talk about her experiences of watching a client die. I think this is something that will always affect me, perhaps even more than suicidal thoughts, sexual assault, and abuse.

All this going on meant I decided not to submit an application for the Clinical Psychology Doctorate that year. However, once qualified as a PWP and with a full caseload I applied for the 2022 cohort and secured one interview. Unfortunately, I have never been more anxious in my life and was distracted by trying not to faint, so my answers were barely full sentences – no surprise that I was not offered a place! Nonetheless, it was a productive experience to prepare for interview and I now have a better idea of what to expect. This journey is a frustrating and complicated one, particularly when relatively few people understand, why on earth, I'm putting myself through the pain of it when I could go down a different career path. Luckily for me my younger sister wants to be an actress so I'm not the only one that our parents despair with!

As I progressed in the IAPT service I was promoted, and now work as a senior PWP. This means that I have a reduced caseload but supervise five PWPs and deliver clinical skills supervision. I have also been able to bring the knowledge I gained from working in a health Psychology area to this role, although the sense of imposter syndrome is real some days! I have loved the opportunities I have been offered, particularly designing CBT-based courses for clients firstly with anxiety, then also comorbid with long-COVID and secondly for those with comorbid irritable bowel syndrome. This experience has also meant I have kept up with the research side of things by analysing participant outcomes and feedback. No day is the same in IAPT, but I quite like it that way!

I plan to apply for training this year but am trying to be as compassionate to myself as I am to my clients and supervisees. As one of my colleagues said to me recently:

"Your time will come - you're exactly where you are meant to be right now".

Lizzy Fadden,
Senior PWP

Dear Lizzy,

Thank you for your story. I'm sorry to hear how anxiety provoking the whole interview process was. I do believe that when it's the right time and we are ready for the next step it feels more comfortably within our stride, and I am so excited for that to be the case for you soon! I really love that the prominence of psychologists in the media has turned people's heads towards the career from a young age.

Well done to you on your promotion to senior PWP!

I agree with your colleague that we can most certainly learn a great deal from the roles we find ourselves in and that they can teach us so much about ourselves, our clients and the world along the way too.

Wishing you so well in this next stage of your career and as ever,

Thanks for being part of my world,   *Marianne*

255

24

- Holly's Story -

What's the Worst that Could Happen?

At 37 I often feel out of place working as an Assistant Psychologist amongst so many fresh-faced students in their early 20's. Then I pinch myself and remind myself that I am worthy of being here, of doing this and that my life experience has helped me get to this place where I can see the end goal of becoming a fully qualified Clinical Psychologist. The journey for me has been long....

By the time I was choosing my GCSE topics I had decided that Psychology was the helping profession for me. It was something I loved and was so passionate about. I was fascinated by people, the way they behave and why they do things. However, my school didn't offer Psychology at GCSE, so instead I opted for Sociology, which I thoroughly enjoyed. A-Levels were where I finally got to begin my Psychology studies and although I still loved learning, the pull of 'student lifestyle' did impact my grades and so I got a B in Psychology instead of the A I was predicted, which meant I did not get my place in my first-choice university. I was devastated that I had to go with my second-choice university, but now see what wonderful experiences and friendships that it brought into my life, and I wouldn't want it any other way.

Being the first person in my family to attend university made this step feel like a big deal. I studied Psychology with Childhood & Youth Studies at Manchester Metropolitan University, which as I later found out is sadly not accredited by British Psychological Society, (BPS).

TOP TIP:

If you are looking into undergraduate Psychology courses then 100% pay attention to whether the course is accredited by the British Psychological Society as this will make your whole journey so much easier!

At this point in my life, I wanted to specialise in working with children and young people[46]. I learned so much about the foundations of Psychology and child development and my love for Psychology continued to grow. However, my university experience and studies were disrupted by grief as only 2 months into my first year I received one of the most devastating phone

---

[46] Hence the course choice.

calls. It told me that one of my best friends had been killed in a car crash. That phone call is one I will never forget and that initial period of disconnection and thoughts of 'what's the point' and being unable to concentrate in lectures or on assignments made me almost feel like quitting. I felt so lost and far away from home. The desire to be close to my friends and family meant I often found myself on a train back home most weekends. Yet I battled on and found new support in some of the wonderful people in my halls of residence. As I have now learned is common with grief, I felt guilty for going out and having a good time, so I still shut myself in my room a lot. Plus, having previously had fond memories of being out with my friend I would often end up in floods of tears if I was out and heard one of her favourite songs. As with grief, time does make it easier to manage those feelings and I started to think more about what she would have wanted, and that life is too short to allow the darkness to take hold for too long.

The next two and a half years of study were a mixed bag of emotions which featured:

- The end of a relationship
- The start of a new relationship
- Studying
- Working part-time
- Partying
- And a variety of physical symptoms telling me that something was not right.

At the time I thought it was simply down to the student lifestyle, but it was always there in the back of my mind that it might be something more. I graduated with a 2:2, disappointed not to be finishing with the 2:1 I was aiming for, but I accepted this was appropriate based on what I could do with everything else that had been happening outside of studying.

After graduating my first real experience of working in the care sector was when I took on a job supporting deaf-blind young adults. It was revelatory for me and I learnt a lot about myself in that role and loved building the relationships with the service users. It really reminded me of the importance of communication in developing relationships and how to overcome challenges in that regard.

I moved back home and got a job I loved working in a Special Education Needs (SEN) school as a support worker. It was a challenge though as my physical health symptoms had been impacting my day-to-day life more and after numerous blood tests and doctors' appointments, finally some answers came: I was diagnosed with Crohn's Disease. In case you're not familiar with it, it's a form of Inflammatory Bowel Disease (IBD), and is a lifelong condition with no cure, just treatments that can help keep it in periods of remission. It can be debilitating with a variety of symptoms, but for me I just felt so relieved to have an answer to what had been causing me all of the symptoms I had been experiencing. To know that it was not all in my head was validating and I very quickly had the attitude of this disease does not define me and I will not let it. Crohn's is something I have but not who I am.

I continued to work in my support worker role where I was gaining valuable experience and whilst doing this I fell in love and continued quickly down the path of having a family of my own in the form of 2 beautiful daughters and a husband. This meant that my priorities changed and my dreams of becoming a psychologist fell to the background. My body had been through two pregnancies and been on numerous medications to try and get my illness under control. This, alongside also parenting meant I was unable to return to full-time work. So, after my maternity leave, I went back to the SEN school part-time and realised that things had changed. I was using all my patience up at work and finding I did not have as much as I wanted or needed for my own children. This settled it for me, now that I had my own children it made me realise that I didn't feel I wanted to work with children with additional needs anymore. This was because I needed to be there fully for my own children.

Alongside this my marriage broke down and I found myself as a single parent. I went through a period of feeling lost not knowing what my future looked like after such big changes. My Crohn's flared up and I was admitted to hospital for a few days because I had lost almost a stone in a week. This was the reminder I needed that I must prioritise my health as I had to stay well to care for my incredible daughters. That is when I found Solution Focused Hypnotherapy. I went from not knowing what I needed, to knowing I needed something. I had some sessions, my confidence grew, I was able to manage my pain better and I felt so many positive changes in my life that I decided this was something I wanted to train in and be able to help others with. I found the highly respected Clifton Practice and in 2017 I completed my diploma in Solution Focused Hypnotherapy (DSFH). I did this over a period of 1 year, alongside taking on some domiciliary care work when my children were with their dad.

This experience led me to have a mindset of saying 'yes' to every opportunity that was presented to me for a year, with an attitude

of 'why not, what's the worst that could happen?' Subsequently
I found myself:

- As an extra in a music video that was being filmed locally
- Completing a survival of the fittest race
- Writing the monthly medical health article for 'The Local Answer'[47] This was a joy as it tapped into my love of writing and being able to help people. It also gave me a new snappy writing style as opposed to the academic style I had been used to.
- Starting my own business offering SFH.

Running my own business was never something I envisaged and luckily through attending local networking events I found some wonderful people to surround myself with and learn from. I have continued to grow and run it part -time alongside working in various care roles including:

- Domiciliary carer
- Reablement support worker
- Dementia care assistant

I have also continued to grow my knowledge by attending conferences and accruing continuing professional development (CPD) points. I have completed some specialist training in Sleep Difficulties, Rewind Trauma Therapy and the Medical Hypnotherapy Diploma. I am still as passionate and excited about using SFH to help people as I was 5 years ago.

---

[47] The Local Answer is a free monthly publication that produces 180,000 magazines delivered door to door including local businesses.

By this stage, health wise, I had tried numerous medications all of which either left me with horrible side effects or just didn't work for me. The only thing that seemed to help keep me in remission was steroids. These have their own side effects and after many courses over a couple of years, a bone density scan revealed I had early onset osteoporosis. The steroids were stopped, and since those results, I haven't been prescribed any. Luckily the brilliant scientists that research medications and a cure for IBD had found an immunosuppressant medication that worked well for my condition. After a successful trial I started going to hospital every 8 weeks for an IV infusion. The fatigue, bloating and pain has never fully left me but other than that my symptoms were pretty much under control. There has been the odd blip over the years where I have had to receive double doses and am now every 6 weeks between infusions, but overall, this has been a game changer.

In 2019 I started working in a private rehab clinic, where I progressed from recovery practitioner, to acting senior and then outreach worker. Whilst working in this environment I completed the Level 3 diploma in adult social care and completed Acceptance & Commitment Therapy (ACT) training. Over the years people I care about have struggled with addiction. Therefore, the substance misuse sector has always been close to my heart. Working within it left me inspired and reconnected my thirst for Psychology.

With this inspiration and my health quite stable I finally took the plunge and applied to study a part-time master's. In 2020 I was completely thrilled to be offered an unconditional place at the University of South Wales in the Clinical Psychology MSc programme. I needed to be able to support my daughters and so studying full-time was not an option for me. Then with the excitement of being a student again (mature or not) along came a global pandemic. The medication I was taking was an immunosuppressant, so I was told to shield. Therefore, I found myself isolated at home, unable to attend university in person and for the first time, quite scared. As I previously mentioned, from diagnosis my mindset has been positive and kept me going through some difficult times, but to see the words 'extremely clinically vulnerable' in a letter from the government and hear the government announcements telling me I must stay home, and shield was difficult as I was being told to accept my condition really is important and makes me 'vulnerable'[48].

In traditional Holly style, I didn't let this fear or difficulty accepting my 'vulnerability' consume me or hold me back. Instead, I accepted that I must shield and therefore wouldn't get the university experience I had been expecting. So, my life became home schooling my daughters alongside home schooling myself! The lectures were provided online, and I was pleased to have the extra time to study. It was during COVID and the first year of my MSc that I decided to get back into the mindset of 'why not, what's the worst that could happen?'. As a result, I said yes a few more times:

- Yes 1 = My Uni emailed about a remote job opportunity funded by the DWP. It was to maintain employment in people struggling with their mental health. I applied and got the role which helped me in numerous ways: extra income, managing a case load and support work delivered over the phone.

---

[48] A word which has never sat well with me but that's another story!

- Yes 2 = I started working remotely as part of a private team supporting people with eating disorders, which alongside addiction has become a specialist interest of mine.

- Yes 3 = Whilst on LinkedIn during summer 2021 I saw a job advert for an Assistant Psychologist with my local NHS trust. It was in a completely new team being set up to support the health and wellbeing of health and social care workers. I loved working at the rehab clinic and so I was not going to leave for anything other than the dream role of Assistant Psychologist. Unsure, I discussed it with my current partner, and he reminded me that I had nothing to lose, and that he believed in me. So, I laughed at myself whilst completing the application form thinking:

a) I had no chance
b) Worst case scenario I wouldn't get it
c) Even then I would still be in a job I loved
d) It would be valuable application and possible interview experience.

To my shock while away glamping with my daughters, my best friend and her daughter, I received an email[49] on the Friday inviting me to interview for the job on the Monday afternoon over Teams. I was gobsmacked, I instantly accepted the invitation only to have the realisation that I would be returning home Monday morning after a long weekend glamping, having zero time to prepare. Of course, fear, imposter syndrome and self-doubt crept in, but luckily being kept busy with my family

---

[49] Thankfully I still had phone signal!

and best friend meant those thoughts did not get much space to grow. Instead:

- I got home a few hours before my interview.
- Showered properly[50]
- Read the job role details again and made notes.
- Reminded myself of the Trust's values.
- Did a mindfulness exercise to feel ready.

The interview went well, but I was still not convinced I had enough Psychology experience to get the role and imagined the 100s of graduates who probably applied and were more experienced than me. Then, the following day, the most amazing phone call happened! It was from my now boss offering me the Assistant Psychologist job! I wanted to scream and shout with joy but remained calm and professional on the phone. She told me that with my experience and background I was exactly what they were looking for. They had no doubt I would be an asset to this newly forming team. The role would be fully remote which meant for the first time in 12 years I would be able to work full-time, again. What an opportunity, something I had only ever dreamed could actually happen.

I handed in my notice at the rehab clinic and made it clear I was only leaving for this amazing opportunity: they understood and were excited for me. As I write this, I realise that next week I will have been in my AP role for a whole year. Thinking about the amazing year I have had; I still can't quite believe it. Some of the highlights are having:

---

[50] Always tricky to feel fully clean in a camp site shower!

- Helped support many individuals working throughout the health and social care sectors
- Attended meetings with so many varied professionals across the NHS
- Assisted in creating a Long COVID staff support group
- Become the project lead for our Long COVID staff support programme
- Completed training in Compassion Focused Therapy (CFT)
- Been part of one of the most supportive Psychology informed teams.
- Connected with other APs locally and nationally
- Presented webinars over Teams to a range of professionals
- Become an Inclusion Ally

When I applied for my MSc, I was only working part-time so don't get me wrong, it has been a strain balancing studying my final year, with working full-time, keeping my SFH business going[51], along with parenting my children. Just to add to the strain, we also moved to a new house 7 months ago and I am currently in the final stages of completing my research dissertation due at the end of next month. Despite all of this I would not have changed a thing. I love what I do.

One thing I would say is that there is a lot written and discussed about the competitiveness within the field of Assistant Psychologists and aspiring ones. I have personally not found that

---

[51] Admittedly for a while I decided to stop seeing private clients as my health was starting to suffer from the pressure I was under.

at all. I think when you are coming into a profession such as Psychology where you want to look after people's mental health and wellbeing, then you are likely to be someone who has compassion and cares about others. When reaching out, connecting not only with other APs but talking and asking other Psychologists how they got to where they are and if they have any advice etc, all I have found is kindness, openness and compassion. If/when you come into this environment, especially the strained NHS, remain compassionate, genuine and honest and you will more than likely be met with the same. I can't help wondering what is next. I'd always thought it would be the Clinical Doctorate, but the more psychologists and professionals I have met in the past year, the less certain I am about that. Deep down I think that is still the ultimate dream, but for now I am content and wanting to learn as much as I can, plus I would like a tiny respite from studying on such a big scale and just focus on my family and my work. So, I think I might not apply this year, but come next September I might just go for it, as my youngest daughter will be in her final year of primary school and after all, *'why not, what's the worst that could happen?'*.

Holly Buckley
Assistant Psychologist

Memo

Dear Holly,

Thank you for your story. Well, if you want something done then ask a busy person most certainly applies to you!

Congrats on your first year as an AP and wishing you well with your thesis. I'll admit I got slightly excited when I recognised your MSc uni name because I did my undergrad there except in those days it was called Glamorgan! So, 20 mins later I have just done a virtual tour with a lovely chap called Brad! Also slightly gutted that by looking over Brad's shoulder it looks like they have pulled the old nightclub down but that's a total aside!

I am so pleased to learn that you've been able to find a treatment which helps stabilise the Crohn's. Be kind to you.

Thanks again, Marianne

25

- Nadia's Story -
If She Could See You Now

Hi, I am Nadia. I am currently working as an Assistant Psychologist. I get asked all the time how I got to where I am today. It wasn't as straight forward as some would think as I've faced a lot of adversity along the way. Here is my story. I hope it inspires you.

I've always wanted to work in healthcare, but I've not always wanted to work in mental health. That changed for me when I started struggling with my own mental health. Throughout my teenage years I tried therapy, but I had quite a few unhelpful experiences that made me give up on it many times.

In 2015, however, due to my declining mental health, I failed my A Levels. I genuinely believed my life would be over. What I didn't know however was that the redirection was going to lead me to greater things.

I left the environment I was comfortable in and started on a very long and uncomfortable journey.

This journey led me to a lot of pain and disappointment.

I felt like everything I touched was broken.

But this taught me how to be content with my own broken pieces.

People I once loved caused me pain, but this taught me to value those who love me.

I spent a lot of time on my own, but this taught me how to take care of myself.

Lessons I've learned

In 2017, I finally decided to give therapy one last chance. My therapist Chrissy genuinely saved my life. I left therapy a changed person. Suddenly, things started to make sense for me.

This sparked my passion for Psychology.

However even this journey, was not an easy one...

Halfway through the first year of my Psychology degree, I woke up and could not feel three of my fingers. Two months later I was having emergency surgery. This meant that even though I am right-handed I did half my degree with my left hand. The struggle didn't end there. The world as we all knew it was about to change. During the pandemic I was writing my dissertation whilst sitting on the trampoline in my garden – anything to get out of the house for a bit! I can now look back and laugh at it but at the time it was far from ideal.

I finally graduated in Summer 2020. I remember sitting with my parents, crying in disbelief. It took a lot to get my degree. 'Finally, I'll be able to get an Assistant Psychologist job at last!'. Or so I thought. In two weeks alone I applied to more than 55 jobs. I was feeling pretty confident because by this time I had:

- 2+ years voluntary experience
- 5 different part-time jobs across the years of my undergraduate degree
- A 2:1 degree

I thought it would be easy.

Rejection.
Rejection.
Rejection.

I didn't even get a single interview. Post-graduate blues hit me like a truck. I felt like I wasn't good enough. One day, I decided to swallow my pride and I applied for jobs I wouldn't previously have thought to apply for. This led to me starting to work as a Teaching Assistant in Severe & Enduring Mental Health (SEMH) schools. Never once would I have thought I would work in education, but doing so, changed everything for me! I used this experience and worked as a Child & Adolescent Mental Health Services (CAMHS) Teaching Assistant on an inpatient ward. This was so rewarding. It was my first insight into inpatient settings. I felt like I could make a real difference here.

But it was hard. It was so hard. Imposter syndrome hit. This wasn't helped by one experience where someone laughed at me. She told me I'd make a rubbish Psychologist. She said I'd probably need a Psychologist myself. As much as I pretended these words didn't bother me, they really ate at my insecurities. Instead of letting my thoughts consume me, however, I used them to make me stronger. My experiences with Cognitive Behavioural therapy (CBT) helped immensely here.

I still remember the first time I heard the words:

"Nadia, you saved my life."

It was from this point I knew I was going to make it in this field no matter what anyone says to me.

Working for CAMHS was an eye-opener. I reflected so much on my own experiences, and I knew I would do everything I could for the children I supported. I thought of that woman who laughed at me then. I wish I could tell her "Look at me now".

Following this, I spent a few months working in Occupational Therapy, supporting men in a rehabilitation hospital. My dissertation had been on male mental health, so it was interesting for me to work in this field and put theory into practice just a year later. Within this role I helped patients set goals for the future and supported them in enrolling onto college courses, work placements and volunteering. I fought their corner when no one heard their voices. I really thrived in this role. I remember before I left, a patient said to me:

'Nadia, I felt like this was not just a job to you, you really cared.'

And I really do.

Battling with my own mental health as a teenager really set me up to become the woman I am today. I would never look down on a person, the way I was looked down upon as a patient. I knew from a young age that there is nothing I would not do to support my clients, in any way that was feasible for me to do so. So that brings me to my question and one to ponder on 'the form.'

Does that not make me a better Psychologist?

Perhaps we need to stop stigmatising mental health professionals who have a history of poor mental health and learn from their journey. As someone who has been through the system myself, and came out on the other side, I really feel like my journey has led me to become the best version of myself possible. And only when I feel like I am the best version of myself, can I give to others.

As I write this now in 2022, and I am working as an Assistant Psychologist. I still remember when I got the call offering me the job. I couldn't believe it. I cried tears of joy! I felt like I was floating on air for days. I really felt like I made it. I thought of Nadia from 2015; 17 years old and feeling like the world was so huge, and I was so small. I wish I could tell her that one day your mark on people's lives will be so big.

I realise now that everything really does happen for a reason. Every single part of the jigsaw is slowly starting to come together, and I am really looking forward to meeting the woman I am becoming.

I wish teenage Nadia could see me now. Because I really did become the adult I needed when I was younger.

I just now that she would be so, so proud.

Nadia Ahmed
Assistant Psychologist

Dear Nadia,

Your story is one of such personal growth and strength too. I'm reminded by some teaching I did during my DClinPsy where scars were discussed and in certain cultures they are celebrated because they mean survival and I get that sense from your experiences too. It feels like post-traumatic growth certainly.

I was totally welling up when i got to the end and I was able to read about your excitement and pride for future Nadia. Well done to you! Wishing you all the best for this next stage of your journey!

Thanks again, Marianne

26

- Julia's Story -

Writing to Reach Me

Two years ago, in the summer of 2020, I wanted to die. Drowning in the depths of my depression after a difficult breakup and smothered by the isolation imposed by the COVID-19 pandemic, I felt that I had nothing left to live for. This wasn't my first foray into mental ill health, and in fact, depression is something that I have experienced episodically for nearly a decade now. It seems to rear its ugly head every few years or so, meaning that while my depression may be out of sight, it's never truly gone.

I've long had an inkling that I would like to become a therapist of some kind someday. Perhaps in 20 years or so, when I'm older, enlightened, and ready to help others along the same path. I liked to think that one day I would be 'better', and at that point I would be able to handle working in mental health and helping others. What I didn't realise is that being 'better' doesn't really exist, and that I was capable of helping others exactly how I was.

I've always loved books and growing up I was a fierce reader, proclaiming aged ten that 'when I grew up, I was going to be an author just like Jacqueline Wilson' who was my absolute favourite. Of course, back in the early noughties I was told that wasn't how the world works and that I needed to find a real job when I grew up, because people didn't just become authors. Fast forward twelve years, and I was beginning my first graduate job as an editorial assistant for a prestigious book publisher. In many ways, I felt like I'd won.

I loved working in publishing and for my short career spanning just 5 years, I worked in editorial in the specialist non-fiction division, working my way up to an Assistant Editor role. I was responsible for editing a number of books at any given time, and nothing will match the excitement of seeing a book that I'd worked on make its way from symbols on a computer screen, into the real world and into my hands. I met the most wonderful people and forged lifelong friendships, but eventually realised that I had to go. Like many people, I had been forced to reassess my values during the pandemic and publishing, when it came down to it, was a business that needed to make money. While I loved the people and working in a building filled with books and book lovers, I knew that I needed to make a change. I didn't want to spend my life making as much money as possible for a company that I would never see the profits of. I wanted to help others like me, whose lives have been touched by mental ill health. I had a new purpose.

After deciding that I wanted to change industries and move into a healthcare role, I tentatively started to branch out and try new opportunities. As a linguistics graduate, I knew that I wanted to study Psychology academically and that university was the place for me to begin. In January 2021, I started the short course in Psychology of Mental Health at Birkbeck, University of London. I studied part-time in the evenings alongside my full-time editing job and absolutely loved it. The content was fascinating, the teaching was great, and the course itself was highly engaging. Most importantly, it confirmed something very important - that this was what I really wanted to do. I was going in the right direction. In order to actually find myself a job in Psychology, however, I knew that I needed to find myself some practical experience. After applying for a wide range of voluntary roles, I was accepted by a crisis helpline and trained up as one of their volunteers. Again, it was a bit of a test for myself before I committed to a full-on career change. Would I be able to cope working with people who are in a high state of mental distress? Would I find it triggering myself? Although I was certain that I would be fine, the only way to truly find out was to try.

In mid-2021, not long after starting at the crisis helpline, I landed my first full-time job in Psychology, and began my current role as a Trainee Psychological Wellbeing Practitioner (PWP) that September. I could write a whole article in itself about how the trainee process has been, and I can definitely acknowledge that it's been one of the most difficult challenges that I've taken on thus far in my career. Balancing clinical work with study over the course of a year was genuinely really hard, and I initially struggled to develop my reflective writing skills. Over time, with practice and support, I've arrived at a place where I'm about to qualify as a PWP, and I have more confidence in my role than I'd ever thought I would have.

I love working clinically and spending time with patients is everything that I hoped it would be. There's a real beauty in what we do as PWPs. Based on the principles of Cognitive Behavioural Therapy (CBT), we deliver guided self-help interventions with our patients and teach simple yet effective evidence-based skills that can be very effective for those suffering from mild to moderate mental health difficulties. Treatments such as worry management and behavioural activation can be life changing, and I really enjoy my role in helping adults of all ages to develop these skills. Learning these techniques has also been useful for my own mental health, and I've been consciously integrating some of these into my life, finding the skills to be useful in maintaining my own wellbeing. I'm looking forward to consolidating and expanding my skills as a qualified practitioner, of which there are many opportunities to do so.

It was around this time that the little girl inside me who desperately wanted to become an author started to rear her head again. By this point I'd already been published in an anthology and a number of magazines, but my creative self was itching to get stuck into even more creative projects. I wanted writing to become a part of my actual job. Making the most of pockets of free time during my PWP training, I continued to nurture my award-winning book blog: juliasbookcase.com. I also continued running my Instagram account of the same name, @juliasbookcase, and started a new account @thatbookishpsych. Alongside this I started to gain commissions writing about mental health and Psychology for a general audience, with the intention of continuing my writing whilst I train as a Clinical Psychologist.

Ever since I'd decided to change careers and start out in Psychology, I'd had this idea that I wanted to become a Clinical Psychologist. Of course, I knew it was ridiculously competitive and a difficult thing to achieve, but I've never been afraid of difficult things. I'd forged a career in publishing, become a professional writer and snagged a place on the PWP training programme. Don't get me wrong, I'm not overconfident or arrogant at all. I just know that hard work and dedication pays off and being determined in my ambitions means that I am so much more likely to achieve them.

So, what's next for me? Well, I'm planning to begin my master's degree in early 2023 whilst practicing as a newly qualified Psychological Wellbeing Practitioner. I've chosen a Psychology conversion course that's accredited by the British Psychological Society, meaning that once I graduate, I'll be eligible for graduate membership of the BPS, which is a requirement for entry onto the Clinical Psychology Doctorate. I'm also keen to find volunteering opportunities in both Psychology research and psychiatric hospitals so that I can fill as many gaps in my knowledge as possible. After that, the plan is to begin applying to the Doctorate and continue on my path to becoming a Clinical Psychologist.

But this isn't my only ambition. I hope to one day return to book publishing as an author and write non-fiction books using my knowledge as a mental health professional.[52] I also hope to continue writing for a general audience as well as other clinicians and hope to one day write a column for a magazine too. I have a long road ahead of me and I don't expect it to be easy, but I do intend to pursue my goals with the grit and determination of that ten-year-old girl who was once told that she couldn't be an author when she grew up. Watch me.

Julia Mitchell
Trainee Psychological Wellbeing Practitioner

---

[52] Chrissie's editorial note: Oh Julia! Please, please do – I'll be a big fan! Whilst I did an undergraduate Psychology degree, after my child Psychology master's and a period of struggling with getting a paid Assistant Psychologist role, I became self-employed! I started doing distance learning tutoring for Levels 2 to 4 in various Psychology and Counselling courses. I'd always loved writing, and even attempted some creative writing as a teenager when I should have been revising for my GCSEs and A-Levels. I did have a brief stint in various honorary AP roles, but these were all contractual and since then I have expanded my business through which I'm currently in Associate roles conducting research with the University of Bristol and editing for the BPS The Psychologist magazine! I have also learnt the hard way that DEdPsy is not for me after being dedicated to the cause from my teens, having applied three times - once interview, once reserve but never a place (!) and now I'm pursuing Counselling Psychology training! I have certainly had a little rant after proofreading your story, I'm sorry, but it was thoroughly relatable and I'm sure will inspire our readers – thank you for sharing!

Hi Julia,

Oh my days! What a story opening! I am so pleased you've been able to come to a happier place now and have been able to use your learning about psychology to help yourself to grow and change as well as those you work with.

You absolutely sound like one determined woman and I look forward to reading one of your books in future - watch out Dame Jacqueline - Julia is a coming!

Marianne, x

27

- Charlotte's Story -

Why Not You?

Ello, I'm Charlie, I'm thirty...three (Gosh, typing that out loud! Eek!) I'm from Stoke on Trent, and still live a stone's throw away. I live with my partner of 9 years, our gorgeous 5-year-old tornado, my Mum and our 11-year-old fur baby Bertie, it's a busy household! Coming from the Potteries, and my parents having worked in local factories all of their working lives, you could say I have a pretty working-class background. I was the first one in the family to go to university (a very proud day all round!) and I want to be pretty honest and say that my journey hasn't been an easy one. I'm not one of those people that knew that they wanted to be a Clinical Psychologist from an early age and if I'm really honest despite having googled (a lot) I still didn't know what a CP *really* did up until I started working in a team with one. Having witnessed family members battle with their own mental health problems from an early age, my compassion for others and interest in wanting to understand mental health and recovery, started to flourish. So, when it came to me applying for university courses, I knew Psychology was a good fit plus it sounded fascinating and had exciting prospects. In 2007, I started my journey quite traditionally by doing an A-Level in Psychology. I completed my undergraduate degree in Psychology and Criminology in 2010 and my master's degree in Clinical Psychological Research in 2011. Although this is now over 10 years ago it really doesn't feel it!

At this time both of my parents had physical health conditions and so living at home to support my parents whilst studying wasn't easy. My dad was quite poorly throughout and as a family we were struggling to get the right help for him. There were a few occasions where emergency services had to be contacted and this was a particularly low point for us. Looking back, I think this was a turning point for me. I felt I had nowhere to turn to; the helplessness and the isolation - I hated it. Those feelings have stayed with me ever since. I knew I never wanted to feel like that again. I think it was then that Clinical Psychology really struck me as a role I wanted to aspire to. It was also what drew me to the roles I took up later down the line where I could do what I couldn't do with my dad, support people to access the right support at the right time.

Despite the difficulties I was having at home I was motivated to make them proud. I loved my Psychology course and whilst waiting outside lectures I often found myself staring at a large board outside of the lecture hall which detailed different types of Psychology roles and had pictures of professionals wearing snappy suits, smiling and talking to people. I would think to myself "how awesome would it be to be an actual Psychologist, so rewarding and so professional!" Unfortunately, I could never quite picture myself doing it, it just felt out of reach. But I continued to put this to the back of my mind as I was enjoying my course. Then about halfway through my third and final year of my undergrad there was a significant moment that caught me off guard. I think this happens to all of us at some point. In my case, I suddenly had the terrifying thought:

"What am I going to do when I finish my course?"

I'd been so embroiled in the university bubble and getting to the finish line that I hadn't *really* thought about the reality of life after Uni.

What would I do? Apply for a full-time job? What type of job would I apply for? Will it be a job that's even relevant to my degree? If not, what has it all been for? Was I going to have to go back to PC World and work full-time?!? Cue the DUN, DUN DUUUN! and the existential dread! I also had a dissertation to finish! That's when I decided that my best option was to do my master's, and luckily, I was in a position to do this and work part-time whilst living with my parents.

Sadly, just before starting my master's, my dad died. Looking back, I'm not quite sure how I carried on, but somehow, I managed to use it as a distraction and power through.[53] After completing my course, I took a much-needed break to process everything. I spent time with my mum helping to redecorate the house. Ever since I can remember, Mum's had Multiple Sclerosis but for a long time you couldn't really tell. You see she

---

[53] Chrissie's editorial note: Gosh Charlie, I feel this. My dad was diagnosed with a heart condition a few months before I started my postgraduate certificate in Counselling Psychology and died just before the start of term two. It was not easy to say the least. So, I just wanted to say that this was very brave of you, well done for doing it.

has the progressive sub-type and so over time I've seen her mobility deteriorate very slowly. She now uses a walker and / or electric chair to maintain a good level of independence and she often has a better social life than me!

During this time away from studying and work I started to reflect on that Psychology careers board in the Uni corridor again. I decided to really start researching DClinPsy courses. I turned to our trusty search friend Google and found various Psychology forums. Hindsight is 20:20 vision and now I wish I hadn't! Every other comment made reference to how overwhelmingly competitive it was and how impossible it was to get on to a course. This certainly didn't help that, 'it's so out of reach,' feeling I was having. Alas, after finding out what the criteria was for one particular course that appealed to me, I felt a little more confident and decided to book a spot at their next open day. Now for the most part, it was great - I finally got to talk to others interested in doing the course, and to trainees and teaching staff, however one of the final talks was from one of the course directors. When I heard the words,

"Not everyone here will make it onto the course,"

I started to get this sinking feeling. It felt like the lecture theatre had turned into the Hunger Games arena. Was I going ever to make it as a Clinical Psychologist? Were the warnings from the forums true? Unfortunately, in terms of lasting impact it was this part of the open day that stayed with me. This, all mixed up with a lack of resources and lowered confidence meant that I didn't think about applying to any courses again until many years later. Somewhere inside me, however, I knew I should keep the path open and get lots of relevant experience, making myself ready for the day when the time felt right to apply.

So, after a quick detour to fill you in on some of my background let me take you back to my job specifics:

- I started volunteering with a local mental health charity called Changes. They help facilitate mental health awareness workshops.
- Not long after that, I got my first support worker role in a private hospital working with adults with severe learning disabilities in a locked rehab unit. This role was a bit of a shock to the system as it was quite a challenging environment at times. I found the frequent use of restraint difficult, but I quickly developed my dynamic risk assessment and de-escalation skills. It was hugely rewarding to support people to lead valued and fulfilled lives.
- From here, I went on to have various support worker roles in the voluntary sector specialising in working with rough sleepers and adults with addiction issues. It was here I saw the impact of disenfranchisement. Social exclusion, substance use, and dual diagnosis were common among the customers I supported in these roles. I learnt that building and maintaining a relationship based on trust was key, e.g., attending consistently each morning with a hot drink. This allowed me to build therapeutic relationships in an empathetic, sensitive, and open-minded manner. I also developed familiarity in uncomfortable, crisis-related situations such as finding emergency accommodation for vulnerable people. I really enjoyed this work - I had the privilege of getting to know people from all walks of life

who trusted me with their stories, often filled with complex trauma.

- I then took a post as a service coordinator advocating for people with multiple and complex needs. This required me to support people to access appropriate support, communicating effectively and coordinating multi-agency meetings with various external agencies, encouraging collaborative working and promoting solution-focused practices. Through their powerful stories, I saw the value of lived experience and peer support and I continue to promote the idea of people being experts through their own experiences. I recognised that Psychology has an essential role in challenging oppression and social inequality, by empowering communities and encouraging systems to change.

It was now 2015 and I realised I find it hard to leave roles. I seem to have this terrible problem of getting very attached and comfortable! Having changed roles almost annually and having enjoyed the learning opportunities each new one offered, I was soon pondering that display board again and that my development would be supported by:

- Finding an NHS post
- Getting some more clinical experience
- Hopefully getting a step closer to finding and applying for that ever-elusive Assistant Psychologist (AP) role!

And so, in December 2015 I stepped into a Support Time Recovery Worker post at an Early Intervention in Psychosis team. This was where I really found my feet – as well as the confidence to get back on track to working towards applying for the DClinPsy. I finally had the opportunity to work in a multi-disciplinary team and ('Hallelujah') had access to qualified Clinical Psychologists! This post was truly eye opening. It helped me to piece together everything I had learned about mental health so far. I finally began to learn how Clinical Psychology manifests in practice, and what it really means to be a Clinical Psychologist within the NHS. I remember talking to the first Clinical Psychologist I had ever met about my Aspiring Psychologist journey so far. I also discussed my hopes for the future, and she must have sensed my lack of confidence in taking the next steps[54]. Essentially, she asked me:

"Well, why not you?"

The 24 months I was in my STR worker role I:
- Took every opportunity I could to work with the Clinical Psychologist
- Got a mortgage
- Had a baby

I then started to apply for courses via the Clearing House. You know - the 'trial run...' I kind of had a sinking feeling of dread that I wouldn't be able to get an academic reference as it had been a long time since I had graduated!

---

[54] Psychologist's intuition?

TOP TIP:

Always stay connected with supervisors and those who could potentially give you a reference!

And so, with trepidation, I sent an email to my master's supervisor. I reminded her who I was and why I desperately needed a reference. To my horror, I got an automatic reply stating that they had retired and couldn't give references. Cue the panic and tears! Alas, all was not lost! I then googled my undergrad supervisor and found she was still working at the university – and even better, we were Facebook friends! When I contacted her, she was more than happy to provide me with a reference.

I don't do things by halves my first application was then made slightly more challenging by a 2 week stay in hospital with Meningitis a month before the deadline![55] Even though I didn't

---

[55] Side note – whilst I was in hospital, I did get a lovely reply from my master's supervisor who understood my position and she did offer to provide me with a reference if I still needed one!

get an interview that year I was just so relieved to have made a start in navigating the applications system.

After a few years of badgering the Early Intervention Service Manager about the team needing an AP post, all the stars one day aligned, and it finally happened! They had secured funding for an AP post within a new 'At-Risk Mental State' (ARMS) service. After a *very* long-awaited interview... I got the job! Even though I may have played the long game, I loved the service and the team so much, I knew it was worth it.

In this post I've had the opportunity to get really stuck into the development of the new ARMS service, and to really make my mark on what the role of an AP looks like within it. I've got a brilliant supervisor and, as well as educating me on NHS processes, she has helped to fill some of the gaps in my understanding of various aspects of both the AP and CP role.

My confidence continues to grow, and I put a lot of that down to my new motto of:

- "Just say yes!"[56]
- "Yes" to the public speaking
- "Yes" to delivering training
- "Yes" to any relevant training
- "Yes" to developing and presenting any new innovative ideas in a bid to getting funding
- "Yes" to getting you seen
- "Yes, yes, yes!"

Just make sure you use your supervision to help you manage all of those yesses without risk of burnout!

---

[56] Within reason!

At the time of writing my story I've been in my AP post for 16 months and I've gone through the DClinPsy application process twice. I've taken two screening tests and despite being very well versed in grounding and relaxation techniques I've really struggled to manage my anxiety both times. To be fair to me the very large countdown timer bar on the screen and my Fitbit asking me, *"you ok hun?"* definitely didn't help! Reducing this anxiety and increasing my confidence in this area is something I still need to work on and practice. I'll do this with some exposure work in my own time. It was at this stage, that my little boy completed his nursery years and started school. It had become apparent that he had special needs about 2 years ago and then we had to go through the gruelling process of getting him the right support in the form of an Education Health and Care Plan (EHCP) for school and an Autism Spectrum Condition, (ASC) assessment.[57] [58] Fast forward to today and he has been diagnosed with ASC and he will be starting at a fantastic Special Education Needs (SEN) school this September and we can't wait! He is happy and healthy, and he is my heart! I also want to give a shout out to my other half. He knows I'd crumble without his constant support; we are definitely on this journey together! I guess I feel that it's important to mention this because despite it feeling like it, life does not and will not stop for clinical training. You also need to make sure that you have a life outside of Psychology, as there will always be days when you just need to take off the Psychology hat, and just do you. So, buy the house, get hitched, travel, have the babies (or the fur babies); whatever desires you have, don't let career progression worries

---

[57] I could write a book about the issues and challenges with both of these processes, Marianne, what do you think?!

[58] Marianne's little note: Yes, definitely! Do it! Keep me posted! ☺

292

hold you back from living and making a life. There will always be another application season! Plus, it's all relevant experience when you think about it - it's how you can reflect upon it which will shape you into the Psychologist you aspire to be! Win-win! Having had the opportunity to really reflect on my journey whilst writing this story, I actually feel kind of sad. Looking back, in those early days at Uni I didn't have the confidence to believe that I could actually be a Clinical Psychologist one day. I'd totally put it on a pedestal out of my own reach:

"Nope, it's not for you Charlotte!"

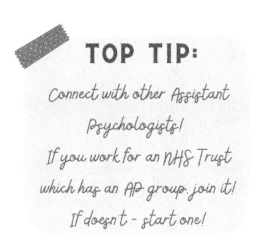

TOP TIP:

Connect with other Assistant Psychologists! If you work for an NHS Trust which has an AP group. join it! If doesn't - start one!

But then again, in my defence, it just wasn't in my world at that time - I didn't know any Clinical Psychologists or even mental health professionals who I could talk to for advice or opportunity, nor did I have any friends who shared my aspirations to be a Clinical Psychologist. That, plus the Hunger Games speech, and the over competitive nature of the beast, I'm not sure how I could have done things differently. More recently I've noticed a surge in Facebook groups, YouTube channels and Instagram accounts dedicated to supporting Aspiring Psychologists, sharing stories and experiences and trainees sharing life on the course. I feel these have a more positive and compassionate vibe to the older forums. I wish I had had access to these years ago. I did just that when I got my AP job: I shared posts on various specialist Facebook groups and was overwhelmed with the responses. We share information, challenges and successes, and lend a compassionate ear when needed. I really value this kind of peer supervision and feel it's particularly important when overcoming the feeling that we are being pitted against each other. It is competitive, but we all have value, and we shouldn't have to feel like we have to climb over the shoulders of others. It's the system itself than needs to change. This is the only way Clinical Psychology will see the inclusive and diverse workforce it says it is striving for.

A few months ago, I became part of the Aspiring Psychologist Membership, run by the lovely Marianne. This has been a wonderful source of support both professionally and personally. Oh, how I wish this had existed 10 years ago![59]
Well now I suppose you're up to date!

I guess I'll wrap up by saying that if any part of my story resonates with you, I want you to know that you are not alone on your Psychology journey. I feel I've been on this path for a long time, and some would say that I'm not that far from the starting block but it's now a matter of when I qualify - not if. I finally I have the confidence to believe I can. So, I'll finish with asking you what I was asked not so long ago:

---

[59] Marianne's little note: Thank you so much for your kind words. It's been wonderful having you on board. I'm so pleased you're finding it helpful. I totally wish I'd started it a while ago too as it's a pleasure to run.

"Why not you?"

Whether you:

- Are considering making the difficult choice to move across the country for a course
- Are a carer
- Have children of your own
- Are mortgaged up to the eyeballs and so your course options are more restricted

Remember that whatever your situation, above all you are human first. Any DClinPsy course and the profession will be lucky to have you. You've got this! ♥

Charlotte Fowell
Assistant Psychologist

DEAR CHARLOTTE,

Thanks so much for your story.
I'm sorry to learn of the loss of your dad. You might well find the work of the charity 'It's Time' helpful. They specifically support people who have lost a parent prior to the age of 30 and the unique challenges associated with it.

Also, totally don't worry about not knowing what a clin psych did until recently - I'm not sure I really knew what one did until I started working as a qualified! In fact, I recall a very cringe-making answer I gave at an interview when asked to define mental health. I still shudder to recall it 11 years later!

Wishing you so well with this next application season. I could do with learning more about the selection tests so let's see what we can do about that!

Thank you!

WITH MY BEST WISHES, MARIANNE

28

- Lorela's Story -
Shine Bright Amico Mio

Whoever you may be, and wherever you are, well done for your immense courage and resilience. A career in this field can be as satisfying and enlightening as it can be stressful and exhausting.

"But what do you know?", the bully in my head says, "realistically you are not even halfway through the process, the hardest part is yet to come!" "I have made it here, and if I am here, there has to be a reason, I deserve it!" is what the other part of me constantly counters in this daily battle within my head.

When you bully your "recent Psychology graduate" 22-year-old self you are bullying the wishful and dreamful 15-year-old that worked so hard to make you who you are today.

So, here is my story. It starts when I was 7 and I spotted the London Eye and Big Ben on my English book. My dreams of moving to England had started. By the time I was 15, I was like any teenager; very full of life and excited for what laid ahead. One day in passing, my parents discussed potentially moving to England and my heart jumped out of my chest. My parents weren't that serious about it, but I was.

After that, I would spend my time googling all sorts of things regarding the British educational system, until one day I googled "colleges in London" and King's College London (KCL) came up. OH MY!! Somerset House, its ice-rink in winter, Bush House, Guy's Campus, oh, how beautiful. That was going to be my future school. If I told you that I was screaming from excitement it would be an understatement, my parents actually thought something bad had happened. It was me, who'd right then and there, decided that I was going to King's, my parents just had to agree with me. Simple right...? Well, not really.

Saying that you will move to another country is one thing, but actually doing it when the country you live in has been your home for 23 years, is another. This is the situation that my parents had already found their younger selves in. At their respective ages of 18 and 25, they had migrated from Albania to Italy in hope of a better future. To say that it was a rough couple of weeks I would not be lying, but my parents have always sacrificed everything for my sister and I and given that she had already set precedent by moving to the U.K., combined with my dogged pertinence about going to King's, they were convinced. We were all moving - HOORAY!!

17th of June 2015. We officially moved to London, my dream city. Safe to say the first two years were not as exciting as I expected them to be. For starters, King's College was a university, not a college/high school, and I was only 15. Secondly, in Italy there are no GCSEs, which means that whatever I had studied there, was of no value here. In addition to that, I was soon going to turn 16 so the local secondary schools would not accept me. I was desperate, suddenly regretting every decision I had made; anxious and panicked, I felt I could not complain. I was the main reason my parents left everything behind. In August 2015, a long 2 months after our arrival, the council education department sent a letter. I was told I could enrol in a programme at my local college, where I had to take English and Maths diagnostic tests. Essentially, it was a programme aimed at migrant teenagers who were too old to go to a mainstream secondary school and kids who had dropped out of mainstream schools. It was not great, but it was my only option.

This programme was sort of a "second chance" that gave students the opportunity to get some qualifications and advance their studies. As my diagnostic test results were very good, I was placed in the highest ranked class. This group was the only one where students had the opportunity to do GCSEs (which was the only way to get to A-Levels and therefore to King's). We did not get to pick our GCSEs, we only got to do six pre-determined subjects which was not as useful when it came to applying for A-Levels. For example, I could not pick any sciences at A-Level as I only did core GCSE Science. At the time, I had no idea what these requirements meant. It was only a few months before GCSEs finished when I was applying for colleges that I realised what a big problem this was. Thankfully, Psychology A-Level did not have any other requirements, so I was able to choose that, along with Sociology, Italian and French.

These two years where I completed GCSEs were not my finest. I was dealing with untreated obsessive compulsive disorder (OCD) which apparently, along with severe anxiety and low mood, I'd had since I was seven years old. To make matters worse, during the exam period I got Acute Sinusitis, and let me tell you, that was an absolute nightmare. I still remember how lightheaded I felt and how during my citizenship exam everything around the room was spinning. I couldn't walk straight, so after the exam my friends had to help me out of the room.

Despite the challenges, I managed to pass all my exams. Unfortunately, no A* or A grades were in sight and the cherry on top of the cake was my tutor telling me how he was disappointed in me, which of course, made everything better. Self-doubt started pitching in, A-Levels seemed harder than I had imagined, my favourite aunt passed away due to pancreatic cancer only a year after I lost my grandpa to lung cancer. Could it get any worse?

I started thinking:

"Psychology is too hard." "I didn't even get one A at GCSE - how will I manage to get one at A-Level?" "If I don't get an A, I am worthless, I cannot go to King's, I cannot prove that I am clever, that I am a good, hard-working girl, like everyone in my family expects me to be."

But did they really?

Nobody had expectations of me but myself. I was suffocating myself with these spiralling self-destroying thoughts. I was asking too much from myself, putting me under useless pressure.

Some amazing counsellor made me realise that. After months of the following thoughts:

- "Should I just drop out?"
- "Should I do an access to science course instead, it may be a bit easier?"
- "English is my third language, I struggle to write essays and to express myself, to be a psychologist you need great communication skills."

I gave up. I was so tired from all the thinking that I just said:

- "I will just finish these A-Levels and try my best, there is not much time left anyways, and whatever will be, will be".

I am so glad I followed this advice because if I hadn't, I would never have passed A-Levels and been accepted into King's.

Somehow, I was still not satisfied though. "I made it to King's, so what? This doesn't mean anything." The self-sabotaging continued throughout university, and the imposter syndrome due to exams being online was LOUD. However, one thing that we do not think of when it comes to ourselves, is that some of us went through university struggling with our mental health. Who else if not us, the Psychology students, understand how challenging that can be! I am so incredibly grateful that I studied this subject, coming from a culture where mental health is not even a concept as I was able to understand and accept my own struggles and the deep-rooted generational trauma that had afflicted the older members of my family which had in turn also affected me.

It is also worth mentioning that online exams were BRUTAL. I mean it. It didn't matter if you had an open book next to you; if you did not know how to apply your knowledge to the question, then that was it. So yes, exams were online, but they were not in any way merely testing memory, so my fellow friends who completed online exams, please know that you absolutely deserve the grades that you got and that the reason for your success is your hard work. And yes, I may have realised this a bit late, (towards the end of my degree really) but it is always better late than never, right?

July 2022. I finally graduated with a 2.1 which felt amazing. Yes, a First class could look better on my future DClinPsy application, but you know what? I am so much more than a degree classification and so are you. We are the knowledge that we have, the experiences that have shaped us, and whether you have a 2:1, a 2:2 or a 1ˢᵗ, it does not matter, it's what makes you, you, that is going to get you on that training pathway; your determination, resilience, and hard work.

Yes, bully in my head, I am less than halfway through, but I am working towards my dream and if ever there is going to be something that will stop me from following my dreams, it is not going to be you. My family and I have sacrificed way too much for something as trivial as you to be a reason for impeding my success.

I have previously let this fear win me over. In year two at university when I could have applied for a placement year I didn't as I was scared that my grade would not average the required 60% or above, (yes, that is how little I believed in myself). I have blamed myself so much for not even trying and giving up so easily. I eventually got 61% so I spent my third year regretting this decision every day.

But what is gone is gone, even if it is awful to have missed such a good opportunity which could have made my life easier in the future. I decided not to beat myself up. It is not my fault if my brain made me believe I did not deserve anything good or that I would not experience something good. I learned a lesson the hard way and it is okay.

I made a mistake, but I learned from it.

August 2022. It is official, I have been offered a place at King's (yes, again) to study Early Intervention in Psychosis, which was one of the modules that I chose in year three and absolutely adored. This MSc also involves a placement (HOORAY) which I am so excited to start. The road that led me here has not been easy, but mainly because I have not made it easy on myself. Mental health is so incredibly important, and that is exactly one of the reasons why I want to be a psychologist. Throughout my whole life I have experienced such brutal and awful thoughts and I know exactly how it feels like to be in need, and to receive the help you deserve, can be lifesaving. I am sure that many trained and accredited psychologists before me and future psychologists have been and will be in a similar position as me, and as sad as it may be, at the end of the day we are human and we find some comfort in knowing we are not alone in our experiences, whether they are good or bad.

So, my wonderful and brave reader, I hope that you found some comfort in my story and realised that in all your challenges you are not alone; it is human to struggle.

I hope that you never stop following your dreams and I wish you all the best in this world.

Shine bright.
With my best wishes,

Lorela

Lorela Qallija
Master's Student

MEMO

Dear Lorela,

Grazie mille per la tua storia!

Wow! That English textbook has a lot to answer for
but what a fabulous story! I also want to say that
regardless of what you may have told yourself in
the past about your writing fluency I think that you
write beautifully.

My French textbook with a picture of a motorway
was not nearly so compelling! (But I do still sing the
song about the French motorway almost 30 years
on!)

Wishing you every success in this next stage of your
career and in your continued journey into self-
compassion and beyond. Do keep us posted!

May King's Be Kind, Marianne

DR MARIANNE TRENT
www.goodthinkingpsychology.co.uk

29

- Shoban's Story -

Allowing Your Interests to Guide You

I can't actually really remember when I first become interested in Psychology. As with some of my biggest passions I can vaguely remember life before and life after, but none of that pivotal light-bulb moment that made me realise what my vocation in life was going to be. It's sort of just ended up seeming like it's always been a part of me.

I'll start with some of the before because what I used to want to do was study medicine. However, that notion was already starting to fall away during high school which is roughly when Psychology came onto my radar. I think I must've been at least 14, because I remember being disappointed that it wasn't a GCSE option.

Fast forward a couple of years and my first step into the world of Psychology was during my A-Levels. I was well aware just how difficult it was to get into Psychology, so alongside this, I was also doing some voluntary work at a Rebound therapy centre[60] and with older adults. College was a very difficult time for me and one that even now, as I write this, knocks my mood down a bit to think about it. With hindsight, I felt so underprepared for the jump in the quantity and complexity of the work I had to do. I think it's fair to say that I buckled under the pressure of it all and whilst I did really well in my EPQ[61], I definitely didn't come out with the kind of grades I would've liked. At the time, it hit especially hard that I didn't do all that well in Psychology because I had been so good at it up until my exams. I had loved learning about it, and I knew that despite what those grades might have indicated, I had a real flair and aptitude for it.

I still managed to get into university to do my Psychology undergraduate degree and almost instantly came out of the pit of misery I'd been stuck in for the last couple of years. This was a really transformative time for me, and I had some of the best years of my life. I got to meet so many different people, try so many different things and for the first time in my life, I only needed to study something I was wholeheartedly interested in. I also gained some more work experience doing some really rewarding voluntary work with Victim Support and the university's nightline service. My final year was definitely one of the most challenging as so many obstacles and personal

---

[60] Rebound Therapy is the phrase that describes a specific model of trampoline (exercise) therapy that uses a full-sized trampoline to provide opportunities for movement, therapeutic exercise and recreation for people across virtually the whole spectrum of special needs.
[61] An EPQ (Extended Project Qualification) is, to put it simply, a BIG independent project for which you'll earn a qualification.

problems were thrown at me. I remember staying up till 8am to finish my final piece of Uni work and even though I spent the rest of the day drifting in and out of sleep, it was an incredibly satisfying feeling to have finished it.

Results day was pretty nerve-wrecking...... until it wasn't. I couldn't sleep much and when I did properly wake up, I spent most of the morning and early afternoon sat on the sofa trying not to think about it all too much. So of course, I spent most of that time, refreshing my emails to see if my results had come through. Eventually, I was sent a breakdown of my module marks and even though I had worked out my grade, I still didn't feel sure and had to wait for the confirmation email. Once the second email came through, the text was too small to read the words, but I could tell where the grade was written, so I quickly zoomed in there and saw the words:

"First Class Honours".

I'll never forget just how good it felt to see those words and to think that in spite of everything that could've knocked me down over that year, I still managed to get through it all.

Soon after, I got my first post-Uni job as a Junior Behaviour Practitioner, working with children with autism. This ended up being pretty short-lived as I found out at the end of my third week that the clinic would be closing down in 6 weeks' time. Although this was initially a shock, it ended up being exactly what I needed.

In my last few weeks, I managed to get my first NHS job, as a Support Worker in a Community Mental Health Team. This also ended up being a fairly brief stint, albeit an incredibly enlightening one that taught me a lot about how the NHS and multi-disciplinary teams operate.

About 2 weeks into the role, I came across a recruitment advert for the second cohort of 'Trainee Associate Psychological Practitioners'. The role was designed to be another entry route into Clinical Psychology[62]. It means being placed in various different services across primary and secondary care and involves training for a year whilst studying towards a postgraduate diploma. I applied almost straight away and the very next day at work, I had several people telling me they had seen the advert and wondered whether I had applied for it. It took some time to hear back, but I got an interview and was offered a place in a Community Learning Disabilities team. I was initially so excited and left wondering how I'd managed to get here already. It all started pretty well, but I didn't drive and very quickly the long and indirect commute combined with the travel required for the job itself started to take a massive toll on my ability to focus and even enjoy the job. It was a shame because if it wasn't for the commute, I'm sure I would've enjoyed the role a lot more and wouldn't have even thought about leaving until after the training at the earliest. I wasn't in a position to move or move forward with learning to drive, so it became clear to me that this was a situation that wasn't going to improve anytime soon.

In fact, the situation had me feeling so exhausted that I started to question what I was even doing this all for and whether I would be better off trying to get any job, even if it was outside of Psychology. Anything as long as it meant that I didn't have to travel so much. I applied for all sorts of things and one of those

---

[62] But I think would work well for those looking to get into other practitioner Psychology professions as well.

roles was a 'Clinical Associate in Psychology' (CAP) apprenticeship. The university host just so happened to be where I'd done my undergraduate degree. The prospect of going back there, as well as working in a Community Mental Health Team (CMHT), again seemed too good to resist. It meant I could go in with some idea of what to expect which I was certain would help me to settle into the role. In addition to this, I would also be in a better position to move and live somewhere close by.

As I write this now at the age of 23 in August 2022, I'm happy to say I have been offered the role and I'm due to start in October.

I'm incredibly grateful to have gotten to this point so quickly; I do often have the classic imposter syndrome of wondering how the hell all this happened.

Looking towards the future, I'm trying to keep an open mind about where I take my career. I certainly hope to stay in the CAP role for a while and it'll be nice to have a job that I can spend a good chunk of time in and get really good at. I have a strong interest in Forensic Psychology as well and moving forward, I look forward to figuring out how I can utilise that in a meaningful way as part of my career.

I like the idea of moulding my career around my interests, but what those will be in 12 months' time could be very different to what they are now, so the approach I'm taking is to just think back to how my past experiences have led me to where I am now and allow that to guide me to where I'll go next.

Shoban Adam, Trainee Clinical Associate in Psychology

Thank You

Dear Shoban

Thanks so much for your story. It sounds like you've built up such a diverse range of experiences across your career so far. Thanks also for giving me the opportunity to google 'rebound therapy' as it's not one I had stumbled across so far!

I hope you really enjoy being back in your old uni stomping ground and that you enjoy the CAP role. For Episode 39 of the podcast I chatted with a tutor on a CAP course and it sounded so brilliant. Such great learning experiences AND a living wage too!

Thanks again,

Marianne

30

- Amber's Story -

My Journey to Educational Psychologist

Schools are central in every community and are critical for children and young people's future. My narrative includes a nurturing and encouraging primary school experience; however, my secondary education was extremely challenging and resulted in me losing my passion for education. When studying Psychology at A-Level my excitement for learning returned. An Educational Psychologist (EP) came to discuss careers options and my journey as an aspiring EP began. After meeting an EP for the first time I went home and told my parents "I'm going to be an Educational Psychologist". They replied "Okay, what's that?" and amusingly they still ask the same question!

Post-graduation was difficult as I watched my non-Psychology peers gain graduate roles, internships, and roles in their industry. I was still working as a barista in a café. I was in a rush to match my peers, but now, looking back this is a journey not a sprint. It wasn't until the November after finishing my undergraduate degree I finally landed a full-time role as an Educational Support Worker (ESW) at a college. I supported young people aged 16 to 25 years with Special Educational Needs and Disabilities on specialised courses. Early in your career don't underestimate the value roles such as Teaching Assistant, Support Worker, and Care Assistant (just to name a few) as they give you instrumental skills, knowledge, and experiences. I learnt so much as an ESW and started to apply what I had learnt in my degree into my practice and reflect on how theories don't apply as cleanly as you expect (or hope). After two years as an Educational Support Worker, I was ready for a change. I knew I wanted to have a specialised master's degree, so I applied and got a place on an Applied Child Psychology course. I dropped my hours and decided to complete the MSc part-time over two years to give myself a chance to enjoy it rather than cram the learning into a year. As I prepared for my MSc, I saw a job advert for a Junior Assistant Psychologist in an Educational Psychology Service which sounded like a perfect fit for me! Originally my plan was to achieve a master's before I applied for AP roles. I printed off the job and person specification and told my mum I was thinking about emailing the service for work experience. My mum questioned why I wasn't going to apply for the role. It hadn't crossed my mind because I thought I was "under qualified". I realised that in the field of Psychology you are only pre-qualified, not under qualified. I applied and was invited to interview. This was my first AP application so I approached the interview wanting to gain feedback on how I could improve for next time. This outlook made me less nervous and possibly improved my performance as I was offered the job! As this role was part-time, I could still complete my MSc. In my year as a Junior AP, I learnt so much about educational Psychology, how

- Amber's Story -

EPs work in practice, academy trusts and what type of practitioner I wanted to be.

The opportunity arose for progression to Lead Assistant Psychologist where I would co-ordinate a team of APs and volunteers who were on placement for their undergraduate degree. Fast forward two academic years and I am now leading my second team. I applied for the Educational Psychology Doctorate for the first time in November 2021 and made the interview reserves list for two Universities. I will be applying again in November 2022. I have had the pleasure to work with incredible, genuine, and passionate individuals on my journey. Be curious with the people you meet, don't be afraid to ask them questions. The route to any Doctorate is lengthy, accept and celebrate the ebbs and flows as part of your journey and only compare yourself to where you have been and not where others are. This is your path, make it your own.

In loving memory of my brother, Luke.
26th March 1999 – 2nd April 1999

Amber Hayday

313

MY MEMO

Dear Amber,

Thank you for your story about striving to become a trainee Ed Psych. I love learning more about different routes to becoming a qualified psychologist and I know our readers will feel the same.

It's a lovely thing to have dedicated your story to your brother and I'm sending my condolences to you and your family. Sometimes it is useful to know about resources for other families who may lose babies and young children so just wanted to mention Dr Kara Davey who does such wonderful work in this field.

Wishing you so well in your training applications this year

Thanks again, Marianne

31

- Ebony's Story -

Reframing the Journey

My professional quest towards Clinical Psychology has been transformed from self-doubt to self-compassion. The remaining paths to be travelled evoke curiosity within me as I embrace the growth ahead of me. Most of all, I am excited about the future, not only for me, but for my colleagues and for what the future of this profession holds. Reframing my Aspiring Clinical Psychologist journey has been crucial for me to reclaim control over my emotions and self-worth, and I have finally been able to find peace and enjoyment in my work.

I had my eyes set on Psychology since I was a teenager trying to figure out my own emotions and mental health challenges. Much to my A-Level Art teacher's dismay, I weaved it into anything I could. I've always felt that understanding our own mind is the most important journey we can embark upon. This led to pursuing an undergraduate degree in Psychology which included a placement year. In this period of my life, I was consumed by knowing all I could about Psychology. Every book

I would read would be Psychology related, every YouTube video I watched was about Psychology and I even created a new Instagram account to only follow and surround myself with Psychology content and other Psychology students. My identity became Psychology. This might seem like a positive, however, I very much lost the sense of who I was as a person. If you removed Psychology, what else would be left?

At this time, I was nowhere near able to apply for graduate jobs or the Doctorate in Clinical Psychology, but when I saw others getting on to training or securing Assistant Psychologist roles or making YouTube videos on Psychology, I naturally compared myself to them and felt like a failure. This in turn led to feelings of resentment and jealousy. From this point, I knew that I had to distance myself from Psychology and look at developing who I was as a holistic person.

> At that time, if you had asked me "what makes you stand out?" I would have frozen, not had an answer and possibly experienced an existential crisis. However, now I would reply with "how long have you got?" before detailing my character, values, hobbies, things that bring me enjoyment and purpose, and most importantly of course, my incredible dog.

After finishing my undergraduate degree, I started my first clinical role working as a Health Care Assistant at a forensic psychiatric hospital. This role was tough (and very frightening!)

to say the least, but it gave me a great insight into the world of mental health nursing, how the mental health and criminal justice systems collide and a sprinkle of insight into the role of Psychology in a forensic context. As soon as I started in this role, I acquainted myself with as many psychologists as possible, we had valuable discussions and I gained lots of nuggets of useful information. So, when a paid Assistant Psychologist (AP) post came up I thought: "I've got this in the bag!" In actual fact, I absolutely did not "have it in the bag". This was my first rejection from a "proper" Psychology role that I felt I had a real chance of at least getting an interview for. It cut deep. I questioned my skills, my values; I even questioned my identity! Who am I if I can't even get an interview for this role where the people screening the applications know me and my enthusiasm? After all, they have met me in person, so this not only felt like a rejection of my skills, but it also felt like a rejection of my character. A few weeks after this I managed to secure a meeting with one of the psychologists who had read my application. This meeting was incredibly eye opening and invaluable. I had completely misunderstood what an application required. I had written one singular paragraph explaining why I wanted the job. I had not spent hundreds or even thousands of words detailing the skills that met the job description or person specification! Looking back, it is unthinkable that I would have ever submitted an application like this one, but I suppose if you don't have peers who are making similar applications or guidance or even feedback, how would you know? This is why I now ask for feedback so regularly in my professional life; who knows what you might learn and how that could help! Following this, I got on to writing a "real" application, which as I'm sure you can imagine, took slightly longer than it took for that one paragraph! Anyway, around one thousand and five hundred words later, a few example personal statements and some networking... et voila! My perfected personal statement tailored perfectly to the job description and person specification. I was now ready to quickly personalise and fire off applications whenever required. Following this, I spent a scary amount of time on the NHS Jobs website, it even took over my social media use at one point. I would constantly be searching for potential jobs, using as many terms as possible and applying for any job that felt suitable. Overall, in this period I applied for around forty Assistant Psychologist and Trainee Psychological Wellbeing Practitioner jobs. Luckily, I had lots of time on my hands due a combination of shift work and the disruption COVID was causing.

In March 2021, I started my first "proper" Psychology role as a Trainee Psychological Wellbeing Practitioner. To say that I was thrilled about getting more than one offer for a Trainee Psychological Wellbeing Practitioner post across different Trusts would be a huge understatement. I had worked incredibly hard for this, and for once, I felt deserving of it. I always thought engaging in learning and clinical work was something I'd enjoy. I say this because I always found when I was working, I wanted to be learning; and when I was learning, I wanted to be working. So, this was the best of both worlds! I was incredibly excited at the prospect of having a job that so many people strive for. A job that would give me more clinical experience than I could ever dream of. However, the year was far from a dream. As it turns out, the role was, as I was rightly warned, very challenging and required a lot of hard work and additional hours. Initially, despite knowing I had worked hard to get this job and I knew I was worthy, the imposter syndrome crept in. Also, I should probably say that in the first three months of this role I ended up moving to a new area, buying my first house with my partner and becoming a dog mum. To say there was a lot going on would be an understatement!

I thought I was handling it just well enough but two-thirds of the way through the course I found my wellbeing becoming compromised. I felt no sense of purpose in the work I was doing and often felt too overwhelmed to function. Thankfully, being authentic and open by engaging in reflection and encouraging an open dialogue with my supervisors, colleagues and line manager really helped me through this challenging time. I was able to figure out my own difficult emotions, figure out what was going on and make a plan for moving forward. Some may see this bump in the road as a negative, but personally I found it enlightening and without it I would not have developed as much as I have. I am proud that I was able to work through this adversity and thrive because of it. Additionally, I learned that embracing my vulnerability and allowing myself to share my authentic self is not only my strength, but also my superpower.

This time, working as a Trainee Psychological Wellbeing Practitioner allowed me to learn and develop more than I ever could have imagined:

- Not only the theory about being a therapist;
- but also, the experience of being able to apply it in practice.
- This further developed my learning and applied skills, and,
- most importantly, by building therapeutic alliances I was able to understand and work through the complexities in these relationships.
- But by far the most invaluable learning made here was learning how to use supervision effectively!

This role gave me a large and incredibly supportive cohort of around twenty-five Trainee Psychological Wellbeing Practitioners (PWP). As peers, we have helped and supported each other more than we could have even known possible, and for that, I am eternally grateful. As well as the role itself, I learned a lot about mental health services and their strengths and limitations. I found it particularly interesting working within an Improving Access to Psychological Therapies (IAPT) service. This is because it was helpful to see this target driven approach to mental health services from a clinician's perspective and to understand the political context in which it finds itself. This allowed me to engage in critical thinking and to engage in conversations surrounding mental health services.

Reflective practice is something that we bang on about a lot in the Psychology world. But it can be difficult to reap the rewards of reflection if we don't know how to do it effectively or how to make it work for us. Although I had read all sorts of books on reflection and tried to enforce it more times than I'd like to admit, I just didn't click with it. Not only was this incredibly frustrating, but it felt like I had failed. Honestly, I didn't learn to embrace reflection in a way that fully worked for me until I started training to be a PWP. This may have been down to the fact that this was the first time that I had experienced multiple structured supervision spaces or that it was a very steep learning curve, but what I know for certain is that when I stopped trying so hard, relaxed more and was able to be my authentic self, wonderful things happened. I was able to discuss and reflect in a way that was helpful for me, and it was praised by others. Since then, reflection has been an invaluable element in my tool kit, both professionally and personally.

It has allowed me to:

- Work through some really difficult times in training
- Understand myself.
- Work more effectively with clients.
- And most importantly, it has helped me develop a healthy work life balance which I have found crucial working in such an emotionally exhausting job.

Reframing my aspiring Clinical Psychologist journey from a journey of comparison to a journey of finding my purpose was revelatory for me. Evoking compassion and self-awareness were crucial to me surviving this part of my journey. Now Psychology is where I get into my state of flow; it is where I thrive. But to make the journey work for me I just needed to reframe it.

Ebony Baker
Psychological Wellbeing Practitioner

Thank ♡ You

Dear Ebony,

Thanks so much for your story. I love the theme of evolution and enhanced self-compassion narrative which runs through it.

I think you're right, supervision in the right pairs of hands can be truly amazing. But using it well and appropriately was never taught to me during any of my formal education. It's something we seem to have to figure out along the way. So, maybe it's time that changed and there needs to be more specific content in this area!

Keep on thinking and wondering and reflecting and it will most certainly take you to wonderful places along your journey and beyond!

Thanks Again,

Marianne

32

- Emily's Story -

You're Allowed to Like Your Job

My aspiration to become a Clinical Psychologist formed during my placement year at Uni. I was working as an honorary Assistant Psychologist (AP) at Hope, a day service for adolescents with complex mental health and social needs. Prior to this I'd always had a long-standing desire to understand myself and others; a drive to help others and the desire to academically excel. I think these factors unconsciously guided me towards a career in Clinical Psychology, before I knew it was a thing!

Since my early teens I've been curious about mental health. I would spend my spare time watching YouTube videos about people with eating disorders and dissociative identity disorder, (DID). For a Year 8 assessment, I wrote a story about twin teenage girls, one of whom developed anorexia. I noticed other girls in my year started cutting themselves and wondered why. Thinking back, I would have benefited more from some introspection into my own mental health, as I now recognise, I was a socially anxious teenager, who developed some strange behaviours and rules for living as a way of coping. For example: I avoided going to the toilet at school at all costs; never wore my hair down and made myself ill with anxiety on mufti days. When I reached sixth form, I felt able to break my rules and re-invent myself a bit, but at times I was still very anxious.

Anyway, my curiosity about the mind was what led me to pick Psychology at A Level. I had excelled at triple science for my GCSEs which led me to toy with the idea of studying medicine, and so I also picked Chemistry, Biology and Maths[63].

I soon decided I didn't want to do medicine:

1. I wasn't that interested in physical health
2. It seemed a hard course to get on to
3. It would require many years of study at Uni[64]

Due to my love of crime detective shows I then decided I might want to study Forensic Chemistry at Uni. I looked at a few courses in my first year of sixth form. I then realised this would involve a lot of Maths[65] and the post-grad job options seemed limited. So, when the sixth form advertised that Oxford university were running a week of summer school for state school pupils, I thought I would apply to do Psychology as a test run to see if I might want to study it longer term. I was fortunate enough to receive an invite! Of course, on the day, my anxiety reared its ugly head, and I ended up crying on the train platform.

---

[63] I enjoyed Science but Maths? Not so much!
[64] Ha! Little did I know what future me would set her mind on!
[65] Which I was struggling with and later dropped.

My lovely Dad offered to ride the whole journey to Oxford with me to help me navigate the changes and settle my nerves. Luckily, my worry was for nothing, I made a few friends and thoroughly enjoyed my week away and decided Psychology was the right course for me.

When it came to picking a university, I recall a course representative from one of the Unis I visited emphasising the benefits of completing a placement year. Being a person who has always struggled to make decisions, and only really knowing that a Psychology degree would be useful in pretty much any job, I thought this was an excellent idea as it would help me figure out what I wanted to do as a career. Therefore, I ended up narrowing down my choices to Unis that enforced a placement year. In 2014 there weren't too many Unis with a good reputation that offered this at the time and so this left me with Bath and Surrey.

As it turned out, I didn't get the grades for Bath. In fact, I didn't get the grades I needed for Surrey either! Luckily, I'd checked the UCAS website before picking up my results, and saw I had gotten into Surrey, which softened the blow to my ego when I later opened up my results.

I would say my university years where when I worked out what my real interests and values are. For the first time I started running and going to the gym. Growing up I'd heard my mum and grandpa talking passionately about their work with children with additional needs and this is likely where my own interest started. To this end I got a job I adored as a support worker at charity called Challengers which provided weekend schemes for children, teenagers and young adults with disabilities. Initially I was working with the kids, but when I realised that working with the young adults meant I'd be able to go out on day trips with them, rather than staying at the centre, I soon jumped ship! Some of the trip highlights included:

- A cocktail bar
- Harry Potter Studios
- Outdoor pursuits
- & Even a few weekend trips away

During the four years in this role I learnt so much about respect and maintaining dignity. I saw firsthand how behaviour enables someone to get their needs met and the importance of reciprocal non-verbal communication, particularly with those who were minimally verbal[66]. I loved enabling the young adults to access activities that they otherwise might not be able to do because of their need for extra support. I developed a bond with some of the more 'challenging' individuals I worked with, and now and then, I wonder how they are getting on and hope they are living their best lives.

The first time I heard the term 'Clinical Psychologist' (CP) was during a second-year lecture to help us decide what we wanted to do for our placement year. When the CP told us about what her job involved I thought it sounded right up my street. But she also warned how competitive it was to get on a training course and how we would be fundamentally changed by it:

"Your relationships will end as you became different people on training".

---

[66] Often indicated with those with an autism spectrum disorder.

This scared me a little, as I had then, and still have now, a wonderful partner who I did not want to break up with. I decided, if Clinical Psychology was what I wanted to do, I could be the exception, but I better give it a test run with my placement, before I made any 'life changing' decisions.

It took me a while to get a placement[67]. I went to numerous interviews for honorary Assistant Psychologist roles and my friends kept getting offered the jobs, but not me. I remember it was getting into April and I still hadn't found one. I was starting to think if I didn't get one soon, I would need to broaden my search. I had one more interview lined up with a charity called Hope. They had two placements on offer, both of which were commutable from home.

I welled up when I got the call to say they wanted to offer me the job.

As placements in health care settings are generally unpaid, I decided to:

- Work 4 days a week for 9 months (September to June)
- Move back home for the year[68]
- Apply for a second job (on top of Challengers) so I could do paid work two days a week

Being the savvy person I am, I got a job at my local leisure centre, so I wouldn't have to pay for a gym membership!

---

[67] You may notice this becomes a recurring theme!

[68] I was fortunate enough that my parents could support me to do this.

During my placement at Hope, I learnt a lot about the role of a Clinical Psychologist and how mental health services function within the NHS. I approached other teams within the trust and asked if I could visit for the day. I ended up:

- Visiting an eating disorder service where I shadowed a group and an assessment
- Visiting a psychosis service
- Shadowed an Autism Diagnosis Observation Schedule (ADOS) and a Fetal Alcohol Syndrome Disorder (FASD) assessment
- Observed an Eye Movement Desensitisation Reprogramming (EMDR) session[69] through a one-way mirror

I really loved how the role of a Clinical Psychologist changed within the different services and hoped I would be able to experience such variety throughout my career, to develop a breath of knowledge and skills, and (maybe one day) find my niche.

Over the placement I also attended a monthly AP group, where I learnt more specifically about the jobs I could get after I graduated and how difficult the process of getting onto the Doctorate was. I didn't really say much in these meetings, I would mainly sit in awe at the knowledge and experience of the APs who attended the group, hoping that would one day that would be me.

---

[69] An intervention for PTSD.

Following my time at Hope I returned to Uni to complete the last year of my course. I enjoyed being back in an academic environment, but after almost 4 years of studying and living like a student, I was desperate to get a full-time job! For some reason, I got it stuck in my head that I needed to get an AP job straight out of Uni. I had done a placement year so surely that was enough to get me the job of my dreams?!

In between travelling and working at Challengers I applied on and off throughout the summer. Unsurprisingly, I struggled to get job. Some of my friends had applied and gotten job offers whilst we were still at Uni, I had attempted this but hadn't been successful. When I was in The Philippines, I got one interview offer which I desperately tried to re-arrange for when I was back, but this was to no avail. Following this, I set about actually knuckling down and putting some effort into my application. I was about to give up hope and start thinking of other options[70] when I was offered an interview for an AP job at an IAPT service. A few weeks later, I was offered the job and in October 2018 started full-time employment.

Unfortunately, within a few weeks of working in this role, I realised this was not the AP job I had dreamed about since my placement year. It turned out I was fulfilling an admin role, for a branch of the IAPT service which was yet to be set up. I basically had very minimal workload, which consisted of booking rooms for therapists, calling clients from the waiting list to offer them an appointment with a CBT therapist, managing the database and if the AP working on reception was busy, *occasionally* answering phone calls. I was bored most days! The most valuable experience I managed to wangle whilst here was

---

[70] Like working as a teaching assistant.

being the third facilitator of a psycho-education group for anxiety and depression.

Before too long, I was using my time to browse for 'proper' AP roles on the NHS Jobs website!

I think this job put a sour taste in my mouth for IAPT. I decided I didn't want to train as a Psychological Wellbeing Practitioner (PWP) as I didn't want to end up in a service as poorly managed as this was. After submitting a few applications, I was invited to an interview for an AP job within a community team for people with learning disabilities (CTPLD). The interview went by in a blur, I was honest about my disappointment in my current job and relied heavily on my experiences at Challengers to answer the questions and clearly my passion shone through. A few days later, I was ecstatic to receive a call offering me the job and I cried happy tears. I was a little concerned about what future employers might think of me only being in this role for 4 months (at a push!) but I decided my own happiness was worth it and handed in my notice.

In February 2019 I started my 1-year fixed term contract as an AP in the CTPLD. I adored working in this team. I felt really well supported, there were lots of opportunities for me to shadow different disciplines.

TOP TIP:

When working within community learning disabilities MDT's you can often shadow: Occupational therapists. Physiotherapists. Speech and language therapists. Dieticians & LD nurses.

My main role involved:

- Carrying out dementia assessments which gave me experience delivering psychometric tests and semi-structured interviews
- Formulating in supervision whether someone might have dementia or if other factors may be contributing to their current presentation[71]
- Writing up associated reports
- Joint therapy sessions with my supervisor
- Service evaluation
- I also contributed to the assessments of whether someone met the diagnostic criteria for Learning Disabilities / Intellectual Disabilities

---

[71] This made me feel like a detective, which with my love of the TV shows I obviously loved!

Towards the end of the year, I was asked if I would like my contract to be extended for an additional 9 months and I jumped at the chance!

In March 2020, COVID-19 hit, and we all had to adjust to a new way of working. I supported in adapting the dementia assessments to be delivered via video call and also created YouTube videos to explain the subsequent lockdown to those with an LD. However, after a while of delivering assessments virtually, they became monotonous. I really missed engaging with people in person and realised I was no longer learning new skills. With the end of my contract looming, and my first unsuccessful DClinPsy application under my belt, I started looking for a new job.

I was surprised to find this really difficult! I thought getting another AP job would be easy, but I was quickly proven wrong. It took me two months of trial and error with my application before I was offered an interview. I then seemed to have gotten the formula right, as this was followed by a few more interview offers. With each interview, I learnt from the feedback and adjusted my approach the next time. On my third interview, I was offered the job! This was an AP role within an older adults community team, a split post between working in their Care Home Pathway (4 days a week) and within the Psychology team (1 day).

This role challenged me in new ways. It involved a lot more responsibility:

- I had my own caseload of individuals who resided in different care home (mainly living with dementia, but some had mental health issues)
- I took on more of a care-coordinator role
- I carried out initial assessment for re-referrals, enquiring about medication, physical health issues, looking at blood test results etc.
- Within the Psychology team, I delivered therapy on a 1:1 for the first time
- I learnt a lot about how physical health impacts mental functioning, had to assert myself as a professional to care home staff and came face to face with the transience of life

Had I had the right support, I like to think would have been able to manage this. However, this was not to be.

I started the role just before the second lockdown (October 2020), which, due to the strict restrictions put in place by care homes, meant I had very little opportunity to shadow my team members and learn how best to do the role. I now recognise that I did not get enough clinical supervision for my Care Home Pathway role and my manager/supervisor left, which led to the team becoming very stretched. As a result, my caseload drastically increased and I got even less supervision. I felt overwhelmed. I no longer enjoyed my job and started to doubt my ability as a clinician. This coincided with not getting any DClin interview offers on my second time applying which led me to doubt my ability to ever be able to become a Clinical Psychologist.

If I couldn't manage an AP role after 6 months, how was I ever
going to manage DClin training?!

After struggling in silence for months, not wanting to burden the other members of my team, I broke down during a supervision and the team were able to offer me more support. Over the next few months, a new manager started and I slowly began to feel more competent. However, I started to realise that I did not really enjoy the field I was in. Due to dementia being a degenerative disease, I found this weighed on me as I saw clients decline and some eventually die. I liked that I was able to help improve the quality of their lives and reduce their distress, but I couldn't shake the thought that ultimately they would just get worse. I started to fantasise about getting a new job.

One summers day, I happened to go onto NHS Jobs and stumbled upon a job advert for a therapy assistant/Assistant Psychologist within my local Community Mental Health Recovery Service (CMHRS). A rush of excitement surged through me. I could imagine myself in this role wearing the name badge! For a while now I'd held the idea that I'd enjoy working with those with enduring mental health issues and doing a more therapeutic role. Now here was my chance to see if this was something that really would resonate with me! I quickly typed up an application and submitted it before I could have any second thoughts. A few weeks later, I was invited to interview and the next day I was offered the job! I could not believe my luck and at the same time, it felt it was meant to be.

This was now a year ago and as I write this I'm still working in this team and wearing that name badge! I absolutely love what I do which is:

- Running psychoeducational groups
- Working with clients 1:1 doing low-intensity interventions
- Checking in regularly with those on our Psychology waiting list
- I also co-facilitate my Trusts' Aspiring Psychologist group, incidentally it's the one I joined on my placement year, and I do speak a lot more now!

I have learnt so much in the last year and I still feel like there is a lot more for me to learn.

For The Aspiring Psychologist Collective and for you dear reader I have tried to make my account mainly about the experiences I have had on my ongoing journey as an aspiring Clinical Psychologist. I chose to do this rather than focus on the ongoing struggle of 'getting onto training'. This is in an attempt to re-story my own experience, as over the last 4 years since graduating I have come to realise that this is a much more helpful mindset. Rather than counting the years of 'not getting on' I thought I would be transparent. I know this is helpful information and questions I'd want the answers to so:

I have applied 3 consecutive times for the DClinPsy, and only this year (my third attempt) did I finally get offered an interview, at which I was unsuccessful. I think ultimately, my anxiety (honestly, I was the most anxious I had ever felt, I could not stop shaking for the whole of the 45 minutes!) was what let me down this year and a lack of awareness of my personal self. These are both things I am working on.

I feel confident about this year's application process as I can see how much I have developed since last year and hope I will be able to demonstrate this in my application this year and get another chance to prove I am ready for a place on a training course. But we shall see. Each year that passes, I am simply more ready to handle the trials of training and hopefully this means I am more likely to enjoy it once I get on!

Emily Friend
Assistant Psychologist / Therapy Assistant

Emily's Top Tips

- Do a placement year - if you can, you can get a student loan to cover the course fees and living costs. This will give you an idea of whether you might want to go into clinical psychology after you graduate. Also, at some unis, this counts towards years of clinical experience. I know a few people who got onto a DClin course straight from their undergrad, as the course they applied to only required 6 months clinical experience and an entrance exam.

- Whilst at uni, offer to support with research projects. I had the opportunity to do this but dithered about it too much and by the time I thought I might be able to manage it, the opportunity had gone to someone else.

- Keep a reflective journal and try to write in it regularly - this is something I was encouraged to do on my placement year for an assignment and then my first supervisor advised I kept one too. They are a great to look back on as a collection of your thoughts throughout different experiences.

- When at uni get a relevant part time job. There are lots of different kinds of roles out there, like support workers, activity workers, working as a crisis line call service. This will give you valuable experiences to talk about in interviews.

Continued.....

- Don't be like me and be so rigid about having to get an AP job. There are lots of other types of jobs out there, like Psychological Wellbeing Practitioner, Children's Wellbeing practitioner, Occupational Therapy assistant, etc which will give you really valuable experiences and skills. If I was to go back in time, I would tell myself to apply for a trainee PWP role when I finished uni as I have always struggled with not being explicitly 'taught' the skills I use as a AP, I have just kind of muddled through and learnt these as I have gone along.

- Never be afraid to ask for extra support (something I have learnt the hard way). In my current role, I asked for additional supervision when I stated working with clients on a 1:1 and I went from having supervision every two weeks to weekly.

- Join an assistant/aspiring Psychologist group! There may be one in your Trust / local area, so enquire about this and if there isn't one currently running, maybe set one up! Being a part of a group of people who do a similar role to you and know what it is like to be a 'prequalified' member of staff, striving to get onto a difficult training course is invaluable, especially if you work in a team where you are the only AP. Or, if you have the time & money, maybe join Marianne's aspiring psychologist group, of which I am a proud member.

- Remember: it is about the journey NOT the destination, so ENJOY it. This is something I am really trying to focus on as I go into the next application season. All the experiences we have just make us better clinicians and prepare us more for whatever lies ahead.

MEMO

Dear Emily,

You have grown and changed and developed so much confidence in just the time since I have known you. I am so excited to follow your journey as you continue towards your 4th DClinPsy application cycle. I do believe that when you are ready it might well feel like your first time though because your ability to reflect and be mindful and connected to the application and interview process will have changed so much since your previous attempts.

You are kind and caring and gentle and you regularly make me laugh, I can't wait to see your next name badge!

Thanks for being part of my world,
Marianne

DR MARIANNE TRENT

www.goodthinkingpsychology.co.uk

33

- Issy's Story -

My Journey into The World of Clinical Psychology

So, a few things to know about me; I got my BSc and MSc in Foundations of Clinical Psychology, I had anorexia and lots of therapy as a teenager, I'm now 25, live with my wonderful partner, have a thriving relationship with my parents and I have a very cute dog. I'm also applying to the Clinical Psychology Doctorate for the first time.

My journey into Clinical Psychology has been both textbook and quite unusual. At school I was a perfectionist and academia has been my family's love language for as long as I can remember.

'I'm proud of you'

in my recollection, were words reserved for academic achievements, close to perfect test scores and aspirations to make something of myself. I'd attended private schools my whole childhood and was incredibly aware that my education was an investment my parents had chosen to make. So, naturally and with a big push from my school system, I decided I needed to make good on that investment and become a doctor, or lawyer, a scientist, or a dentist. Of those things doctor sounded most appealing, and most *me,* I always positioned myself as a caregiver, a listener and a fixer.

This led me to two key experiences in my formative years; my first interaction with the mental health system, as a patient and the last-minute decision to risk disappointing my family and my teachers by stepping away from my place at medical school and instead to go through clearing to study Psychology at university. Let me rewind a bit to give you a bit of my background and what ignited my passion for Psychology. When I was 14 and a service user myself, I experienced:

- Wait lists
- Dismissive professionals
- Having to jump through hoops and meet the thresholds of suffering to access support

I learned that these are all particularly big issues in eating disorder services which is where I found myself. Eventually, my family felt it necessary to fork out the money to access private care rather than wait weeks for a bed, which would then likely send me to the other end of the country, far from my support system. This privilege changed the course of my recovery and the support I was able to receive at the right time. It's something I often reflect on working in services today. Still, I sat scared in waiting rooms, felt powerless in my care plans and experienced the good and the not so good of mental health care services. Importantly, I got to experience a positive therapeutic relationship and all which that encompassed.

Reflecting on my privileges has been a pinnacle part of becoming an Aspiring Psychologist. Deciding to switch courses and take a path towards Clinical Psychology, I began working in inpatient hospitals with incredibly vulnerable people at some of the most difficult times of their lives. Looking around a CAMHS eating disorder unit, I remember thinking how easily this could have been me. Far from home, isolated from friends and family members, rigid routines, difficult staff and patient dynamics, constant alarms going off... while not all patients are the same and therapeutic pathways will be different, surely this environment was only making many of these kids sicker and sadder and to feel more hopeless? I'd been treated in a day unit, 15 minutes from my home. My mum could come to appointments with me and we waited in a grand waiting room, filled with glossy magazines, the walls covered in beautiful artwork, natural light beaming through the skylight windows. And I got to go home to my own room, my own bed and to my own dog! Family therapy wasn't easy and developing then; recovering from anorexia was by no means a privilege, but in this setting, this quickly and this close to home... it certainly was. To this day I can't help but wonder how long it would have taken me to get better in the broken NHS eating disorder pathways, if at all... And I'm not just talking financial privilege, I had parents who showed up for me and came to family therapy sessions with me, friends who rallied around me, took the time to understand what was going on for me and how as a system we could work together to help me get better.

I think some element of survivors' guilt plays into my passion for work today. Being able to reflect on this lived experience and to think systemically about what is maintaining mental illness has allowed me to be a better clinician. The skill to be able to think critically about privilege has continued to develop though my work. As a white cis heterosexual woman, born into a family who had the time and money to invest in my education, going to private schools, I cannot brush aside difficult conversations and ignore where my blind spots may (do) lay.

As Aspiring Psychologists, Healthcare Assistants (HCAs), Assistant Psychologists, Healthcare Workers, Support Workers and more, we have to be self-reflective enough to acknowledge our potential to do harm. Mis-pronouncing patients names for example is incredibly harmful, invalidating, and teaches that person that you are not a safe space. Enacting microaggressions of racism, classism, perpetuating stigma, invalidating what you might not understand... all examples of ways we as people, who carry biases, might inflict harm on the very people we are supposed to care for. Becoming a reflective, compassionate, culturally aware Psychologist isn't going to be just about reading all the right books or listening to the right podcasts. Much of the work must start with you, looking back over your upbringing, your life experiences, and dissecting areas you might hold bias. Start with the social GGRRAAACCEEESS, developed by John Burnham in 1993. Think about what areas you identify with and have experiences to reflect on, what areas are tricky for you, what biases or misconceptions you may hold. If you have a positive and safe space with a supervisor or colleague, talking through each section can lead to powerful and meaningful discourse and enable you to expand your awareness and maybe support your colleagues in their own learning too.

Working in the Clinical Psychology field and holding lived experience of mental illness can be tricky. I find this is particularly the case when working in emotionally demanding settings as they can drain resources for self-care. For me, having an open and honest conversation with my supervisor or line manager early on about my lived experience has been helpful, I often start even earlier; at interview! Acknowledging that I am in the very privileged position I can be in work, seeking other job opportunities doesn't have the same urgency as someone who may need to line up their next months' rent – I would rather not get a job than work in a team where stigma and bias means lived experience is looked down upon. Sometimes after an interview I'd ask:

> *"What are your thoughts and approaches to managing a staff member with their own lived experience?"*

It's a way I dip my toe in the waters and gauge how safe a space this team might be for me to work in. I've also asked about visible self-harm scars or tattoos simplifying mental health difficulties. Nine times out of ten, the responses are reassuring, and for that one interview when they aren't? I thank my lucky stars I dodged a bullet, or I decline the position (again acknowledging the privilege I hold to be able to turn down a salary). Once I've started in the role, I typically use one of my first supervisions to discuss my lived experience, where it may show up for me in the role, how to spot any bias or over-identification or projection and how to keep open line of communication with my team. This takes the pressure off, makes me feel seen and understood and allows me to use my insight during team formulations or reflections without worrying constantly about accidentally exposing myself; whereas, early on in my career I'd be so anxious and worried about my boss or colleagues finding out and judging me or assuming I wasn't cut out for the job. Beyond disclosure and fostering a positive supervisory relationship, find ways to engage in your work and look after yourself. This might be engaging in activities you enjoy outside of work, setting regular times to see friends and switch off, scheduling your annual leave so you have periods to look forward to and recharge... It should also look like setting boundaries in your personal life, professional relationships, and your relationships with the service users you support. When Psychology is your work, your hobbies are entangled in all of your relationships – it gets pretty draining, pretty quickly!

Here's what some healthy boundaries look like for me across many of my roles so far:

My Healthy Boundaries

1 I don't talk about work with colleagues outside of work hours.

2 When I'm overwhelmed, or something significant has happened outside or inside of work or I'm on a path to burn out, I set a supervision session to discuss with my manager.

3 When I've had a difficult day and am noticing that I don't have the emotional capacity to show up as my best self & need some alone time to recharge - I communicate this with my partner.

A career in Psychology allows me to feel fulfilled by work and with careful and considered use of supervision, reflective practice, and healthy communication with colleagues I look forward to every day going into work, no matter how tricky. I hope you can or do find the same too.

Isobel Bros
Assistant Psychologist

MEMO

Dear Issy,

Thanks so much for your story, I especially love your healthy boundaries & your nod to John Burnham and his GGRRAACCEESES. I was lucky enough to be taught by him on a number of occasions and he's wonderfully charismatic and humorous in abundance too.

It sounds like you are being wonderfully compassionate to yourself and that is so incredibly important. Wishing you so well for your future.

Thanks again, Marianne

DR MARIANNE TRENT
www.goodthinkingpsychology.co.uk

34

- Matt's Story -

"Would You Like Ice with That?"

My name is Matt. I'm 26 years old and live in Liverpool with my partner and our two cats, Leo and Esme, who are very spoiled. At the time of writing, I currently work as an Assistant Psychologist (AP), but by the time you read this I'll be on the DClinPsy course at the University of Exeter! Let's not rush to the punchline though, there's plenty of experiences that came before that, so follow me.....

My interest in Psychology really began at A-Level. I had a good teacher (shoutout Miss Cochrane) who made the lessons dead interesting, and her way of teaching essay writing skills really clicked with me, so I got decent grades. Interest + decent grades = me thinking I had a knack for Psychology and planted the idea of studying it further at university. Before this idea though, I had been set, for years, on wanting to study 'Theoretical Physics' and by the time UCAS applications had to be submitted, I was torn between choosing this and Psychology. I really deliberated. I was passionate about Psychology but given how long I'd been focused on Physics; it wasn't an easy task to get me to consider another course. So, I chose the science-y one! Then I didn't get the grades I needed; how different life would have been if I had! So, faced with the clearing process and self-doubt that Physics might not be for me after all, I came back to the idea of studying Psychology.

And so it was that in summer 2014 I accepted an offer to study Forensic Psychology and Criminal Justice at Liverpool John Moores University and never really looked back! I enjoyed learning more about Psychology and never felt like I was doing something my heart wasn't in. In my final year, I went to a couple of events which explained the various roles we could go into with our degree and the routes associated with them. At first, I was interested in pursuing a career as a Forensic Psychologist, but after having the qualification process explained to me, I was a little put off. Especially when I was introduced to the DClinPsy course the week after. The facilitator talked us through some routes and highlighted the most popular at the time being graduate > Psychological Wellbeing Practitioner (PWP) > DClin. I think this is the point where my mind became set on getting on becoming a Clinical Psychologist.

In 2017 I graduated with a 1st and then promptly moved in with my partner in Winchester. Struggling to find relevant work quick enough, I went back to my comfort zone of working in Hospitality. After 6 months I landed a job as a Recovery Worker in a care home for people experiencing long term mental health issues such as schizophrenia, bipolar, and personality disorder. Our work revolved around:

- Supporting with developing daily living skills
- Managing and improving wellbeing
- Boosting social inclusion
- Crisis support

I loved this job. It taught me more than I could've imagined about working in mental health and helped shape me as a person too. We only ever had a maximum of 8 service users (SUs) at one time, so it gave me the opportunity to work very closely with people. Staff got to know SUs incredibly well and were involved in almost every aspect of their care and lives. We were working in these people's *homes* after all. Working so closely with people like this made it important to maintain boundaries, be clear about what was and wasn't appropriate, and what was expected of both staff and SUs. The importance of boundaries and the role staff cohesion plays in their maintenance is one of the key things I learned in my time in this role.

Despite my love for this job, at some point I started to feel like it was plateauing. Most of the work I was doing was social care related, and while it's incredibly important and linked to psychological wellbeing, I wanted to develop specific skills in psychological work. After working there for a year, I was lucky enough to be asked to step up to deputy manager. This reinvigorated me and felt like a new challenge I was excited for, so I was happy to accept. Despite the extra responsibility and stress it brought, I enjoyed this role even more! I basically did a lot of the same stuff as a Recovery Worker, with some extra tasks on top and some decision-making responsibilities. I learned a lot about leadership, the pressure from both internal and external organisations, and even more about myself as a person. Still, I again got to a point where I felt disillusioned with working there, but this time it even bled into existential questions about working in mental health at all. Of all things, being somewhat motivated by money, I started looking into recruitment. I was ready to turn my back on Psychology altogether. In Summer 2019, after 6 months as deputy manager, I left the job to move back up to Liverpool. I had very mixed feelings as I had loved the job and team but felt like I needed more.

So, back in Liverpool this time with my partner (and our first miaow - Esme!) we thought everything was going to be better. The rent was cheaper; I was gonna get a job in recruitment and make more money, she was gonna start teacher training. Life looked good!

Naturally nothing went to plan but I was lucky enough to get a bar job for a local restaurant quickly. Over a period of about 4 months, I attended several recruitment interviews. There were some glimmers of hope, but ultimately, I was unsuccessful. I started finding myself thinking about Psychology more and more and that I had made a bad decision in trying to leave. Even when I thought about a successful career in recruitment, I had begun feeling like I wanted to come back to Psychology. I wanted to learn more about it, about therapy, about current research etc. I missed it. So, again, I found myself torn. I began applying for Assistant Psychologist (AP), trainee Psychological Wellbeing Practitioner, (PWP) and recruitment roles and figured whichever came first I would throw myself into. If I loved it, great! If not, as scary a thought as that was, I could always change career paths afterwards.

Drum roll please...

All my job applications failed. I now felt useless and as though my whole life would be spent at the restaurant. I could see it now, my gravestone etched with "Would you like ice with that?" I doubted I'd even have an obituary. It would just be a "Help Wanted" ad advertising my position. Safe to say that all hope of any decent career had crashed head-on into rock bottom, and I didn't know how to fix it.

But not to worry--I didn't have to fix anything! COVID came along and broke the world instead, and I was forced out the restaurant like everyone else. I'd officially gone another level below career prospect rock bottom. Sick. Faced with no income, I contacted my old manager at the care home back in Winchester. I suggested I come to help out there on a week-on-week-off basis so I could still see my partner. This would mean doing all the sleep-ins, but I wasn't really in a position to be picky, and I had nowhere else to sleep anyway. She was desperate for staff and she and her deputy were shielding, so she agreed and wanted me to come back immediately. The week-on-week-off idea went out the window almost instantly. In the most bizarre and demanding circumstances, there was too much to do and not enough people to do it. Between the 70–90-hour weeks, daily life changes, moving and living alone, and barely seeing my partner (or Esme) at all, the next 7 months were challenging. And yet they were also some of the most interesting, rewarding, transformative, and even (weirdly) some of the most enjoyable months of my life. I learnt a lot about myself, leadership, resilience, and problem solving. It's also impossible to explain how important the support from colleagues was during this time, especially Tamsyn[72], who was also acting as deputy manager with me. The experience also reaffirmed my interest in mental health and Psychology, and it was during these months I applied for my master's.

I applied for 2 courses: Manchester and Southampton. I had planned to move back to Liverpool, so Manchester made sense, but Southampton was purely down to peer pressure from Tamsyn. I had no idea how things would work if I got into Southampton, but I knew doing a master's together after our experience in the care home would make the course easier and more enjoyable, and that was enough for me to apply. So, apply I did... hungover on the day of the application deadline with Tamsyn's considerable help. God only knows how I got on, but I did, after being rejected from Manchester. After a few years of feeling a bit stagnant, I was so happy and excited and finally felt like I was making some progress in my career. Luckily for me too, the course was entirely online! I was able to move back to Liverpool and continue studying with no issues. This also meant we could get Leo which, don't tell Esme, is the biggest positive really.

After my master's I started applying for AP roles again and noticed an immediate difference in the response I was getting. I was finally getting interviews! Hooray! I'm not sure how much of this was down to the MSc or the experience in a care home through a pandemic. Regardless of the reason, I was made up.

---

[72] Tamysn has consented to her name being used here

Despite coming close, I was unsuccessful in my first two AP interviews. I got really good feedback and made sure to make good use of it but was still unsuccessful in my 3rd interview. In an amazing stroke of luck though, there was another team, the Asperger's Team, who just about to start recruitment processes for an AP. When they were told by my interview panel how well I had done at interview they said they'd be delighted to offer me the job. I obviously jumped at this!

Compared to my previous roles, working as an AP was a real change. It felt much more independent and being part of a Multi-Disciplinary Team is a brilliant way to learn about other professions and how they interlink. I have heard of some real horror stories with some supervisors in AP and trainee posts, but I have been incredibly lucky to have two excellent supervisors who have been absolutely invaluable to me for my development, confidence, and getting onto the Clinical Doctorate.

Speaking of which, that application process. Grim. Proper grim. Writing the personal statement felt like such a gamble, with so much conflicting advice from different places. I decided it was impossible to try and take it all on and just trusted my supervisors. After all, one of them had gotten 6 interviews in 2 years when she was applying so she must have been doing something right. I decided I could only do so much then it was up to the DClin gods, so I "finished" writing and then submitted. Oh my god. I got 2 interviews. Obviously very excited, I started to imagine what life would be like if I actual got on the course. A group chat was made for interviewees, and someone had said that their supervisor told them that, from the interview stage, they have a better chance of getting on the DClin than they did of getting an AP job. This makes sense when you think one AP post might have anywhere from 5-12 or more people applying, whereas the DClin interview 3 people per place on average. Oh my god x2. Day of the first interview, having done hardly any prep because nothing would go in, I booted up Zoom and greeted what I hoped were my future tutors in a full suit and a gaming headset. Online interviews are weird. The interviewers were so nice and supportive but wowee did I mess it up. Honestly, I stumbled and stuttered, I waffled, I straight up didn't know some things, I even forgot what variables I used in my master's project when I brought it up purely by choice to try and get back to some level of comfort zone. By the time I finished I had already adopted the mindset of "oh well that was terrible, but it was a really good experience". Deffo wouldn't have been able to do that if I didn't have another interview in the horizon. So, I started putting energy into that and didn't give too much thought to getting onto the first course. Then one day at work, I get the outcome email from interview 1. "Dear Matt, I am delighted...". They're delighted to reject me? Rude. Oh wait... what? I was in utter shock reading I had gotten a place! My supervisor was with me at the time and jumped out of her chair. I had a lie down on the floor under the table. When I felt less sick and dizzy, I went to call everyone and tell them the news I was so certain I wouldn't get to share. Then began the bizarre process of coming to terms with moving.

Moving felt so strange because it was relatively short notice, and I knew what it meant. My partner wouldn't be coming with me. She was doing well at her job and wasn't able to find another down in Exeter in the timeframe she had. She is planning to follow me down next year, but a year long distance is a bit of a sour note to otherwise incredible news. Worse still, because I'm renting and in a house share, I can't even take Leo or Esme. At least the house I'm going to has Bella, a black lab, to keep me company in the meantime.

That brings me pretty much up to date with my journey! I'm sure there'll be plenty more interesting stuff from the DClin onwards, maybe I'll do another chapter if Marianne does an Aspiring Psychologist Collective 2.0. I know you'll want to know if nothing else, whether we get any more cats!

Matthew Williams
Trainee Clinical Psychologist

MEMO

Dear Matt,

Thank you for your story and for helping us gain a very vivid picture of what zoom interviews were like! It clearly shows that we can afford to be human and drop some of the rubber balls so long as we don't drop the glass ones - especially around those tiny cat toes!

Wishing you so much luck and happiness on your course and with your partner finding a job so you can all live together once more.

I will certainly keep you posted about 2.0!

Thanks again, Marianne

DR MARIANNE TRENT

www.goodthinkingpsychology.co.uk

35

- Libbi's Story -

Looking at your Reflection(s)

I moved schools in year 10 and in doing so accidentally fell into Psychology. To begin with, I was asked to study Religious Education (RE), and then in year 11, Psychology. It was an unplanned perfect match! I remember learning about the Stanford prison experiment, how the brain stores memories, Phineas Gage and doing our own psychological 'experiments' such as the Stroop test. It quickly became my favourite lesson as I was never bored. I also quite liked Maths, so the statistics/research topics didn't bother me. I just loved the idea of understanding human behaviour so picking the subject for my A-Level and then my undergraduate degree were easy decisions.

During my degree, I began working in various part-time retail and waitressing jobs. Alongside this, I babysat and did a personal assistant role for people with learning disabilities. My final year of study took place in lockdown and as a result I became terribly bored of the same four walls! I suppose the one good thing about it was that I had a LOT of time to think. It was around this time I decided I'd like to be a Clinical Psychologist and wondered how I would go about this. After a few google searches, I realised the importance of gaining experience. Thanks to lockdown many places were recruiting staff, and so whilst

357

finishing off my final year and doing my dissertation, I began a part-time support worker role in a care home for adults with mental health difficulties. During this time, I also completed the Childline induction training and volunteered on their helpline.

Following my graduation, I had my eyes set on the much-coveted Assistant Psychologist role. I had seen many posts on Psychology Facebook groups about how harrowing the search to get one can be. After many applications (and many rejections), I decided to search more generally for a role within the NHS. After a few interviews, I eventually got a role supporting a qualified Occupational Therapist (OT) as an OT assistant on an older adult mental health/dementia unit. I worked with the OT to deliver a timetable of activities to promote meaningful engagement for the patients on the ward. This included crafts, gardening and... - bingo! A rather fun job indeed! I also linked in with the Assistant Psychologists on the unit to see what they were up to. I was able to help them out with their cognitive stimulation therapy (CST) group which was set up for people with dementia to help them maintain their cognitive abilities and evoke memories. This was the first time I felt I was doing something 'psychological', although on reflection, I had already been building up important skills for the Psychology world such as:

- Building relationships with patients
- Multidisciplinary team working
- Understanding NHS processes

After a few months in this role, I got my first interview invite for an Assistant Psychologist role. I remember how nervous I was as I wanted it so badly. Overall, the interview itself went okay, but my brain has a habit of picking up on the bits that went 'wrong'. After a stressful 24 hour wait, I was relieved to be offered the job!

So that's how, just a few months after graduating, I found myself as an Assistant Psychologist on a 24/7 mental health 24/7 crisis line. Something I'd thought was impossible! During this time, I began a part-time master's in Applied Clinical Psychology. If you are thinking that sounds like a lot of work..... you're right! After only a few months on the crisis line, I began to feel slightly burnt out. This wasn't helped by the fact I didn't always receive the qualified supervision I should have done. I'd also realised that in the long term, doing a whole month's worth of night shifts didn't feel doable for me. So, once again I started searching for another AP job but this time in a more 'typical' role. Thankfully with a paid AP post on my CV, it seemed a lot easier to score points in the paper sort. After a few interviews and two offers, I decided to take a role working within young person's eating disorder service. At the time of writing this in September 2022, I am in this role and absolutely loving it. I am also relishing the more flexible hours and work life balance! I have completed the first two years of my master's and I am looking forward to embarking on my final year. Juggling work and study and life is not easy and I failed one of my modules which I then passed during the re-sit. Thankfully the final year has fewer modules and so alongside working for a good team in a role I really enjoy I am looking forward to this next 12 months.

My advice for Aspiring Psychologists:

Explore Reflective Practice

During my undergraduate degree I attended a (now defunct) reflective practice group. Alongside my work roles, I strongly believe this was a key ingredient that led me to get the jobs I have. If you're struggling to find a group, there are many videos on YouTube about reflective practice in Clinical Psychology. There are also many models you can use to help you reflect. Some of these include The Gibbs reflective model (Gibbs, 1988) and the social GGRRAAACCEEESSS model (Burnham, 2018). I have found reflecting is a process – any thought could potentially be a reflection. Therefore, if you are wondering *'what on earth is reflection?'* you have probably already done it. But reflective practice is learning to think about your thinking, the situations you have been in and how they felt. This is SO helpful for your own personal and professional growth.

Get Experience as Early as Possible

Any experience working with vulnerable people will help set the foundations for gaining roles that are more directly within Psychology (such as Assistant Psychologist, Psychological Wellbeing Practitioner and many more). Some examples of good experience to search for on NHS Jobs or Indeed, is 'support worker', 'healthcare assistant', 'wellbeing coach', 'caring assistant', 'occupational therapy assistant', and 'activity coordinator'. If you can volunteer, helplines such as ChildLine or the Samaritans are also extremely useful for gaining experience communicating with people who are distressed.

Explore Your Options

Take time to think about your current experiences, what you want to strive for and why you want it. This links back to the reflection bit - if you don't have a clue, try different things! I also like to have a plan B up my sleeve if things do not work out the way I want them to re. Clinical Psychology. I have noticed through meeting different people that there are lots of roles where you can have very similar duties to a Clinical Psychologist without the title – from my

360

experience, I have met a mental health nurse who was also a CBT therapist; a clinical lead within a Psychology service that had a different core profession (such as social workers, occupational therapists or learning disability nurses) and a family therapist whose background was in teaching.

References:

Burnham, J. (2018). Developments in Social GRRRAAACCEEESSS: visible-invisible and voiced-unvoiced 1. In *Culture and reflexivity in systemic psychotherapy* (pp. 139-160). Routledge.

Gibbs, G. (1988). Learning by Doing: A guide to teaching and learning methods. Further Education Unit, Oxford Brooks University, Oxford.

Liberty Braben
Assistant Psychologist

Libbi. Libbi. Libbi. *Thank You*

Thank you so much for sharing your knowledge and advice so freely with our readers.

I love what you have said, and I know people will find it really useful.

I most definitely agree with you that reflecting is key for any aspiring, or for that matter, qualified psychologist. I have found some very interesting revelations come out of my reflecting sessions. If I'm driving and I'm struck with a great reflective morsel I've even been known to ask Siri to create me a note! It's a game changer for sure!

Wishing you well with your final master's year and beyond!

Thanks for being part of my world. Marianne

36

- Rebecca's Story -

In Accordance with Your Values

During my time at college, I was fortunate to attend a talk about Clinical Psychology training at the University of Hull. The Hull/York fast-track is the only one of its kind in the country, allowing students to gain a place on Clinical training straight after their undergraduate degree. I had lived in Hull all my life thus far and knew I wanted to move away for university, so this led to me to study to Psychology at the University of York, with the fast-track route as my goal. With the Doctorate in mind, I used my time at university to gain relevant experience.

During this time, I:

- Worked as an agency support worker at the weekends
- Volunteered for NHS activity groups during half-terms
- Joined the committee of a relevant university society
- Became an e-mentor for Sixth Form students with barriers to university education
- Volunteered abroad for a month as a mental health activity worker

I cleared the first stage of the selection process which was being selected to undertake the specialist third-year Clinical Psychology modules. The places on these modules are capped each year. I then also secured an interview at the end of my third year. Unfortunately, I was unsuccessful. I was devastated; this was my first big rejection (though there were many more to come). At this stage, it felt all the more monumental as I had no back-up plan – it was what I had been striving for since college! This meant that I also had very little knowledge of the traditional route to Clinical training. I spent that summer applying to Assistant Psychologist (AP) jobs and was fortunate to gain a split-post role as an Assistant Psychologist/support worker supporting adults with autism and learning disabilities.

Over the next few years, I worked in two further AP posts, one at a specialist school for young people with Autism and learning disabilities and one in an NHS community mental health team for older adults. Securing AP posts was never an easy feat and didn't seem to get much easier even as I gained experience in the roles. For every interview I received at least five rejections, and each role saw me working in a new location, meaning I moved away, moved back home, then moved away again. I was tired, and my efforts felt fruitless. After two DClinPsy application cycles, and zero interviews, I went into the third round of applications with high hopes but low expectations. By this point I had met other Aspiring Psychologists, qualified psychologists, and had a better understanding of the career path and how competitive it really is. I was enjoying my work as an AP and understood the importance of being ready for training and not rushing the process, though I still had regular moments of questioning my skills and suitability for such a competitive career path. Of the four courses I applied for in the 2021/22 applications, I received two interview invites after successful shortlisting tests.

For the first time in three rounds of applications, I had finally gotten the chance to interview. Looking back, I put a lot of pressure on myself, and made pages and pages of notes in preparation for how I might answer questions and reflect on my experiences. Going against my longstanding fear of role plays, I took up an offer from a qualified Clinical Psychologist to have a mock interview. It went terribly! The questions were nothing like what I had prepared for, and on a few questions, I was stuck for anything to say at all. While I felt embarrassed at the time, it was a useful experience as it allowed me to think about question styles and themes that I hadn't previously considered and gave me the opportunity to seek feedback on my performance. In March I had my first REAL interview, and felt that overall, I could have done better. I was placed on the reserve list, and this did not transpire into a place. I had my second interview in May. Since March I had learned to calm my nerves a lot and pushed myself to expand on my answers where I would normally have stopped. This interview was successful, and I was offered a place on the course!

Acceptance and Commitment Therapy (ACT) has been a key part of my journey, so I wanted to break down how I have incorporated the ACT model and the impact this has had.

I kept a reflective journal which helped me to notice:

- How unprepared I felt during previous applications, and that the biggest thing I needed to work on was confidence.

- My mindset was key... this is where ACT entered. I read Russ Harris' *ACT Made Simple* and this taught me about the 6 core processes of psychological flexibility versus psychological rigidity.

I have deliberately kept the rest of this account quite fluid in style which maps on to my reflective journal thoughts. I hope this means you can finish the questions and join up some dots for your own processes.

Contact with the present moment vs. dominance of conceptualised future

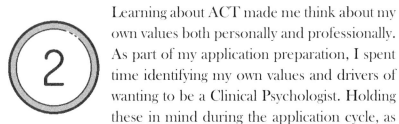

With the nature of the Doctorate being so competitive and highly sought after, it's easy to become fixated on this future goal at the expense of enjoying the journey. Engaging in mindfulness practices with clients helped me to reconnect with the present and learn to embrace the opportunities I was afforded on a daily basis. I often forgot what a struggle it had been to secure my AP posts, and I was reminded to celebrate this accomplishment and to appreciate the value of the experiences offered in my daily work.

Values vs. lack of values

Learning about ACT made me think about my own values both personally and professionally. As part of my application preparation, I spent time identifying my own values and drivers of wanting to be a Clinical Psychologist. Holding these in mind during the application cycle, as well as in my AP work, helped to ensure that I was acting in line with these values, such as applying to courses that aligned with my interests and preferences.

Committed action vs. unworkable action

Identifying my values was the first step, the next was putting these into practice, by living in line with these values. Setting realistic and concrete goals to keep myself accountable was a helpful part of this process.

Self-as-context vs. attachment to conceptualised self

Reflecting on my own practice and development through supervision and keeping a reflective journal helped me to let go of unhelpful narratives and 'imposter syndrome'.

De-fusion vs. cognitive fusion

Cognitive fusion refers to being stuck in unhelpful thoughts, so using my reflections helped me to distance from self-limiting thoughts and beliefs.

Acceptance vs. experiential avoidance

I acknowledged the impatience that I was feeling and leaned into the uncertainty. This was an ongoing battle, and was more difficult at some times than others, but this change in mindset was crucial in helping me to manage application anxiety and build resilience.

I hope some of my musings will be helpful to you in your own journey and thanks for reading.

Rebecca
Trainee Clinical Psychologist

With Thanks to you Rebecca.

Thank you for your story.

I loved your ACT vibe and also how you're making it so clear to the reader how and why you've been offered a training place. The ability to be reflective, inquisitive and to grow as a result of your ponderings can be truly transformational. I think it is most definitely the key thing to convey in any DClinPsy application. It's not necessarily what you've done but how it's shaped you and how you have grown as a result!

Wishing you so much success, happiness and growth in your doctoral training.

Thanks again. Marianne

37

- Shaunak's Story -

~~Not~~ Good Enough

I am so pleased and proud to say that I have been offered a place on the Doctorate in Clinical Psychology at the University of Hertfordshire. As a proud British Indian man, reaching this point at the age of 33, I cannot help but notice a mixture of emotions and then feel confused by them when pondering the prospect of starting clinical training. I guess this makes sense, as reaching this point has not been straightforward. This is my story until now.

Throughout my childhood, I lived in 3 countries and several cities which has offered a richness of experiences, providing opportunities and privileges that I am grateful for. I will always remember getting onto a yellow bus or rickshaw in the morning so I could go to school. Whilst my experiences were eye-opening, I also had to adjust to different cultures, educational systems and communities, which was not straightforward. Assimilating to different societies at times was confusing, making me feel lonely and othered. I was fortunate enough to overcome these difficulties through the support of my parents, which

368

enabled me to stay on the "tracks of life" and obtain the grades needed to study an undergraduate degree in Human Resources. I would like to emphasise that I do not think any of this would have been possible without them and my siblings.

When studying Human Resources, I was fascinated with the idea of how organisations can develop cultures that inculcate growth in their people by using interventions to promote and facilitate their wellbeing and development. However, I quickly realised how these principles are not routinely used in industry and how, in many cases, a more pragmatic path is followed. Despite feeling slightly disillusioned by this life trajectory, I persevered, obtained a good grade and worked briefly in industry. I was proud of these achievements, but in 2012, shortly after graduating, I switched the train tracks of my life and started a Psychology conversion course.

During my Psychology conversion course, I was introduced to various concepts and how psychologists and academics work collaboratively to make sense of the human mind. Listening to cognitive psychologists decipher cognitive processes and how they correlate with neural substrates fascinated me. I just wanted to read more! Through time, I became more interested in how psychological theories can benefit societies through clinical applications and the understanding of self. For instance, I was fascinated by how the build-up of amyloid plaques in Alzheimer's patients can cause deficits in rehearsing, retaining and recalling autobiographical memories and yet are able to recall semantic memories especially earlier in the onset of the disease. Whilst learning about this disease was fascinating, I was also saddened by the distress it caused to patients and their families, which I experienced both personally and professionally.

The above experiences convinced me to pursue a career in Applied Psychology as I wanted to continue studying the human mind but also learn ways to ease psychological distress. When embarking on this venture, I was naive in how the profession represented my community and the competitiveness of pursuing it. For these reasons, I found it hard to get my "first break"; a role where I felt valued by others, where I could develop as a clinician, and one in which I felt supported by others. When faced by this adversity, I often questioned if this career was for me, which often made me feel confused and not welcomed by the profession I wanted to join.

To keep the dream alive, for nearly 8 years, I travelled and worked across the UK. Throughout this time, I did my utmost to ignore the experiences of being othered, and through patience, I managed to find some kind and amazing people from whom I learnt a great deal and who helped me to believe. My first experience of working in Applied Psychology was for a research project developing National Institute for Health & Care Excellence (NICE) guidelines in the North of England. Whilst it was interesting to learn how research is carried out in the National Health Service (NHS), I was more drawn to how my supervisor was able to make clinical decisions whilst showing compassion and kindness to others. I was truly inspired by her, and I think observing her spurred me on even more to pursue the goal of getting onto clinical training. For these reasons, during my working tenure, I was inspired to show the same kindness to others but often found this difficult as I was faced by countless rejections and was often told,

" You don't have enough experience for the job".

In many ways, my first NHS experience was dispiriting; I felt like an outsider as I was not able to get any first-hand experiences of working clinically, and I felt stuck in a fixed-term research role.

Despite this blip, I managed to get my first clinical role in the South of England at an Improving Access to Psychological Therapies (IAPT) service. The job was eye-opening, as I learnt about cognitive behavioural therapy. However, I also found working in a data-driven service made me feel I was becoming increasingly unkind and demotivated about working in the NHS. A little over a year later I left the role and then worked in an outpatient unit in South London. This was my first experience where a kind supervisor introduced me to compassion-focused therapy (CFT). Working together was inspiring and made me consider how showing kindness and compassion to others can instil hope. It also demonstrated the importance of modelling these behaviours to others. Whilst I was actively learning how to use this model in my clinical work, I realised how I found it difficult to be kind to myself and how my experiences had given me the need to show others I am capable (so I could beat my injunction of not being good enough). This often made me feel a range of difficult emotions, which fuelled familiar experiences of feeling lonely and scared. It was sobering to know these experiences are common in immigrants living in their adopted home, which was something I noticed when living in an incredibly diverse part of England. This helped me to normalise my experiences of wanting to fit in and not standing out. While working at the outpatient unit was eye-opening, I felt my 8-month stay was enough. I left begrudgingly but knew I was ready for another opportunity.

I then moved on and over the next two years I worked in various services in North East England:

- Neurodevelopmental pathway for children
- Learning disability
- Psychiatric liaison

During this time, I was faced with two adversities:

1) Learning to live with chronic pain which had arisen gradually following a road traffic accident. This had a noticeable impact on my ability to function, and then there was learning how to cope with pain during the COVID-19 pandemic - where ways of support and coping were gone in a flash.
2) Whilst learning to manage life with pain was difficult and exhausting, I often felt lost and not valued in my roles. I think these difficulties amplified my need of wanting to fit in and beat my injunction of not being good enough.

Sadly, this was not the greatest time for me, yet I kept persevering, and in September 2020, I was fortunate to be offered the opportunity to train as a Clinical Associate Psychologist (CAP) in Sheffield.

During this training, I was fortuitous enough to be able to continue considering my own narrative as a British Indian man living with chronic pain and how it can play out in my life. The process of also receiving personal therapy really helped me to own my experience but also provided a newfound sense of appreciation of my clients' suffering and experiences. My supervisors and tutors in Sheffield made me feel safe and supported. I do not think this increased insight and my ability to deliver psychological interventions would have been possible without their support. Interestingly, this was the first role where I was given a permanent contract.

When I applied for the Clinical Psychology Doctorate for the final time, I had lost count on how many times I had applied, and truthfully, when preparing for the interview I did not have much hope. At the time, I was experiencing a massive flare-up in pain and on the day decided:

"I will just be myself and see how it goes."

The interview happened, and then the waiting game started for the feedback email, but oddly enough, I was okay with it. I felt as though I did everything I could have done during the selection process. When I opened the email to find out I had got on, I just could not believe it and was in shock. I then called my brother and shared the news. His response was priceless, and to be honest, sharing the news with him and then my parents was more joyful than being accepted on the course. It was almost like a massive weight was lifted that I had been holding for so long. I was so happy.

Since accepting my place on the course, the excitement has not gone. I am so glad that I have had my supporters and my parents that have helped me to keep the dream of pursuing a career in Applied Psychology alive. I can't wait to begin the journey of training as a Clinical Psychologist, so I am able to empower others so they can make change. I wanted to share my story so I could show others that dreams really can come true!

Shaunak Deshpande
Trainee Clinical Psychologist

Thank You

Dear Shaunak,

Thank you for your story which was so wonderfully reflective and aware. Your wonderful way with words made it seem almost lyrical and hypnotic in parts. I have to confess that you have also taught me a new word: 'othered' and it's not lost on me that as a white, blonde, British woman, it is likely my own experiences which have rarely made me feel 'othered' which meant it was missing from my lexicon. I shall cogitate on that for some time.

So many congratulations to you on having been offered a place at Herts! I have still never parted with the 2 course offer letters I received, nor with the feeling which came with them. I hope that you'll have incredible experiences during training and that your CFT practices will continue to flow for you as it makes the journey so much kinder. I think your cohort and your clients are so lucky to be getting you in their worlds.

With my best wishes, *Marianne*

38

- Lucy's Story -

Unfinished with No Regrets

I am a 29-year-old woman living with my 7-month-old daughter in South London. I didn't study Psychology but did a conversion master's a couple of years after graduating. I was told so many times how competitive Clinical Psychology was that I was completely put off and decided to become an Educational Psychologist instead! I worked in various roles in Special Education schools for several years, during which time I moved from London to the North West and got married. In March 2020, I left my very relevant job to travel in the Middle East (great timing!!) and ended up unemployed and locked down. Since all schools were shut, I decided to give Clinical Psychology a whirl, and by some miracle I landed an AP job in the NHS and shortly after a place to study the DClinPsy on a local course. I was on cloud nine; my years of striving were over, finally I'd made it – hooray! Or had I? I fell pregnant with a very lovely and wanted baby, and somewhere along this road my marriage ended. I had to choose between pursuing my dream career and staying in the North West and moving back home to

375

South London to be nearer family support. I chose life over work and so have gone from being a 'nearly psychologist' to an Aspiring one again. I have zero regrets though and I am so grateful for every step in my journey. It's an unfinished story but I hope you may feel better for hearing it.

LUCY,

Thank you so much for helping me to get your story across the line at the final hour. Even in its note form I just loved it and thought it was really powerful. I'm so glad you agreed it was too!

So many congratulations to you on the birth of your baby. I know you've recently returned to work and I hope that's going well. I recall a few times where I was so tired, I sat and had a cry with my head resting on my desk. I hope you're not finding days like that, but if you are please know that they don't, and won't, last forever.

Wishing you so well with this next stage of your career and the most wonderful moments as you watch your daughter grow,

WITH MY BEST WISHES, MARIANNE

Sep 2022

39

- AJ's Story -

The Game of Life

When asked if I had a story to tell, my thoughts drifted to how the fuck do I do that? Would anyone even like it, and is it any different to anyone else? Then I remember what I tell everyone else, that you're your own worst critic. What's the worst that can truly happen? (Don't worry my mind can tell you, but it can come for a ride instead).

Let me start with some facts about me:

- So, I'm AJ, 29, male (nice to meet you!)
- I will be entering my 4th year of applying to the Clinical Doctorate
- I'm currently engaged and living with my partner
- I've worked as a Healthcare Worker, Assistant Psychologist x3 and now a Research Assistant

I started on an unusual route to Psychology (Not that I knew it at the time!). My story starts with having an interest in computers and games, winding through to how my focus shifted, following my MSc conversion to some very uncomfortable and ethically wrong job roles. I then started to learn about views of men in mental health, overcoming difficulties with my dyslexia/dyspraxia, and balancing difficult feelings with the process and remembering my values. Hopefully my story will help others, maybe even you.

My interests in playing games and hoping to be the next top player in online games, kept me sane(ish) for the most part of my education. For me it offered the perfect escape, where you can be someone different. What's not to like? I'd had to re-sit my A-Levels and then had to go to college as my grades weren't good enough so it's fair to say that traditional academia wasn't my strongest skillset at that time. Since computing was all I knew, and I'd managed to get odd jobs working with computers, I thought a degree in Software Development was for me. I would say I wished I had a time machine to go back and change my path, but upon reflection, I probably wouldn't be who I am today without the struggle. In my 2nd year of university, it took a toxic relationship ending, losing a lot of my joy in life even in games, and a gentle nudge from my guidance counsellor (my sister, don't let her know I've said this she won't let me forget!) to step out of my comfort zone. With the nudge I decided to work at a camp abroad. Oh boy, did that change my life. I realised I had an addiction to gaming, and that without screens I could be social and enjoy life. I also realised I could still reinvent myself in real life too (some call it the 'outside game'). Thus started my career change via a MSc Conversion. This eventually led to me working as a Healthcare Worker in probably the least safe secure **CAMHS** unit in the country. The young people deserved so much better. It is safe to say that this nearly ended my career there! I was then able escape to what I thought would be the beginning of my Psychology career as an Assistant, but my supervising Clinical Psychologist went **AWOL** in my first week. Fast forward through my previous workplace getting closed by the **CQC** (no surprise there!) and I'm then seconded to a private forensic inpatient for **LD** adults, where I learnt a lot from the amazing clients. However, this was certainly not a level of any game I'd wish to re-visit. It turns out I learned pretty quick that my supervisor took pride in people breaking down in supervision. A fine example of the type of feedback I was offered being on an occasion when I had been unsuccessful after interview for a mother and baby unit, and I was told:

"as a male did you really think you were going to get that role?".

I knew I really needed to get out of private healthcare so then to be able to move into the **NHS** after 5 unsuccessful interviews, was a huge relief. So much so, after my first supervision with such a wonderful psychologist, I was shocked to the point I blurted out:

"is supervision supposed to be like this?".

I learnt so much in just a few months, and even felt supported to be a voice in the team, it was incredible. I really felt myself flourish, after what felt like my career wasn't going to get any better.

My journey then goes more into the pain of the clinical procedure, the anxiety, the impact of basing my life around the process (how partner's put up with us, I don't know!). But also realising that just because I'm an assistant doesn't mean I need to stay silent, that you can try to improve assistant roles, encourage universities to improve transparency in the process (ongoing battle at the moment!), and speak to your supervisor about it. For a long while, I felt this need to be thankful for any scrap that was given to me due to the competition, and it took me a while to realise I'm worth more than that (and so are you!). Don't be afraid to ask for CPD time, search and ask for any training you can, and if you're in the NHS, contact your research team for opportunities. Finally (promise I'll stop writing now), something I'm still very much learning, don't let the destination consume you!

AJ
Assistant Psychologist

Note to Marianne

Hopefully I haven't talked too much for a brief summary or missed the deadline. Either way, it's actually been quite nice to write out some of the story so far!

AJ

Note to AJ

Thanks for helping me pull this together at the 11th hour - I loved your story. So sorry for what you endured with what sounds like loads of sub-standard treatment. I can only imagine what the clients were going through if the staff treatment was this bad! Thanks for giving our readers hope that good things can follow bad! Wishing you well with lucky application #4!

Marianne

40

- Preetasha's Story -

Follow Your Own Path
(Just Breathe)

I have been interested in many careers during my time; from a Disney Princess to America's Next Top Model (despite being British and well, seven years old), and from lawyer to detective, to acting, writing, and then a dentist? I was around 16 when I gained an interest in Psychology. It didn't fit with my then "dentist dream" but I was curious about people, and I picked it as an A-Level as a little treat to myself. It didn't take too much A-Level chemistry for me to realise that being a dentist was my parents' dream, not mine[73]. It's a bit tricky to tell your parents that you're no longer going along with their plan for you, it's even trickier when you have Indian parents. Luckily for me, I was a teenager who was pretty stubborn, and they got over it. That might well be the advice you needed to hear; you

---

[73] 24-year-old me does in fact wish she had listened to theirs and the dentist's advice to carry on wearing my retainers!

are allowed to follow your own path. In fact, my mum now constantly tells me how interesting my job sounds! It was Clinical Psychology I gravitated towards and I ended up doing Psychology at University of Hull. You see, they have a fast-track DClinPsy scheme I liked the look of. The irony is that ultimately, I never even applied for it!

So why did I not apply? There are several things that I feel led to this decision, with my limiting self-belief probably the overarching reason.

I did enjoy uni, (although perhaps a bit too much at first!!) Then my dad suddenly passed away towards the end of my second year, and everything changed. My last-minute submissions that I had previously still scored highly on, became anxiety inducing nightmares, and the thought of sitting in an exam hall was enough for me to panic. I decided to repeat the year to give me some time to breathe, and I thought that going over familiar content would be much kinder than navigating a whole dissertation. This was a decision that did not go down well with staff ("your grades are great though") but I stuck to my guns, and it absolutely paid off – I finished with a First! As good as the advice you receive along your journey may be, ultimately you know yourself better than anyone, and in this case, I knew that I needed that extra time to process my grief.

So why didn't I apply for the fast-track? Well as I said, my new struggles with anxiety had a big effect. Not only did I begin to doubt myself and my ability, but I would also compare myself to others on my course. The ones who were interested in Clinical Psychology, lived, and breathed it, whereas I just wanted to enjoy life again. Did I want it enough? Why wasn't I as determined as the others? Am I limiting myself by going down this route like I nearly did with dentistry, or am I just using that as an excuse? Do I even want to go straight into another three years of university? I think it is important to mention the whiteness of my cohort here, but that is something that deserves full focus and so is a story for another time. Ultimately, I thought that the safest bet was to keep myself open to other careers and if the Clinical route was for me, I could still take the long way round.

I did struggle at university, not necessarily with the content or course material but more so the pressure of deadlines, having to submit on time, and the thought of what lies after graduation. This is what prevented me from doing a master's straight away. I wanted time away from the pressure, to get some experience, and decide what I wanted to do with my life. I, of course, submitted a fair few applications for Assistant Psychologist (AP) posts around the country just in case I got lucky (and never heard back!) I also thought about my other options. Maybe the most impactful of all...I got diagnosed with ADHD. It was a lightbulb moment, everything suddenly just made sense to me. Again, I could talk your ear off about this but, long story short, I realised that any struggles I had were not just a character flaw. And weirdly I got back some of my confidence in pursuing Clinical Psychology. I realised that all the comparisons I had made between me and my peers were ridiculous, and actually I had done pretty well all things considered.

So, let's get back to the journey. Graduating in the pandemic was not fun for anyone, and it took me a while to get my first job. It was as a support worker in a specialist Dementia care home. This is an area that I have a big interest in, and I think it was that passion that got me the job. I'd recently completed a (free) online course on Dementia and this definitely helped in both my application and interview. I also highly recommend support work as an entry level Psychology role as some of the lessons and skills that I was able to learn are on par with ones learnt in my later roles.

My new plan was to work here for a year, and then begin a relevant master's in September. That didn't happen. Instead, I managed to get an AP post (I know!)
I actually had no intention of applying for any AP jobs until I'd completed my master's – because this just seemed like the 'done' thing! But I had a meeting with my manager who asked me to look into Psychology related roles within the company, and of course I got tempted to see if there was anything else out there. There was. I finally heard back for an assistant post, had my first interview, and got the job! (I'm not ashamed to admit there were tears!)

I can't recommend working as an AP highly enough, but I don't doubt there are so many other roles that are just as valuable! I was lucky enough to get my post through an improving access scheme. It was a six-month split-post in an adult Community Team Learning Disability (LD) and a community children & young people's (CYPS) LD positive behavioural support (PBS) team. It's funny because when I first started, I was so worried that people would think I had gotten 'special treatment' or something and I'd always leave that part out when speaking about my job. I don't know when exactly things changed, but now I'm so proud to be a part of such an important initiative. This really spurred my interest in diversifying Clinical Psychology and since then I have had the privilege of being involved in different projects that allow me to work towards this. There is so much to get involved with when you know where to look (social media is a great place to start!) And there's no harm in asking.

I should warn you about six-month posts however, but they'll be over before I get a chance to. As much I couldn't imagine where I'd be without the experience I gained from this, I also could not describe a more stressful time as the months very quickly count down to unemployment.

I know they always say that the first one is the hardest, but my next post did not come easy. Don't get me wrong, I was pretty much getting interviews for the majority of posts I was applying for (and I was getting good interview feedback), but I was just missing out on the roles. They always say to be prepared for rejection in this field, but I don't think you can ever completely prepare yourself. It's easy to start blaming yourself (I would know) rather than the system and wondering why you aren't enough. But it's not you. There are so many amazing, capable people out there, and you are also one of them!

It's very easy to lose yourself in the competitive world of an Aspiring Psychologist. There is so much emphasis on competition, being perfect, and knowing everything (which no one ever does). It's also so easy to compare yourself to the person who's read all the right books cover to cover and is on draft 20 of their Doctorate application. That doesn't mean that's the right way for you.

If there is one thing you take from my story it is to trust yourself, believe in yourself and just... breathe (although that is three!) And please don't be afraid to ask for support. For me, I could not have got to this point without the support of the people around me – both personally and professionally. I was the only person out of my undergraduate friends that wanted to stick with Psychology so until my first AP role I didn't really have support from people who *got* the journey (no offence!) Having this now is invaluable. So please don't be afraid to reach out and ask questions – in my experience everyone has been more than willing to help out!

As for me, I should've listened to my own advice and trusted it all to work out. All of those rejections led to me securing a permanent (!) AP post in a tertiary sector service that I have always had such an interest in. As cheesy as it sounds the right role will find you.

As I'm writing this, I'm now ready for my practice year at applying for the DClinPsy. Me a year ago may have thought what's the point in applying yet and putting myself through the heartache, but where would that have got me?
So that's my story. It's absolutely just beginning and I'm sure that it won't be slowing down anytime soon. I'm so excited for what's next, and hope you are too!

Preetasha Toor
Assistant Psychologist
Aspiring Clinical Psychologist

With Thanks to you Preetasha,

Thank you for your story. I am so pleased that you found your path and that it makes you smile in a way that dentistry never truly did! Speaking as someone currently completing their 3rd course of orthodontics, I hear you on the retainers!

You write beautifully and I know your words will be an inspiration and also likely a salve for those who read them.

Wishing you only the best and most compassionate wishes for you in your first (& possibly only?) rodeo for the DClinPsy application cycle!

Thanks for being part of my world! Marianne x

41

- Antonia's Story -
Reflecting on my Reflections

O ver the years, it's felt like I haven't been able to make headway through a career in Psychology, and that ultimately, I wasn't going to make it. However, as time has gone on, the more I have felt the need to look back and remind myself how far I have come and celebrate what I have achieved.

- I didn't think I'd be able to go to university, but I got a place,
- I didn't think I could apply myself to study at master's level, but I did,
- I didn't think I would ever get my first job working within the NHS, and now I am there.

Yet despite these successes, when I think about taking the next step in my career and ultimate goals, it can still feel so out of reach. This is where reflection has been such an important part of my journey, because when I get overwhelmed with these feelings of doubt, I reflect on my experiences, and all the evidence that through perseverance and following roles that excite me, I am very capable at achieving.

I thought I would discuss some key facts about me and my experiences which I think are notable for their impact upon me and my desire to pursue this career of ours.

Growing Up in a Big Family

I grew up the eldest of 9 girls (all of our names go in alphabetical order too, which has been a very useful conversation starter over the years)[74]. I loved growing up in this busy environment, my family home was always full of energy, silliness, and laughter. When I lived at home, there was always something interesting going on, someone to play with and someone to talk to. Even now as an adult, when I visit home, it's such a welcoming environment. As I was the eldest, I also had a more caring role and loved helping with my siblings where I could. This meant I did things like personal care, craft activities or homework. I found that my role as a big sister also became about giving advice and comfort. This massively developed my empathy and passion to work with children and young people in the future. Like many families, mental health challenges presented throughout for multiple family members. Sometimes this meant being on the receiving end of harsh words and difficult situations. Despite this, I still have strong bonds with

---

[74] Chrissie's editorial note: A real-life Bridgerton family! Love this.

my family members, and we are each other's biggest cheerleaders. Looking back, these experiences fuelled my interest to learn more about mental health and Psychology, which has led me to pursue a career in Clinical Psychology, although perhaps like you, it hasn't been a typical, straight forward journey so for.

I found school quite difficult, looking back it just didn't really 'click' for me. Thanks to my grandparent's support, I got good GCSE results. My grandfather was a teacher, and my nan was good at English and amazing at textiles. However, at Sixth Form I really struggled, and the

more I battled the more I thought learning wasn't something I could do well. This was made more difficult when I would compare my experience with my younger sisters, who seemed to have an easier time at school. At the end of Sixth Form, I went through the process of researching universities anyway and applied for the one subject I found interesting: Psychology. I got two conditional offers and one unconditional one, which came as a complete shock. Finding out that I could go to university felt like a turning point, as it made me appreciate that I could apply myself to something and achieve a desired outcome. I remember some of the first lectures we had were about the history of Psychology and another on reflections. I was hooked! Those three years flew by and after a lot of all-nighters, much caffeine and the support of my partner, family, and housemates, I graduated with a First and was fully inspired to start pursuing a career in mental health.

After University

Alas, this inspiration soon faded. Straight out of university, I started applying for AP positions. I applied for so many but was unsuccessful. This was quite a confidence knock; I knew I had found something that brought me so much warmth and excitement to learn about and talk about. I desperately wanted this role as I saw it as the only option of getting my foot in the door. I was applying to other roles too, and I managed to secure a job in a school. I had previously done some work experience there and in fact it had been my first school until year 4[75]. Initially I ended up landing a wraparound care supervisor role from 3-6pm. Over time this developed into additional hours during the school day as a Teaching Assistant (TA). I was then offered the summer club job, which I took as a massive compliment as it involved planning and organising a lot of fun and engaging activities for the kids and being 1 of 2 members of staff who ran it full time. This role gives me a lot of butterflies thinking back to it now. I had so much fun working in this school, and I was so privileged to work with such amazing children that made

---

[75] Use those connections wherever you can!

it a joy to come into work. This role led me to a developed interest in Intellectual Disabilities (IDs), attention deficit hyperactivity disorder, (ADHD), Autistic Spectrum Conditions, (ASC) and emotion dysregulation. However, I had also reached a point in my Psychology journey where I felt that progression towards Clinical Psychology wasn't going to happen for me, I just wasn't 'good enough'. So, after reassessing, I thought about what I was enjoying and decided to follow that. This led me to pursue my Postgraduate Certificate in Education, (PGCE). I thought I would enjoy being a teacher as I loved working 1:1 with children. But, to my surprise I hated it! I felt that I was constantly trying to slip into my old TA role, identifying that there were children in the class that needed 1:1 support and trying to offer that, but then not leaving enough time to finish the lesson for the rest of the class, this caused me a lot of stress and doubt that I never expected. Looking back, I know that with time I would have built the experience to manage my time better and find ways to support the children in the class effectively, but I found I was dreading the days I had to teach and willing my weeks away. I realised that I needed to listen to how I was feeling: The passion for teaching wasn't there. I decided that job satisfaction was non-negotiable. So, just before my third placement, I withdrew from my course. I felt instantly lighter!

Moving to Scotland

4

So, by this point it's January 2020, and when I mention that date, I am sure you'll know what I will mention in this section. Anyway, before that unfolded, I felt quite unhappy, my relationship had been long distance since June 2019, and I have no idea what to do next. I still didn't believe Psychology was in reach for me and now I had to decide if not teaching, then what? This period was quite difficult, dealing with feelings of failure, frustration and questioning what I wanted to do in life. I finally decided 'screw it' and after discussing it with my partner we decided to move in together. So, I started planning to move to Scotland which is where he was living. Of course, whilst planning this, the pandemic situation became more serious and lockdowns meant that not only could I *not* move to Scotland, but also that I couldn't then visit my partner or even go into work! Although this is where having such a big family was incredible; we all hunkered down in the family home. Although we had periods of worrying for and feeling isolated from other family members and significant others, we came together to be each other's support system and were lucky to be able to make lockdown a more positive experience. This also gave me a lot of time to think about what I wanted to do next. I knew I enjoyed learning about Psychology and mental health, so I decided that I wanted to pursue a master's degree. This was not something I had previously considered doing for financial and self-doubt reasons, but my desire to go back to university and learn about something that excited me won. As the plan was to

393

move to Scotland, I did some research on the courses that were within travelling distance of Edinburgh (I remember believing that we would be back to normal by the time the course started in September 2020) and landed on the Mental Health of Children and Young People: Psychological Approaches course run by the University of Edinburgh. A couple of months later, I found out I had been offered a place, so I found a job working in a care home, moved up to Edinburgh and began my course, I loved every second and graduated with a Distinction! The course itself was supposed to be a mixture of online and in person teaching, but in the end the university moved the course to fully online. This was quiet disappointing as there were social aspects that I felt I missed out on, but there were some positives as well. I got involved in some mental health and university research projects and working from home meant no commuting, which allowed me to organise my time so that I could do volunteering in between working on my assignments and still have time in the evenings to unwind.

Work Experience

After studying, I looked for some experience working with children and young people. I found two bank positions, one working as a nursery practitioner and the other as a sessional children's support worker. Both roles reaffirmed my love for working with this population, but I also loved working with families and supporting them towards more positive outcomes. This gave me a lot of encouragement to start thinking about what I wanted my next step to look like, and because of this, I started looking at a timeline of my experiences and reflecting on the skills I gained from each. I then applied these reflections when applying for full-time roles. As a result of this, in February 2022, I finally landed my first **NHS** role as a Child & Adolescent Mental Health Services **(CAMHS)** clinical support worker. This has been an incredible experience. The role is somewhat undefined and is as brand new to the service as me. But I like this because it has allowed me to explore the capacity of the service and develop the role so that it meets the needs of the team and of those accessing the service.

"

6

Reflecting on
My Reflections

"

My focus now has been reflecting on my current role and everything that I have learnt so far and pursuing opportunities within my team to further develop my knowledge and experience. I am also looking to the future and looking at options I never previously considered. I always thought Clinical Psychology was going to be a straightforward journey from Degree to Assistant Psychologist, to Doctorate. Now I am excited about pursuing work I am passionate about, I am still looking at Assistant Psychologist posts and plan on applying to the Clinical Doctorate, but I'm also considering Clinical Associate Psychologist, (CAP), Clinical Associate in Applied Psychology (CAAP)[76], Children's Wellbeing Practitioner, (CWP), and Education Mental Health Practitioner (EMHP) roles. I've also learnt the value in self-compassion during this journey and making sure that pursuing this career doesn't consume my whole life, and that I organise my time, so that I have time for myself and enjoy it.

Antonia Clarke
Aspiring Psychologist

---

[76] The CAAP is a role in Scotland.

Thank You

Antonia,

Thanks for your story. Your family sounds like a frenetic but love-filled experience. My Grandmother was the youngest of 10 girls and I often wondered what that would have been like!

I am wishing you so much luck, love and happiness for the rest of your journey. Who knows in which direction the road will take you, but I hope you have fun as you set about gaining more numbers and pictures in your career for points 7 & beyond!

Do keep me posted on your progress,

Marianne

42

- Hope's Story -

Tears of Joy Coming Soon

I'm Hope, 30 years old, recently married and living in Surrey. It's currently June 2022 and I'm delighted to say I've just accepted my offer of doctoral training at Southampton. I know I've already skipped to the good bit, but I promise you that this only came following a long, challenging, but incredibly rewarding chapter in my journey. This twisting and turning fable was made all the more complex but enjoyable when I had my son aged 22. I was a lone parent and moved to the Isle of Wight, leaving my busy London fashion career behind so I could be close to my family. When my son was 6 months old, I got a pastoral job in a school. I had no relevant experience but transferable skills (it's like that on a small island!) I then started my BSc in Psychology with Open University, and for 4 years I worked full-time, studied and raised my son alone. During that time, I moved back to London, continued to progress to management in education and after my undergraduate degree, I completed a part-time MSc in Neuroscience at King's College London.

The pandemic hit us all hard. I am aware that my struggles were somewhat trivial compared to others, but I did my thesis in lockdown, while home schooling and working full-time. When I was awarded a Distinction for my toils, I was so proud. For a little while I'd considered becoming an Educational Psychologist – I even applied once but didn't get anywhere. There soon followed two equally unsuccessful DClinPsy applications. So, despite the obvious challenges of being a lone parent in London on a band 4 salary I knew I needed to change tack! I decided to apply for Trainee Psychological Wellbeing Practitioner (PWP) roles and happily was successful. I LOVED being a PWP. I progressed quickly and during my training I took the lead role in the quality improvement project which at the time of writing I am still running. After qualifying, I became perinatal champion and three months later I was supervising the next trainee intake. My work is varied, interesting and really rewarding. I'd thoroughly recommend it.

This year, in my third round of applications to the DClinPsy, I received 3 rejections – in some cases, identical emails to previous years. I was so disheartened. What more could I do? But happily, my last response was from Southampton and their response was an interview offer. I read the email while sat in my car before school pick up. I cried with joy in the playground that day. I had the interview I had waited years for. Many of my colleagues were offered numerous interviews but I knew the stakes were high and the odds were against me. I know you read this on the forums and across social media, but one interview is enough. I was offered my place this year and will be a Trainee Clinical Psychologist by the time this book is published.

I started this journey in 2014 as 23-year-old lone parent. Eight years of huge challenge and huge reward. I worked full time in 4 posts during those years gaining the experience I needed, studied in any spare moments to get my BSc, MSc and PGCert. Life is much easier now; I met my now-husband in 2019 so I will have a babysitter for my future essay writing 😄.

Hope
Trainee Clinical Psychologist

Hope,

Thank you for your story and so many congratulations to you on gaining your DClinPsy place!

Thanks also for following up with me on the day of the queen's funeral when I was eagerly trying to dot i's and cross t's! You received my email about final submissions and replied. It turns out the email inviting you to write had gone astray but I adore that we have been able to pull this together in such a quick time frame because I know that your story is one that so many will feel heartened and encouraged by,

Wishing you and your family every success in your lives in Southampton!

Thanks again, Marianne

43

- Veronika's Story -
My Lessons in Life

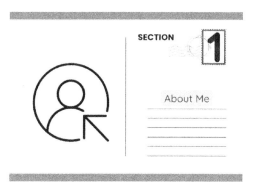

Every story has a protagonist – in this case, a little bilingual[77] 9-year-old girl from a small Slovak town called Nove Zamky. Her mom is from the Hungarian ethnic minority of Slovakia, her daddy is Slovak. She is an only child, sweet, sensitive. When she is asked what she wants to become when she grows up, she has an excellent plan – a different occupation per working day: ballerina, archaeologist, gynaecologist, teacher, and musician. Yes, in case you were wondering – this was me. ☺

---

[77] Spoiler alert - she doesn't yet realise she will one day be tri-lingual!

As a child, I've had endless enthusiasm to learn and explore. Even thought at school I did not fit in perfectly and experienced bullying, I still found my own ways to joy outside of school.

As a teenager I:

- Chaired the Student Parliament and organised various student events
- Competed in contemporary ballet
- Was a Scout
- Organised children's camps
- Played in a local Christian band
- Hiked mountains
- Worked in stables with horses, and went horse-riding

My family lived humbly, but my mom's extraordinarily creative ways of beautifying our life always made it seem like magic. My teachers considered me a talented student; even though I'd never actually studied, I was able to slip through with good grades. Every time someone asked me what I wanted to 'become' – I would get annoyed and worried. I was gravitating towards everything! I was certain that I wished to become a wife, a mummy, and have 'a job'. I know, traditional – but you need to remember, I come from a post-communist country. My parents were still fully socialised in a system where mediocre was praised with everything outstanding weeded out – unless you were ready to pursue it in the name of the communist party. They were not allowed to travel, learn English, watch Western shows, or believe liberal ideologies. At least not openly. Reflecting on the above, it just made sense that none of my relatives ever spoke English (they have recently learnt), nor lived abroad. The possibility of speaking a fluent third language had never really crossed my mind, nor did relocating to a different country. What I did have was a family heritage of hard work, resourcefulness, and resilience. Considering the turmoil of the 20th century, I am proud to originate from ancestors of great internal resources facing all adversities with dignity while retaining their humanity.

Alongside this though I also had my mother's unwavering love and belief in my ability to find a fulfilling path at last.

Significant events that most likely changed the trajectory of my life were:

- The 2008 economic crisis,
- My mom developing multiple serious health issues;
- Both my grandparents passing away in a very short space of time.

While too busy living my teenaged life to notice at first, soon the realisation hit:

"I am rather alone".

The boy I was in love with left, my youthful hopes for becoming a cute wifey got crushed, and the financial support from my parents had disappeared. This was one of the defining moments of my life. I was in a dark and lonely place full of self-doubt, anxiety, and fear. At the age of 17 - this is when I made the decision to 'do it' by myself. After my 3rd year at high school, a friend suggested I try finding a seasonal job in England and make some money. This sounded like an excellent adventure – flying for the first time and trying my luck elsewhere. I won't even start getting into the difficulties of finding a job without speaking English. But I did not give up. I was there, working 16-

hour shifts in a foreign country where I didn't speak the language, packing M&S home shopping parcels. There and then I realised I can do anything. I discovered a new world of possibilities which inspired me to explore further.

I've decided to lay out my story for you as a series of life lessons that I have learned along the way. I hope you'll enjoy them and maybe they'll evoke within you the idea of also reflecting upon your own lessons thus far.

My exploration of a potential career path and acquiring education consisted of 3 downs for each up. I graduated from high school in Slovakia with 4A Highers and enrolled in a Pre-primary Education undergraduate course at Comenius University Bratislava. I'd tried to juggle being a fresher, working odd jobs (no student loans in Slovakia), and still getting good grades. Retrospectively, I don't understand how I persevered. I guess I must have utilised lesson number one, and some of my family work ethic perhaps too.

My Lesson #2

Honour where you come from and do not shy away from developing an authentic identity that is aligned with your personal values

By the end of the first academic year, I decided to save money and permanently relocate abroad. Longing for higher quality of education and desperately needing to be in an open-minded environment helped me to collect the necessary resources to make the move. After a chat with a friend studying in Scotland – I jumped on a plane with a single piece of hand luggage and started my new life in Edinburgh. Within the first month, I'd got 3 jobs. Even though my English was still way below the International English Language Testing System's (IELTS) required standard of '5' which means 'Modest User', I exploited every opportunity to speak to people, assimilate new information and make friends. I'd actually never studied any IELTS in my life, but it was clear as day to me that I was no English whizz. To allow me to jump into the education system ASAP, I miraculously enrolled in a fast-track Higher National Diploma in HR Management at Edinburgh College. This was because by this time, it had occurred to me that if I wanted to be an independent woman, I needed to study business! The closest they offered was HR and being great with people I thought this would be excellent!

Continuously having to hold down odd jobs greatly compromised my educational experience. This may be one of the reasons why I feel strongly about addressing inequalities based on socioeconomic backgrounds. In the September 2021 issue of BPS The Psychologist magazine, qualified psychologists from working class backgrounds discuss their struggles around joining a typically middle-class vocation and re-adjusting their identity in the process. One of the interviewees says:

'The funny thing is, I didn't know I was working class until I started university and then my working classness stood out.'

The article touched me in places I did not even know I've had. It resonated with me so strongly, I kept this issue of the magazine on the top of the pile and occasionally still come back to it, like today. I don't talk about it much, but it IS emotional.

" My Lesson #3

Seek out supportive and compassionate mentors who you can look up to

"

During the HND, I'd taken on employment with a charity as a support worker. This was my first time being in touch with mental health in a professional capacity. Finding this job was an accident. In fact, I didn't have a clue then what it meant to be a support worker, and trust me, some parts of the job were extremely difficult. My limited English and my terrible accent were often in my way. My financial struggles were definitely in my way. My lack of support systems were tricky to say the least. But both at Edinburgh College and at work, I was lucky enough to have a couple of great role models. I found them caring, and they placed trust in my skills and abilities which encouraged me to step into my role as a student and support worker with confidence.

My Lesson #4

Work for supportive organisations whose culture fits you well

In the meantime, I experienced a personal trauma which set me back a thousand years emotionally. Amid this chaos, I still managed to finish my HND and start an undergraduate degree at The University of Glasgow; MA (Hons) in Business and Politics. Housing issues, financial issues, and relationship issues did not help in learning much in the first 2 years of my undergraduate studies. The other kids were enjoying their fresher's week while I was worrying about topping up my electricity key. This made me angry and exhausted. By this time, I managed to find a remote job – a customer service role – all I needed was good broadband and a laptop. An absolute life saver. The organisation was kind, fun, and everyone was helpful. They can't have a clue that they had lifted me out of an extraordinarily difficult situation. I stayed with them for 6 years. This company was a start-up full of encouraging people genuinely interested in my personal experience. Working for them has put me through university. As an Engagement Operator I have learned a lot about how to speak to people, how to communicate compassionately whilst problem solving, how to adapt my tone of voice to what a given client preferred, remote working, and taking initiative to update my product knowledge regularly. I've met some very nice and inspiring people here.

My Lesson #5

Build connections with like-minded people who can grow into becoming your closest friends and form your strong support system

While my personal life was in shambles, I accepted a Living Support Assistant voluntary role at a student accommodation. Here I provided out of hours advice and support to residents regarding first aid, mental health emergencies, accessing medical help, emotional support, course worries, and exam stress while applying active listening skills and signposting students to relevant services. The Living Support crew was a cool bunch of people – I've had some nice times around them and one of the crew members slowly became one of my closest friends – Ana[78], studying neuroscience. Ana has also had a self-made and a unique journey, we clicked from the start. She knew THE struggle too.

My Lesson #6

Find opportunities for practicing your leadership skills

This was around the same time I completed the Certificate in Teaching English to Speakers of Other Languages (CELTA) Teacher Training. I've always had a natural affinity for facilitating groups, empathising with people, and teaching – so I though this will be a great opportunity to develop my skillset further.

---

[78] Ana has consented to her real name being used here.

My Lesson #7

Sometimes, showing compassion and acceptance can seem like a small step to you compared to the huge difference it will make in the other person's quality of life.

After the second year at Uni, I went through a heart-wrenching breakup which affected my grades. As a result, I was only able to progress to my Honours degree with Politics. Of all the subjects I'd initially enrolled in this though it was my least favourite. Frankly, it was not for me at all, but I couldn't afford to quit, so I clenched my fists and carried on. I've had my moments of appreciation for the subject, sometimes even enjoying constructing an argument for a given essay, but my mindset did not allow me too much leeway when it came to the usefulness of these activities. The two great things stemming from my Politics degree were a six-month Erasmus+ International Exchange in Indonesia and a kind and forgiving dissertation supervisor. My supervisor helped me rise above my inability to appreciate politics and was graceful enough to accept me for who I am and what I was capable of at the time. This made an insanely massive difference in my quality of life, and I couldn't be more thankful for that. Again, great mentors RULE!

My Lesson #8

> You may encounter challenging events that affect you more than others. These experiences may leave you feeling deeply unsafe and often helpless. This can lead to emotional trauma which may affect an individual's sense of self, their sense of others and their beliefs about the world. It is important to reflect on such events in your life and ask for professional help if they affect you negatively.

The exchange in Indonesia could form a separate book on its own. I managed to use my stipend to stop over in Dubai, Abu Dhabi, Goa, and New Delhi. Yes, I've travelled India by myself as a 24-year-old woman! Challenging but worth it. Arriving to Indonesia, the heat alone was unbearable. Never having been outside Europe, blending into this diverse, improbable society required a high level of adaptability. Witnessing controversial issues like the adverse treatment of people with various sexualities, a completely different world view, the urban-rural divide, and the big divide between rich and poor – deepened my awareness of how essential role context and cultural awareness plays out in society. My coping skills were tested when I had a cancer scare and for the first time in my life, being put under general anaesthesia to have a biopsy. Fortunately, no malignancy was found. However, the traumatising experience of being alone, on the other side of the world, believing for a week that I may die – it was INTENSE. Years later I would still get anxious at any sign of illness and have an emotional response linked to a fear of cancer.

> **My Lesson #9**
>
> What gets you through pain and suffering – is connections with people. You may know them for a day, or a lifetime – it's people who make everything bearable. People who show up for you, mentors, guides, small sparks of light at the end of the tunnel

About 1 month later, while riding my motorbike heading to a surfer-beach, I had a road accident. Thankfully, local villagers found me unconscious on the road and delivered me to the local village hospital where due to shortage of resources, my extensive wounds were sanitised by alcohol while I was held down unanaesthetised screaming in pain. My friends came to the rescue three hours later and we embarked on a 4-hour journey back to the city. Have I mentioned the...pain? I had a surgery under general anaesthesia again in the international hospital having treatment similar to burn victims. It was a bit like torture. My doctor and I became friends in the process and once I managed to walk again, I spent time with her family during Ramadan, eating Iftar together. Her family gifted me a beautiful hijab, my first Qu'ran, and they were fun too. This was the same surgeon who had biopsied me a month earlier – I was a returning customer so we'd had time to get close. I also made a couple of other very close friends here. A Bulgarian girl – Slava,[79] was like my stepmom; a tiger-mom protecting me and fighting for me every step of the way. My sweet, loving friend Rafi[80], who would be studying for his exams next to my hospital bed until 1am, and Alila[81] – a caring and capable businesswoman with an unbelievable level of integrity. And there were many others <3. The surgery and months of recovery humbled me to

---

[79] She is happy to have her name used here
[80] He has also consented to being within this story
[81] Once again, she is happy to be here

submit to the healing process patiently. I consider this to be one of the most defining experiences of my life. Not only have I developed immensely as a person, but I also had the chance to better comprehend the variety of shades of what we call the human experience. And the nature...and the kindness of strangers...and the food, oh the food. A little piece of my soul stayed in Indonesia after these 6 months.

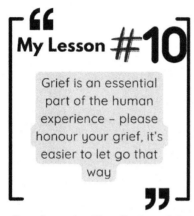

My Lesson #10

Grief is an essential part of the human experience - please honour your grief, it's easier to let go that way

The semester after returning to Scotland was one of the most depressing times of my life. Everything seemed dark, cold, lifeless. My parents and I buried grandpa and grandma during this time. I missed being there when my grandma died. I still feel guilty about it. She died and I was not there, I did not have the chance to look after her or say goodbye. Neither have I had the chance to grieve properly being consumed by moving back to Edinburgh and the flat hunt.

My Lesson # 11

Financial resources don't make one happy, but they make misery a whole lot more comfortable and may even open otherwise closed doors.

I decided to remain in Edinburgh as it felt more homely and moved in with a close friend. In the meantime, my parents gave me what I considered a nice large sum from my grandparents' inheritance. I cannot express how thankful I am for this great gift – it was the luckiest timing as well. I was just about to disintegrate mentally.

My Lesson # 12

The best ideas come to you in the shower.
AKA: If you can't see the forest from the tree, just step back for a moment

After returning to Edinburgh, I managed to pull together a dissertation project, pass all my exams, and I then swore to never return to the U.K. ever again. I decided I needed to fly to the African continent – to the Canary Islands - to rehabilitate myself and convince my nervous system *'we're safe now'*. I just wanted to eat fresh fruit, lay on the beach soaking in sun, sleep all day and all night, and finally be at peace. Although at this point I was still holding down the customer service job, I was working +/- 20 hours per week remotely throughout my university degree. At that time, I knew what I did NOT want to do – and that was ANY of the things I'd tried so far! I decided to take some space. I rented a studio in my hometown as a base and travelled for a year. I visited 9 countries and lived in Austria for a while. I took up a new hobby, snowboarding, and gradually started recovering emotionally. Maslow's Hierarchy of Needs comes to mind – when you feel safe, and have shelter, and don't have to overwork, and have time to develop warm, interpersonal connections – suddenly a new layer of needs becomes accessible – self-actualisation. I admit, it is highly possible that without my grandparent's inheritance I would have never been able to take space, recover and open my heart to new interests. The COVID-19 pandemic meant I had to stop travelling. Suddenly, I had plenty of time to face the state of my mental health. As terrible as the pandemic was for many people – for me, personally, it allowed me to turn inwards and explore what was overshadowed by a loud busy life in the past. This is the time when mental self-care slowly but surely infused my life. I stopped beating myself up for not having my career all worked out, which led me to a 180 degree turn to take life by the day. It was one of the best 2 weeks I've ever had (yes, it only lasted 2 weeks). Until one morning, when I woke up rested, at peace, with a certainty as if I knew it all along – I will become a mental health professional. Did I know how? No. Did I care? Also no.

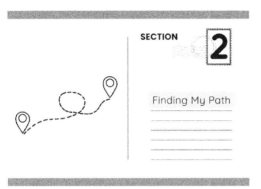

SECTION **2**

Finding My Path

I started conducting desk research on potential career paths in mental health and by chance I stumbled upon the option of completing an MSc in Psychology of Mental Health – at The University of Edinburgh. Though I previously decided to never return to Scotland, this was different. I just KNEW it was the right idea – and I applied. Nothing less, nothing more – I applied. 3 months later, I received my acceptance letter, but I was at peace all along. I knew that this was 'IT' and for the first time in my life I felt absolutely undoubtful that this was my path. I'm aware that not everyone has the privilege to be able to afford an expensive master's degree. Considering my earlier years, I can strongly empathise.

My Lesson # 13

If you start doing what is authentic to you - things just start falling in place

I packed up and moved back to Scotland. I felt like a different person – I was actively and happily taking part in the student life; I STILL had my online job which paid for my living expenses and this time around I was eligible for the student loan which made my life just a bit cushier. It made a big difference. The people I studied with were equally passionate about the same things as me. With every module, every essay, every conversation I just continued growing fonder of the subject. I was honoured to receive a sound foundation on various theoretical and conceptual aspects of Psychology delivered by both experts in psychological science and Clinical Psychology. During my degree, I also developed a taste for research. Emerging from a post-communist traditional education system, critical thinking was way out of my comfort zone at first. But being part of an inquisitive open-minded environment sparked the desire to skilfully analyse, evaluate, and conceptualise information. This culminated in the dissertation writing process–exploring Third-wave therapies. I conducted a large quantitative cross-sectional study in the pursuit of understanding the ingredients of change during Acceptance and Commitment Therapy (ACT). ME! This has blown my mind.

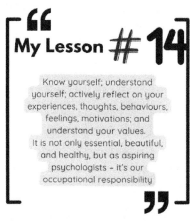

My Lesson # 14

Know yourself; understand yourself; actively reflect on your experiences, thoughts, behaviours, feelings, motivations; and understand your values. It is not only essential, beautiful, and healthy, but as aspiring psychologists - it's our occupational responsibility

I started hanging out with more and more 'Psychology people' which always sparked intriguing conversations that challenged me to my core. At this point, one of my friends confronted me with the idea of leaving my comfortable customer service job and getting into support work to gain experience with clinical populations. This was difficult and scary to me. At first, I decided to keep both jobs - I'd developed an aversion to risk as a result of my earlier experiences. However, two jobs and numerous assessment deadlines did not go together well. I ended up getting worse academic results than I was capable of achieving. My old self would just start beating myself up for this. However, reflecting on it now, I know clearly why I did what I did. When I start to blame myself, I do my best to show compassion to myself. I apply compassionate salve to my wounds; I just recognise the thought, move on from it, and show some tender caring love to the person I was then - who is part of who I am now. If there is one single theme you take away from my story – learn to self-reflect, incorporate it into your daily routine, and always be kind to yourself.

My Lesson #15

Actively seek opportunities for growth

What helped me most in my self-reflection journey was a COSCA (Counselling and Psychotherapy Professional Body, Scotland) Counselling Skills Certificate (SCQF[82] Level 8), which is a foundation course for most Postgraduate Diplomas (Level 11) in psychotherapeutic modalities and counselling. I tend to continuously seek opportunities for growth – so after graduating from my master's degree, the certificate was my next move. It was one of the most valuable educational experiences I've ever participated in. I was lucky to encounter an excellent tutor who was a great personality fit for me, I was blessed with a bunch of compassionate, attentive, empathetic classmates, and an interactive skills-based curriculum that taught me as much about myself as about the person-centred counselling approach, if not more. I just graduated last week – cheers to me. Figuring out the next step is

---

[82] Abbreviation for Scottish Qualification Framework.

like a swan – all graceful above the surface while paddling hard under the water. Doing your due diligence is something you'll need to get used to if you wish to progress in any career. Understanding the industry, its career pathways, networking, asking questions. Unfortunately, to me, it does not seem to be enough to love Psychology; you must also understand the context it operates in. It's a separate learning curve altogether.

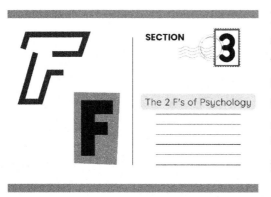

SECTION 3

The 2 F's of Psychology

I came up with this concept of 2 F's last week while doing some research on the experiences we sometimes call 'psychosis'. The first '**F**' stands for *FASCINATION* for the subject – Psychology as theoretical science, and Psychology as science in practice. I am genuinely fascinated by how Psychology is created, the existing knowledge base, and how it is practically applied in different contexts. For that reason, I'm aspiring to become a Clinical Psychologist – a scientist practitioner.

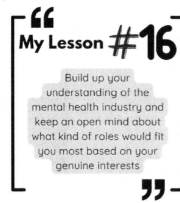

My Lesson #16

Build up your understanding of the mental health industry and keep an open mind about what kind of roles would fit you most based on your genuine interests

It took me a while to get my head around the various mental health professions out there. People who are excited predominantly about the creation of the science gravitate towards Research Assistant positions and PhDs and people mostly intrigued by the utilisation of the evidence base in practice could be interested in a psychotherapist path, or becoming a psycho-educator, counsellor, mental health advisor etc. There is a likelihood there are numerous mental health roles I've never heard of yet – like the recent Clinical Associate in Applied Psychology (CAAP) role which sounds very interesting. Again – due diligence, attentive curiosity, and networking are your best friends. The Assistant Psychologist (AP) role is just one of many roles you can love, enjoy, learn in, and reflect on.

My Lesson #17

Transferable skills are awesome. Learn to frame them in a way that reflects your understanding of mental health professions

After I graduated from my master's degree – having acquired some support work experience during my degree (and earlier, when I didn't know what Psychology was), I wanted to experience how it feels to work with clients one on one. For this reason, I joined an NGO as an Employment Advisor. This role was beneficial for 3 reasons: 1. It aligned with my values – I was providing employability and wellbeing support to people mainly from disadvantaged backgrounds; 2. The employability advice I was giving informed my own future employability immensely – my job was to know how to land a job; 3. I've had a chance to reflect on how I felt working one on one with people all day every day.

My Lesson #18

" Frustration is part of the game – it is unlikely to go anywhere. Probably the best option is to accept it. And maybe, then it will become slightly more comfortable, just name it something funny and have a laugh together. Use humour to make grim-looking things colourful "

If you think I forgot about the second 'F' – don't worry. It stands for **FRUSTRATION**. Since my graduation, I've submitted 24 Assistant Psychologist applications. The submission process is fast, often the roles are online for only 3-4 days before the quota fills up. I used to be visiting the NHS website scouting for new adverts every day. The excitement-rejection cycle can be challenging. I've had 3 interviews, of which 1 was unsuccessful and one was a reserve. In the meantime, I was also keeping an eye on the general mental health job market, tried to network with other professionals, and asked as many questions as possible. By the end of it, I was jokingly saying they just accepted me this time because they got tired of always seeing my name coming up on every applicant pool. Truth to be told, every one of my newest applications was a bit better than the previous one. I kept learning, researching, developing, and my applications reflected this.

I must say, the feeling when you get the acceptance email after an AP interview is exhilarating. This is week 4 in the job for me at the time of writing. I'm part of the Rehabilitation Psychology team at the Royal Edinburgh Hospital with NHS Lothian. My team works with individuals in inpatient wards who experience multiple disadvantages in all aspects of their lives. The individuals frequently have treatment resistant illnesses, have had adverse early life experiences and have been unable to engage successfully with mainstream health and social services. I work as part of a Multi-Disciplinary Team (MDT - Clinical Psychologists, consultant psychiatrist, junior doctors, nursing staff, occupational therapists, community rehabilitation team). I find this type of work enriching. Every profession within the MDT infuses patient care with their own expertise which seems to be a wholesome way of collaboration. I have two amazing mentors who go out of their way to make me feel welcome and comfortable. I've learned more about the work of a Clinical Psychologist in 4 weeks than ever before. It feels like this new universe of opportunities just opened for me here and I wish everyone had the chance to feel what I feel when I go to work in the morning.

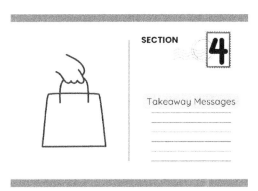

SECTION 4

Takeaway Messages

If you made it to this point, thank you for honouring me with your attention. As you may have noticed, my heterogeneous past experiences show the struggle to find my true path. I've invested a lot of effort into refining what I stand for, understanding my core values, and finding the vocation I'm fully aligned with. To be precise – about 15 years' worth of effort. The key to my strengthening dedication to mental health was most likely my lived experience. I came to understand and appreciate having to work on my own mental health daily. This awakened my interest in Psychology and has grown into a fascination with theory and practice. Though often frustrating, the journey is rich in various highs and lows and if I learned one thing from it all – there is no such a thing as 'bad' anymore. Now I call it 'challenging' – challenging feelings you learn to work with, challenging experiences you learn to process, and challenging situations you learn to take charge of. Psychology will inform your journey to make it into a wonderful adventure.

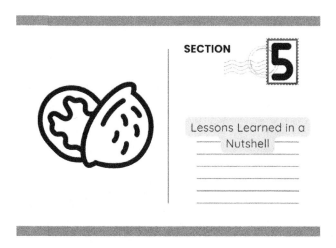

SECTION 5

Lessons Learned in a Nutshell

1. Your own mental health and its cultivation is above all else. Make sure you show yourself care, compassion, and self-love every day.

2. Setting time aside to reflect on your experiences is something you will have to do regularly if you wish to join a mental health profession – it is often uncomfortable but highly rewarding.

3. Even though you love Psychology, there will be times when you will get frustrated, and will need to build a skillset to work with this challenging feeling. There will also be situations when you will need a good amount of resilience and grit to carry on despite facing difficult situations.

4. People around you are your support network – people make everything better and surrounding yourself with people with whom you can have healthy and mutual genuine connections is going to give you a strong base to withstand many challenges.

5. Remind yourself regularly to enjoy the journey - the outcome is only the cherry on the cake. But the cake itself is what you'll be eating all the way through, so make sure you choose a tasty cake.

6. Life doesn't stop happening just because we're Aspiring Psychologists – there will be pain, breakups, useless landlords, friends moving on, death, boredom, turmoil, bad luck, annoying supervisors, financial struggle, personal mental health issues... just to name a few. What matters though is that it is **YOUR** life. You will have the opportunity to create an empowering narrative for yourself, with you being the main protagonist of your own story. And no one can take that away from you.

Veronika Kassova 15/08/2022
Assistant Psychologist

Dear Veronika,

Wow! Wow! Wow! I just adore the way you think! Thank you so much for the care and attention you have given to the task set. I know that when I was an aspiring psychologist this is EXACTLY the sort of stuff I would have found incredibly thought provoking and helpful.

You write beautifully and I am in awe of just what a stunning job you have done regardless of English being your third language!

Congratulations to you on your new Assistant Psychologist job. I hope you continue to grow and reflect and soak up gems of brilliance from the people you meet along the way.

I am going to use your story as the final one in the Collective because I think you've summed everything up so beautifully. Thanks for being part of my world and extending your knowledge and guidance so freely to our audience. A little personal thanks too for your enthusiasm and support of the podcast - it's so appreciated.

thanks so much!

Marianne

Acronym Busting

One thing we do well in Psychology is to abbreviate terms and use the acronyms regularly. Whilst we have used the full terms and added brackets in this book, we thought it might be helpful to have a handy reference guide for them too.

(T)APP	(Trainee) Associate Psychological Practitioner
A Level	Advanced Level (Stage 2)
ABA	Applied Behavioural Analysis
ACEs	Adverse Childhood Experiences
ACT	Acceptance & Commitment Therapy
ADHD	Attention Deficit and Hyperactivity Disorder
ADOS	Autism Diagnosis Observation Schedule
AP	Assistant Psychologist
ARMS	At-risk Mental State
AS Level	Advanced Subsidiary Level (Stage 1)
ASC	Autism Spectrum Condition
ASD	Autism Spectrum Disorder
BABCP	British Association for Behavioural and Cognitive Psychotherapies
BPS	British Psychological Society
BSc (Hons)	Bachelor of Science with Honours
CA(A)P	Clinical Associate (Applied) Psychologist
CAMHS	Child and Adolescent Mental Health Services
CAT	Cognitive Analytic Therapy
CBT	Cognitive-Behavioural Therapy
CFT	Compassion-Focused Therapy
CMHRS	Community Mental Health Recovery Service
CMHT	Community Mental Health Team
CPD	Continuous Professional Development
CQC	Care Quality Commission
CST	Cognitive Stimulation Therapy

CTPLD	Community Team for People with Learning Disabilities
CV	Curriculum Vitae
CWP	Children's Wellbeing Practitioner
CYP	Children and Young People
DBT	Dialectical and Behavioural Therapy
DClin(Psy)	Doctorate of Clinical Psychology
DID	Dissociative Identity Disorder
DWP	Department for Work and Pensions
EHCP	Education and Healthcare Plan
EMDR	Eye Movement Desensitisation & Reprocessing
EMHP	Education Mental Health Practitioner
EP	Educational Psychologist
EPQ	Extended Project Qualification
ESW	Educational Support Worker
FASD	Fetal Alcohol Syndrome Disorder
GCSE	General Certificate of Secondary Education
GDPR	General Data Protection Regulation
GP	General Practitioner (Doctor's office)
GRACES	Gender, Geography, Race, Religion, Age, Ability, Appearance, Class, Culture, Ethnicity, Education, Employment, Sexuality, Sexual Orientation & Spirituality.
HCA	Healthcare Assistant
HND	Higher National Diploma
HR	Human Resources
IAPT	Improving Access to Psychological Therapies
IBD	Inflammatory Bowel Disease
IELTS	International English Language Testing System
IPA	Interpretative Phenomenological Analysis
LD	Learning Disability/Disabilities
MDT	Multi-disciplinary Team(s)
MoD	Ministry of Defence
MRes	Master of Research

MSc	Master of Science
MSc	Master of Science
NHS	National Health Service
NICE	National Institute for Health & Care Excellence
NVR	Non-violent Resistance
OCD	Obsessive Compulsive Disorder
OT	Occupational Therapy
PBS	Positive Behavioural Support
PGCE	Postgraduate Certificate of Education
PgCert	Postgraduate Certificate
PhD	Doctor of Philosophy
PICU	Psychiatric Intensive Care Unit
PTSD	Post-Traumatic Stress Disorder
PWP	Psychological Wellbeing Practitioner
QCF	Qualifications and Credit Framework
RA	Research Assistant
SEMH	Severe and Enduring Mental Health
SEN(D)	Special Educational Needs (and Disabilities)
SFH	Solution-focused Hypnotherapy
SMART	Goals – smart, measurable, achievable, relevant, time-bound
SPSS	Statistical Package for the Social Sciences
STR	Support Time Recovery worker
SU	Service User
UCAS	Universities and Colleges Admissions Service

Acknowledgements

First and foremost, I would like to thank all of the contributors within this book who believed in this project and were excited about it too. They so freely gave their time and compassion, and dedication are at the centre of every story. The nation is incredibly lucky to have such dedicated and caring professionals helping them to feel better. Being even a tiny part of your story and your world is just the most incredible privilege for me.

I thanked most people in my last book and so I'd like to thank them all over again too! That totally sounds like the "Anybody else who knows me" from Radio 2's Pop Master doesn't it?[83] Since becoming fully self-employed my personal network of qualified psychologists has been even more important to me. Thanks to 'The Actual Psychologists', you most certainly know who you are and thanks for our super safe space. Thanks also to Kara, Jade and Dr Berger. Also, to Alex thanks for the cackles, the shared values and for your incredible talents in trauma work.

Thanks to my family for good humouredly responding to my repeated: "I've got to work on the book". Thanks also for giving me Uno, Hide and Seek and snuggles on the sofa as really good reasons to connect with you rather than with my laptop. Thanks especially to Damien for our protected time of an evening, sorry the latter stages of this book have squeezed it on occasion! I also

---

[83] I've been a proud listener to Radio 2 for about the last 18 years so hopefully some of you are too!

adore our grown-ups only Saturday dinners with Lisa T! We totally struck gold when we met 13 years ago and it's lovely being on this wild ride of life with you.

Michelle and Christian Ewen, my media cheerleaders, thank you. I adore having you on this wild ride with me and you're not just brilliant at what you do but so attuned and caring. If you'd like to check them out, you can do at: https://writeontime.co.uk/ Thanks for helping me so brilliantly with the press release. I am excited to see this beautiful book bird fly and enrich people's journey to becoming qualified psychologists.

Thanks to my 'team,' Hannah and Chrissie. Hannah has been a whizz with helping me with the consent process and also making my social media a lot easier to navigate! Chrissie, thanks for persevering with the god-damned OneDrive file. That was fun right? Thanks also to Kyah, and congratulations to you on gaining your place on Clinical Training. I shall miss you so do stay in touch!

I'd also like to thank *you* dear reader for sticking with us right to the final pages. Reading the Acknowledgements, that's dedication that is! Wishing you all the best in your journeys. I do hope that you have found this a helpful resource. If you have, please do tell others about us, and do consider leaving us a review on Amazon and Good Reads and do take photos of you holding or reading your copy of the book and tag me in! I would also love to know whether the advice and guidance in this book is *actually helpful* for you in shaping your future direction so do please keep me posted by connecting with me on socials. If you've got ideas about what you'd like next or ideas for podcast episodes, then let me know!

The End

Website: www.goodthinkingPsychology.co.uk
Instagram: @DrMarianneTrent
Facebook: Good Thinking Psychological Services
YouTube: Good Thinking Psychological Services
LinkedIn: Dr Marianne Trent
TikTok: @DrMarianneTrent
Twitter: @DrMarianneTrent
LinkTree: https://linktr.ee/drmariannetrent

Index

Q

R

S

T

U

Also by Dr Marianne Trent

The Grief Collective: Stories of Life, Loss & Learning to Heal

I hope you enjoy this snippet of The Grief Collective. It will give you a good idea of what the book is like and of how helpful it will be for you or someone you care about. It's also a fascinating insight into real human stories and an excellent way of developing empathy for grief if you have not yet experienced its impact within your life.

Whatever the reason for you seeking The Grief Collective, we are confident that the answer is waiting for you within its pages.

In the *Clinical Psychologist Collective*, I introduced you to Holly as the sneak peak chapter. On the next few pages, I'd now like to introduce you to John.

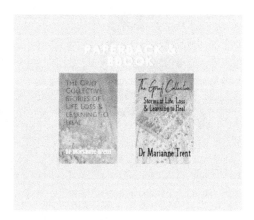

15

John's Story

When I was around six, I would have this recurring dream. In the dream I saw an image of my parents, on their wedding day. My mum in a white gown freckled with flowers; my dad with his auburn hair, parted to one side. As quickly as it had appeared, the image would suddenly stretch and tear and burst into flames, and I would wake, frightened by what I had seen.

When I was eight, they both died. My dad in the January of 2000, in a car accident. Two months later, my mum followed when the breast cancer she had beaten only two years before, had returned.

The experiences were different in that one was expected, and one was not. There had been nothing to anticipate when my dad died; it just simply happened one Friday evening, when he didn't come home. Whereas when my mum was dying, it felt as though everyone walked around our home as if the floor were covered in eggshells. Whispered conversations in hallways, a nurse leaving as I arrived home from school. Despite this, I don't think I understood that she would die. I don't think I believed that she could die. I sat with her on the evening before she did, in the wooden rocking chair that swayed by her bed, staring at my mum for what would be the last time.

There are certain memories that come to mind when I think of them. The way they left dregs of red wine in their glasses on a Friday evening. My mum's infectious laugh, almost witch like. Sitting on the back of my dad's motorbike, as we drove through the woods. Despite these memories, whenever my parents come to mind, I inevitably come back to their deaths and how robbed I feel by it.

When I was younger, I would imagine that they had not died. That in fact, they had gone into hiding, and lived in a cottage on a small hill, hidden by trees. My mum made marmalade there, as my dad worked on the garden fence. The reality of death does not hit you as a child. The permanence of death does not register with a child.

I am fortunate that I have an older sister, and naturally we faced this loss together. We have managed (somehow) to remain best friends throughout the years. These days, when I find time to see her, we inevitably find ourselves drinking white wine, reminiscing about our childhood, and listening to my mum's favourite songs. This will usually involve singing our hearts out to Shania Twain, to the annoyance of the neighbours. Ultimately, she is the only person who can know the gravity of this loss. She told me once how she lay with my mum as she died. How she fell asleep next to her, and how when she woke, the bed was empty and all that remained was the scent of talc.

Grief has seemingly affected us both in different ways. In the years following, my sister turned to alcohol, to drugs and to men

438

who treated her badly to manage her anger and loss. Comparatively, I remained constant, if not something of a wallflower. Yet, as the years went on, I felt as though I was holding myself together with elastic bands, as if I were constantly running, dodging bullets. I knew that my grief would not leave me unscathed forever, and when I turned twenty-one, I welcomed anorexia home, like a crow who had pecked at my window for a decade. What followed were painful years of weighing cereal, shivering in the summer, and crying over bowls of soup. Eventually, I was able to recover, to move forward on a path which was not defined by where I had been and what I had lost, but where I chose to go next.

I lived with my grandparents after my parents had died and I am certain that they did not expect to inherit an eight-year-old boy as they neared sixty. It would be unfair to say anything other than my life with them has been good and that I have been loved. However, as I have grown older, I have felt the lack of my parents' presence more and more. I think of how my mum would have loved a gay son. How my dad, with his love of motors, would have loved buying me my first car. How I would have cried on my mum's shoulder when I broke up with my first boyfriend. How they both would have sat in the audience, proudly, as I graduated. But instead of what might have been, I cling to the very few memories that I do have.

A fortnight before her death, my mum took me to have my ear pierced. The stud they tried to place in my tiny ear wouldn't fit, so she took her own diamond earring out and placed it in my ear instead. I wore this to school the next day.

Now, when I tell people that I grew up with my grandparents, something almost rehearsed spills out of my mouth – I'll say how 'fine' it had been and how I've been given everything that I could possibly need. People often accept this and probe no further. But on a rare occasion, I will confide in a friend, usually over wine, who will ask about my parents. I will tell them what I remember, which ultimately comes back to the details of their deaths. The knock on the door as policemen delivered news of a collision. The smell of talc in my mum's room. The curdled milkshake she had left on the bedside table. By the end of shedding my history, I am usually in tears. In that moment, I think that perhaps I can let go of the weight that has lived in my chest for twenty years and that I have carried since I was a child.

And in that moment, I think I will be okay.

Reading More

I hope you have enjoyed this free trial chapter of *The Grief Collective*. The whole book contains 54 stories in total and it is a wonderfully helpful and inspiring read. For more information or to buy a copy for you or for someone you care about, search for 'The Grief Collective' on Amazon or head to www.goodthinkingPsychology.co.uk/thegriefcollective

If you do go on to buy the book and you enjoy it, we would be ever so grateful if you could stop back at Amazon and/or Good Reads and leave a review. Reviews help Amazon know that people like products and they are then shown higher up in search results for topics. This helps us to be able to bring *The Grief Collective* to a wider audience to be able to support more people to cope with grief and to support those who are experiencing grief.

Thank you.

The Clinical Psychologist Collective Book

"This is the perfect read for anyone looking to get onto a doctorate in Clinical Psychology."

"This book highlights key information you need to know from your undergraduate degree right through to qualifying."

"You'll be sure to learn something from this and reflect on your own journey too."

The Clinical Psychologist Collective:
Advice & Guidance for Aspiring Clinical Psychologists

Dr Marianne Trent

The Aspiring Psychologist Membership

MEMBERSHIP TESTIMONIAL

I'd 100% recommend it! I've already talked to three other aspiring psychologists about how amazing the training was!

The Aspiring Psychologist Membership

The Aspiring Psychologist Membership was launched in February 2022.

It is a wonderfully supportive, compassionate community where we are doing great things in terms of increasing people's confidence, skills and knowledge.

We have regular group Zoom sessions where we focus on key areas of importance to Aspiring Psychologists.

MEMBERSHIP TESTIMONIAL

I would definitely recommend the membership as it made me think about CBT in a different way

Good Thinking
Psychological Services

We also hold monthly Zoom sessions on:

- CBT skills and formulation
- Research Skills/Clinic
- Wellbeing & more

MEMBERSHIP TESTIMONIAL

I am really enjoying all the opportunities for additional learning within the membership

The Aspiring Psychologist Membership

For more information or to join head to:

www.goodthinkingPsychology.co.uk/membership-interested

The Aspiring Psychologist Podcast Review

Here is a snippet of a review of the podcast which is featured in the British Psychological Society (BPS) magazine, The Psychologist:

One of the benefits of this podcast is the normalisation of thoughts and feelings you have whilst working in a Psychology setting. This podcast does not only cover useful topics like non-disclosure, boundary setting, and risk, but it also talks about aspects of being a Psychologist which aren't usually spoken.

Marianne covers topics like "not being in the mood", "how to support an Aspiring Psychologist" and "being a parent whilst training". This is the most useful aspect of the podcast; it ensures that we know we are not alone. It can also help normalise struggling with confidence around self-disclosure, worries over whether you can be a parent and a psychologist, or knowing that just because you are an Assistant Psychologist you don't have to be 100% perfect all the time; it's normal to sometimes not to be in the mood!

Another thing to love about this podcast is how accessible it is - it's absolutely free! For a long time, the tips and tricks of Clinical Psychology have seemed like the world's best kept secret! Not only does the podcast allow Aspiring Psychologists to learn and develop their knowledge of clinical practice, but it also promotes inclusivity, compassion, and a safe space to reflect on whether a path in Psychology is something you wish to pursue.

The Aspiring Psychologist Podcast, with 37 (& counting) episodes, explores how to pursue a career in Psychology with tips and advice on how to develop as a clinician and how to navigate your way to pursuing a career in Psychology. There are many episodes with guest speakers from different areas within Psychology, and other professions such as specialists in leadership and nutrition! This podcast perfectly couples with The Clinical Psychologist Collective book, which explores people's unique and varied routes to get onto the Clinical Psychology Doctorate (and also other Psychology doctorates, e.g. counselling, educational etc).

To listen to the podcast on your favourite podcast service head to https://the-aspiring-psychologist.captivate.fm/listen. Episodes can also be streamed via the YouTube channel, "Dr Marianne Trent".